A2
LEVEL

Psychology

the study guide

Nigel Holt and Rob Lewis

Crown House Publishing Ltd
www.crownhouse.co.uk
www.crownhousepublishing.com

First published by
Crown House Publishing Ltd
Crown Buildings, Bancyfelin, Carmarthen, Wales, SA33 5ND, UK
www.crownhouse.co.uk

and

Crown House Publishing Company LLC
6 Trowbridge Drive, Suite 5, Bethel, CT 06801, USA
www.crownhousepublishing.com

Image credits
Page 12: © Valva Vitaly, Fotolia; Pages 24–27, 50, 97, 108, 118: © Les Evans
Page 30: © Michael J Tarr; Page 91: © Olly, Fotolia; Page 191: © Christopher Dodge, Fotolia

British Library of Cataloguing-in-Publication Data
A catalogue entry for this book is available
from the British Library.

ISBN 978-184590101-1

LCCN 2011925284

Printed and bound by in the UK
Stephens and George Ltd, Merthyr Tydfil

Contents

UNIT 4

THE AUTHORS

Nigel Holt works at Bath Spa University and is an active researcher in perception and cognition, and also e-learning. He has substantial experience as a senior examiner for A level psychology and regularly talks to teachers and students around the UK. Nigel is the co-author of a leading university-level introductory textbook, as well as co-editor with Rob Lewis of the Insights in Psychology series.

Rob Lewis is an extremely experienced teacher and examiner. He has over twenty years experience of teaching A level psychology, and for most of that time has also been an A level examiner. He is regularly involved in INSET and CPD events for teachers and currently holds a senior examining post at a major examination board. Rob can currently be found working in the Cardiff School of Education at UWIC.

ACKNOWLEDGEMENTS

We can only thank Kate and Nic and be grateful for their patience during the production of this series of books. Let's just say that it hasn't always been a lot of fun and their support has been unwavering and indispensable. This time we really *do* promise to make sure that we take time off and do our best to remember that home and work are two separate things…. Once again we thank the ever-vigilant JR and the patient folks at Crown.

KEY FEATURES

Each chapter covers a section of the A2 specification, presenting the key information needed for exam success. Full explanations and descriptions aren't provided, although you might find what is offered is sufficient for your understanding. Whilst this book stands independent of the full A2 Level Psychology textbook, you could find it useful to refer occasionally to the full book for a more in-depth treatment.

Ask an examiner

You will notice occasional green boxes in all chapters. These are there just to provide a little advice and guidance in areas where we think a friendly pointer from experienced examiners might be helpful. Sometimes these pointers will be reminders of something you are already very familiar with, but often they offer important tips and warnings about the exam, based on our experience as examiners.

Question time

It is important for you to understand how you will be tested in the examination. To this end, chapters have lots of carefully placed Question Time boxes, giving examples of the types of questions you could be asked. The range of possible questions is limited by the specification, as is their format. This means that if you plan these essays as part of your learning you really will have covered most questions you are likely to be asked.

Get to know your exam

We've included a chapter called 'Get to know your exam' at the back of this book. Our aim with this is to get you familiar with the examination, including advice on the kinds of skills that are being assessed. This chapter also includes some useful advice on how to prepare for your examination. You would be well advised to read this chapter sooner rather than later.

Further help and advice

Your best source of help and advice should be your teacher. However, if you feel you need some further support, you will find no shortage of people, places and resources out there. But proceed with caution. For example, websites are the obvious place to look but these can become out of date very quickly and the quality of material is either poorly monitored or not monitored at all. You could easily end up receiving advice from someone who is really not qualified to offer it, or using supplementary material that is out of date or even plain wrong. We don't want to put you off: we just want you to be aware of the risks. The website we feel most confident of recommending for further revision material is the official AQA one: www.aqa.org.uk. On here you will find copies of past exam papers (with mark schemes) which you can download and practise, and we recommend you do so as soon as possible.

ISSUES, DEBATES AND APPROACHES IN PSYCHOLOGY

Reductionism

Reductionism is the belief that we can explain behaviour by breaking it down into smaller constituent parts. It comes in many forms – e.g. physiological reductionists might reduce all causes of behaviour to our genetic inheritance, whilst reductionism at a social level considers the influence of others on behaviour.

Only looking at one level of explanations can lead to those explanations being incomplete – e.g. whilst we may gain an understanding of the biology of a mental disorder, we will not fully understand it without considering social influences. The complexities of human behaviour and experience are overlooked.

However, understanding the whole organism is too complex a problem; it is easier to test smaller parts of the whole. This is a scientific approach which has been very successful in increasing our understanding of aspects of behaviour.

Determinism

The determinism debate revolves around the extent to which our behaviour is the result of forces over which we have no control or whether people are able to exert free will and decide for themselves how to behave.

Deterministic explanations have been criticised because they reduce a person's responsibility for their own behaviour.

However, determinism is scientific, since science is interested in laws that determine events. Some argue that this should also be the goal of psychology.

The problem in psychology, however, is that behaviour is not absolutely determined – the everyday observation that people are unpredictable tells us that.

The nature/nurture debate

This revolves around whether our behaviour is predetermined by our genes or whether it is a result of learning from the environment.

The nature view argues that individual differences in behaviour are due to inherited differences in such things as neurochemistry, hormones and brain structure. The nurture view on the other hand states that we are born a 'blank slate' and all knowledge and behaviour is the result of experience.

Any view which takes an extreme position one way or the other can be criticised as being overly reductionist and as underestimating either genetic or environmental influences.

Nowadays it is accepted by most that both nature and nurture are important and discussion now revolves around the relative contribution of each.

Gender bias

If research is biased towards men or women then it doesn't provide a clear view of the behaviour being studied.

A male-dominant (*androcentric*) view can be biased so that male-female differences are exaggerated (*alpha bias*); or so that differences are minimised (*beta bias*), meaning that unique female life experiences are ignored. Gender bias may also be seen in how research results are reported (null results – i.e. that there are no gender differences – are less likely to be reported than ones which suggest a difference). There may also be a methodological bias – e.g. the sample or task may be biased towards one sex.

It has been argued that differences that do exist are subtle and appear when results are averaged over many participants. However, these differences may be exaggerated to emphasise them and contribute to male gender supremacy in society.

Cultural bias
Cultures differ in many ways and have a major impact on individuals within them. This means that findings of research conducted in one culture may not apply directly to another. To misapply research findings in this way would create bias, and such cultural bias serves to exaggerate cultural differences and misunderstandings.

Where one culture is judged in terms of the norms of another, there is *ethnocentric bias*, which can distort cultural differences.

Most psychological research is North American and uses largely white participants. Applying findings from such research to other cultures would be to take an *emic* approach. It has been argued therefore that research should only be conducted from the perspective of the culture in which it has taken place. This is called an *etic* approach (the investigation of a culture from within the culture itself), and is a way to reduce ethnocentric bias.

Research is not culturally biased because it has only looked at one culture; bias comes from the conclusions drawn from the findings. In many circumstances it may be reasonable to draw general conclusions, however – e.g. when there are assumed to be universal similarities such as in the functioning of the nervous system.

Ethical issues in research
Research has not been conducted ethically where there has not been sufficient care for its participants.

It is almost impossible to conduct psychological research which does not in some way raise an ethical issue. There are ways of dealing with many ethical issues, but rarely ways of completely eliminating them. Ultimately, psychologists must ask themselves whether the ends justify the means: i.e. all research with either humans or animals must be considered in terms of the value of the results when compared to the costs (both moral and financial).

Some departures from ethical norms – for example deception, where participants are not fully informed – are acceptable within a cost-benefit framework, and do not reflect badly on the research itself. The value of research becomes questionable when there is clear evidence of a significant departure from professional ethics or codes of practice. Whilst there are examples of this in psychological research, they are very rare.

Approaches in Psychology

APPROACH	STRENGTHS	WEAKNESSES
Behavioural *Basic assumption*: All behaviour is learned, e.g. through classical and operant conditioning.	The approach is able to explain a great many behaviours using few concepts, so is parsimonious. It uses a scientific methodology to explain behaviour.	The focus on observable phenomena means that important influences on behaviour are overlooked. The emphasis on the role of the environment in learning and behaviour (nurture) means that it does not take into account the impact of nature.
Biological *Basic assumption*: Behaviour is the result of our biology.	Provides scientific explanations based on sound methodology. Research has resulted in many effective practical applications – e.g. drug therapies.	Because of a reductionist approach, other levels of explanation (e.g. social) tend to be ignored. It has difficulty explaining aspects of behaviour that are not readily observable – e.g. emotion. Human behaviour is very complex and influenced by many factors, so there is a risk of oversimplification with just this approach alone.
Cognitive *Basic assumption*: Behaviour is the result of mental processes.	Focuses on hard-to-investigate aspects of behaviour using rigorous scientific methodology. Led to useful practical applications, such as therapy.	Can oversimplify very complex behaviours by just focusing on very specific aspects of cognition. Uses hypothetical constructs to explain behaviour – e.g. motivation is said to influence memory, but neither is directly observable. Theories are based on mostly artificial laboratory research, so may lack ecological validity.
Psychodynamic *Basic assumption*: Behaviour is the result of unconscious forces.	The theory provided a framework for understanding psychological phenomena that is not available by strictly scientific means. Encouraged psychologists to consider the importance of unconscious processes influencing behaviour.	The theory is untestable and therefore unscientific, so explanations based on the theory are similarly flawed. Explanations are very deterministic, in that a focus on the unconscious forces means that conscious deliberate behaviour is overlooked.
Social *Basic assumption*: Behaviour is heavily influenced by the presence of others.	Research often uses real-life situations to study behaviour. This means that explanations can have high ecological validity. Real-life research leads to real-life application of theory.	Research is often at the limits of what is ethically acceptable – e.g. deception is usually required. Because research is often very situation-specific, the findings may not be generalisable to other contexts and situations.

Biological rhythms and sleep

You are expected in the examination to show both the skills of knowledge and understanding and the skills of analysis and evaluation in relation to the topic Biological rhythms and sleep.

Where opportunities for their effective use arise, you will need to demonstrate an appreciation of issues and debates. These include the nature/nurture debate, ethical issues in research, free-will/ determinism, reductionism, gender and culture bias, and the use of animals in research.

You will also need to demonstrate an understanding of How Science Works. You can do this through the effective use of studies in your answer (as description or evaluation) or, where appropriate, by evaluating methodology and findings.

WHAT YOU NEED TO KNOW

BIOLOGICAL RHYTHMS

- Circadian, ultradian and infradian rhythms, including the role of endogenous pacemakers and of exogenous zeitgebers
- The consequences of disrupting biological rhythms, e.g. shift work, jet lag

SLEEP STATES

- The nature of sleep
- Functions of sleep, including restoration theory and evolutionary explanations
- Lifespan changes in sleep

DISORDERS OF SLEEP

- Explanations for insomnia, including primary and secondary insomnia and factors influencing insomnia, e.g. apnoea, personality
- Explanations for other sleep disorders, including narcolepsy and sleepwalking

SECTION 1: BIOLOGICAL RHYTHMS

Biological rhythms are bodily cycles that repeat themselves over a period of time. These are assumed to be controlled by endogenous (internal) pacemakers, which are in turn influenced to a greater or lesser degree by exogenous (external) cues (sometimes referred to as 'zeitgebers').

CIRCADIAN RHYTHMS – 24 HOUR (DAILY) CYCLES

Many aspects of our behaviour change within the 24 hour daily cycle, including temperature, hormone secretion and sleep.

Endogenous control

The most important internal clock in most animals has been identified as the suprachiasmatic nucleus (SCN), located in the hypothalamus.

Evidence from research

Stephan and Zucker (1973) – damaging the SCN of rats influenced a number of circadian rhythms, including drinking and wheel-running.

Support

Inouye and Kawamura (1979) – animal SCN tissue kept alive in an organ culture so that it was isolated from all other brain activity continued to exhibit circadian rhythms.

Ralph et al (1990) – took the SCN from a hamster which had a circadian rhythm mutated to a shortened 20.2 hours, and transplanted it into another hamster with a normal 24 hour circadian rhythm. On recovery, the recipient hamster exhibited a circadian rhythm very similar to that of the donor.

Endogenous control or exogenous influence?

Light is regarded as the primary zeitgeber for the SCN. Without this zeitgeber, cycles become 'free-running', i.e. not tied to a 24 hour light/dark cycle. Thus, zeitgebers *influence* rather than *control* rhythms.

Evidence from research

Aschoff (1975) – people kept in underground bunkers (eliminating zeitgebers) kept a natural cycle of activity, suggesting an internal clock.

Support

Michael Siffre (1972) – spent 205 days deep in a cave. He was free to light his work-place when he wanted but had no knowledge of the light/dark cycles in the outside world. His sleep/wake cycle adjusted over time to approximately 25 hours.

Richter (1968) – recorded the rest-activity cycles of a blinded squirrel monkey for over three years. Whilst its cycles became 'free-running', the rest-activity cycles themselves varied by only a few minutes during this time.

Discuss the role of endogenous pacemakers and exogenous zeitgebers in one or more biological rhythms. (9 + 16 marks)

When learning about the three biological rhythms you must *do it in the context of evidence for and against endogenous pacemakers and exogenous zeitgebers. Questions will require you to know about* both *of these.*

INFRADIAN RHYTHMS – OCCUR LESS THAN ONCE IN EVERY 24 HOURS

Endogenous control of infradian rhythms

Evidence from animals kept in carefully controlled conditions shows that annual cycles may be internally controlled.

Evidence for endogenous control

Pengelly et al (1978) – body weight of hamsters kept for 3 years in 24 hour light and at a constant temperature fluctuated as it would have in natural circannual rhythms.

Support

Alexander and Brooks (1999) – kept cobra snakes at 25 degrees and in unnatural 12 hours light/12 hours dark daily cycle for 7 years. Skin Shedding was linked to the natural cycle outside the laboratory.

However, evidence for exogenous influence

Goss (1977) – Sika Deer antlers shedding is closely associated with the lengthening of days as summer approached. Fawns kept in carefully controlled light conditions could be encouraged to grow and shed antlers by controlling the levels of light they experienced.

MENSTRUAL CYCLE

Occurs once a month, and is a series of physical and hormonal changes related to fertility.

Endogenous pacemakers

The cycle is controlled by hormones released by the pineal gland in the brain. Reiberg (1967) found that a woman living in a cave showed a shortened menstrual cycle, indicating that in the absence of exogenous zeitgebers a cycle is maintained.

Exogenous zeitgebers

Many people believe that women living or working closely with one another synchronize their menstrual cycles. It has been suggested that *pheromones* released by the women initiate the synchrony, although there is no sound evidence for this.

Evidence for exogenous influence

McClintock (1971) – her research suggested that women living together in university halls of residence synchronise their menstrual cycles.

Weller and Weller (1993) – menstrual cycles of women living together as mother and daughter or in lesbian partnerships tended to synchronize.

Russell et al (1980) – encouraged menstrual synchrony by applying cotton pads to the upper lip which had been held in the armpits of other women.

Evidence against exogenous influence

Yang and Schank (2006) – 186 Chinese women living in university accommodation showed no menstrual synchrony at all.

Wilson (1992) – suggested that research was methodologically and statistically flawed.

QUESTION TIME?

(a) Outline two or more *biological rhythms*. *(9 marks)*

(b) Assess the role of endogenous pacemakers in any one of the rhythms outlined in (a). *(16 marks)*

ASK AN EXAMINER

Research into three examples of infradian rhythms is presented here, which gives you plenty of material to gain marks to write about this rhythm specifically, or to select it when responding to a general question which enables you to write about one or more biological rhythms.

HIBERNATION

A response to a harsh climate, this lasts up to 7 or 8 months. Metabolism, kidney and heart function all change during hibernation.

Endogenous pacemaker

It is thought that hormones control the changes in body function, allowing animals to prepare for harsh winter months.

> **Evidence for endogenous pacemaker**
> Dawe and Spurrier (1968) – blood from hibernating squirrels encouraged hibernation in awake donor ones within 48 hours of the transfusion.

→

> **Support**
> Myers et al (1981) – substance from the plasma of hiberating squirrels injected into the brain of the macaque monkey (an animal that does not normally hibernate) encouraged heart and temperature changes related to hibernation.

Exogenous zeitgeber

External indicators like harsher weather and shorter days indicate to animals that they should begin to hibernate. For eample, black bears normally hibernate in the wild. In captivity, where there is regular food and shelter, they do not. This suggests that the food and shelter cues (external) are important for hibernation to occur.

SEASONAL AFFECTIVE DISORDER (SAD)

Some people suffer annual bouts of depression during the winter months. The problem appears to be related to levels of light.

Endogenous pacemakers

Many researchers point to a key role played by melatonin – levels increase during darkness and release is suppressed by light. It has been suggested that SAD occurs because of increased melatonin secreted by the pineal gland during the darker winter months.

Exogenous zeitgebers

Because a lack of light seems related to the onset of SAD, treating people with light may be helpful.

> **Evidence for exogenous influence**
> Eastman et al (1998) – exposure to bright light as a treatment significantly helps those who suffer with SAD, with a partial or full remission of their symptoms.

> **Evidence against endogenous control of SAD**
> Postolache et al (1998) – full remission of the kind that happens in the summer does not occur with light treatment. This may be due to a number of things such as the UV content of the light.
>
> Other external issues influencing SAD may be personal finance issues experienced during the winter and reduced social contact.
>
> Some research suggests that people with SAD secrete melatonin normally.

Outline and evaluate research into one or more biological rhythms. (9 + 16 marks)

Exam questions often give you a choice about how many things to write about – 'one or more', 'at least one' etc. Doing more than one means that you write less about each. This is especially useful for the evaluation marks – the more things you describe, the more things you have to evaluate!

ULTRADIAN RHYTHMS – OCCUR MORE THAN ONCE IN EVERY 24 HOURS

The different stages of sleep are collectively an ultradian rhythm, as is the 'basic rest activity cycle (BRAC)'. These are largely under endogenous (internal) control.

Stages of Sleep

Sleep largely consists of several 90 minute cycles of REM and NREM sleep. NREM (stages 1 to 4 of sleep) differs from REM in terms of physical and brain activity. Stages 3 and 4 are known as slow wave sleep (SWS). REM (rapid eye movement sleep – also known as dream sleep) occurs after stage 4.

Evidence for endogenous control

Jouvet (1972) – damaging the brain stem of cats in the area of the locus coeruleus removed REM sleep.

Support

Webster and Jones (1985) – the quantity of destroyed cells sensitive to the neurotransmitter *acetylecholine* was related to the amount of REM lost.

Hobson et al (1975) – REM/NREM cycle is generated by contrasting activities of REM-on and REM-off cells in the brain stem.

Little evidence for significant exogenous influence – sleep cycles are largely under endogenous control.

Basic rest activity cycle (BRAC)

Rest and activity tend to fluctuate in cycles. It is thought that sleep itself is an aspect of night-time BRAC. In theory, the system that controls sleep cycles at night also controls cycles during the day.

Evidence for BRAC

Klein and Armitage (1979) – performance on cognitive tasks through the day fluctuated on a 96 minute cycle, similar in length to the sleep cycle.

Hiatte and Kripke (1975) – the BRAC may be a feeding cycle, driven by how often we have to eat. Balloons inflated inside the stomachs of participants allowed them to monitor stomach contractions and they found an 8 hour cycle. Evidence, they said, that the BRAC was driven by food requirements.

Evidence against BRAC

Okudaira et al (1983) investigated wrist, ankle and forehead activity for 24 hours and found no rhythms at all in their study of bodily activity.

Neubauer and Freudenthaler (1994) gave a cognitive task every 10 minutes for 9 hours and found no evidence for a performance cycle.

Conclusion?

There is evidence then that there are ultradian rhythms at day and at night, but there is very little support for the notion that the same BRAC system controls daily cycles as well as nightly sleep cycles.

It is possible that an exam question could require you to write about a specific biological rhythm – that is, circadian, infradian or ultradian. We've organized this section so that you can clearly see research evidence related to the role of both endogenous and exogenous factors in each rhythm.

THE EXTENDED WRITTEN RESPONSE

OUTLINE AND EVALUATE RESEARCH INTO ENDOGENOUS PACEMAKERS AND EXOGENOUS ZEITGEBERS IN TWO BIOLOGICAL RHYTHMS.
(9 + 16 MARKS)

Circadian rhythms occur over a 24 hour cycle. In the early 1970's, researchers discovered that the endogenous pacemaker responsible for this rhythm was located in a part of the hypothalamus called the suprachiasmatic nucleus (SCN). Stephan and Zucker (1973) found that damaging the SCN in rats affected a number of circadian rhythms, including drinking and wheel-running. In other research, Inouye and Kawamura (1979) kept SCN tissue alive in an organic culture and found that the cells continued to show circadian rhythms.

Further support for an endogenous pacemaker in the SCN comes from Ralph et al (1990). They transplanted the SCN of a hamster with a mutated 20.2 hour rhythm into the brain of a hamster with a normal 24 hour rhythm. On recovery, the hamster began showing behaviours following the shorter circadian rhythm of the donor. This research might be accused, however, of being a little too reductionist. It is focusing very much on the cellular activity of a very small part of the brain, and does not seem to be considering the importance of environmental influences on rhythms.

There is research suggesting that environmental factors are important in maintaining a circadian rhythm. Without light as a zeitgeber, after 205 days living deep in a cave, Siffre found that his sleep/wake cycle had shifted from 24 to 25 hours. It seems that light has an influence on the rhythm of the SCN rather than a control. This is supported by many studies, for example by Richter (1968) who found that whilst the circadian rhythm of a blinded squirrel monkey became free running, circadian cycles varied by no more than a few minutes over three years.

Another biological rhythm is the infradian rhythm. This is when cycles are greater than 24 hours. Some of these are annual cycles, which appear to be under endogenous control. Pengelly et al (1978) kept hamsters in constant light and temperature for three years and found that body weight fluctuated according to a natural annual rhythm. There does seem to be some exogenous influence, however, as Goss (1977) found with Sika deer. He could influence annual shedding and growing of antlers by manipulating levels of light.

Another infradian cycle is menstruation, a monthly series of physical and hormonal changes related to fertility. This is endogenously controlled by hormones released from the pineal gland. Reiberg (1967) are found that a woman who lived for a time in a cave in the absence of exogenous zeitgebers maintained a regular monthly menstrual rhythm.

What's it really asking?
You need to outline (i.e. no huge detail) and evaluate RESEARCH into *both* factors. You don't need equal balance between the two, but make sure that there is a clear reference to endogenous *and* exogenous factors. Since you also need research into TWO biological rhythms then it is best to organise your answer around this. Beware – failure to address all parts of this question will result in partial performance – you lose lots of marks!

After the first descriptive paragraph outlining research, we move onto evaluation. Notice that in this first part of the answer we are just focusing on the circadian rhythm.

I&D
Notice how we've explained why the research might be considered reductionist – the term hasn't been 'plonked' in.

In this first part of the answer, we've just focused on circadian rhythms, and we have tried to make really clear when we are talking about endogenous pacemakers AND exogenous zeitgebers.

We move onto a second rhythm here, starting with an outline of research to ensure we get all those descriptive marks. We quickly, however, move onto evaluation.

Research by McClintock (1971), however, suggested that women living or working closely together in a university hall of residence tended to synchronise their menstrual cycles. She further suggested that this synchrony is caused by the release of pheromones. This is supported by Russell et al (1980) who claim to have encouraged synchrony by applying cotton pads to the upper lip of volunteers which had previously been held under the armpits of other women. Unfortunately, there is no good scientific evidence for such pheromones.

Wilson (1992) has pointed to serious methodological and statistical problems in this research, however, for example indicating that measures of synchrony are flawed. Indeed, in the largest study of its kind, involving 186 women living in university accommodation, and avoiding the flaws of previous research, Yang and Schank (2006) could find no evidence of menstrual synchrony.

> There are a lot more marks available for evaluation than description, so we must get the balance right. The answer ends here with a paragraph of extended evaluation

Comments

The essay specifically asks for research and asks for it to be evaluated. Where research is outlined here (and remember, 'outline' does not require great detail) it is followed by further research used as evaluation. Five studies are outlined for the descriptive marks and, whilst each alone is fairly brief, together they add up to something altogether more substantial.

Of course, you can't put everything you have learned into your answer as you will run out of time, so you have to be selective. This is a tricky question, requiring several things from you – a focus on research, endogenous pacemakers and exogenous zeitgebers, as well as covering two rhythms. This is why planning and preparation are so very important.

CONSEQUENCES OF DISRUPTING BIOLOGICAL RHYTHMS

Biological rhythms are synchronized to the light-dark zeitgeber. Animals (including humans) can adjust to slow changes in this zeitgeber. However, rapid changes can disrupt biological rhythms, with consequences for health and behaviour.

Jet lag

Jet lag is caused by flying across time zones. e.g. because it is five hours behind the UK, flying from London at 1pm means that you would arrive in New York at 3.30pm, even though the flight time is 7.5 hours. This causes a conflict between zeitgebers, which tell us one time, and our biological clocks, which are telling us it is another.

Generally, eastward flights (e.g. New York to London) cause the greatest problems (there is phase advance – backward shift – in the 24 hour cycle). In effect, our body finds it harder to adjust to a shorter day than to a longer one.

Effects of jet lag – evidence from research

Spitzer et al (1997) – Jet lag shows itself as cognitive disturbances including reduced alertness, clumsiness, memory problems and general tiredness.

Cho (2001) – Jet lag causes increases in cortisol, the stress hormone. Repeated increases in cortisol can effect the brain physically. The research showed smaller temporal lobes and poorer visuo-spatial performance in women who had less time to recover from regular flights than in those who had longer to recover.

Evidence for consequences of jet lag – sporting performance

Sasaki et al (1980) – a Russian volleyball team flying east into the Japanese timezone for a tournament performed badly for the first few games but then improved. This was put down to west-east jet lag and the difficult phase advance correction. The research, however, ignored individual differences and variations in team performance as well as ability of opponents.

O'Conor et al (1991) – athletes flying west for training suffered on average a day less with jet lag symptoms than athletes flying east.

Recht et al (1995) – baseball teams in America from the east coast who flew west for games did better than teams from the west coast who flew east.

Evidence for consequences of jet lag – risk of cancer

Rafnsson et al (2001) – of 1500 female flight attendants, those flying for over 5 years had double the risk of breast cancer.

Kojo et al (2005) – Could find no increased risk of breast cancer that could not be attributed to other risk factors, such as family history.

Filipski et al, (2004) – Simulated repeated jet lag in animals and found accelerated cancer tumour growth in jet lagged animals compared to animals reared normally.

Gauger and Sancar (2005) – suggest it is light rather than rhythm disturbance that causes cancer. Light reduces levels of melatonin, which in turn is linked to the development of cancer.

QUESTION TIME 'Research has consistently shown that whilst biological rhythms have endogenous pacemakers, some rhythms are significantly influenced by exogenous zeitgebers.' Discuss the role of exogenous zeitgebers in biological rhythms. (9 + 16 marks)

IDea It could be argued that some of the research into the consequences of jet lag on sporting performance is too reductionist. It focuses solely on the disruption of biological clocks caused by crossing time zones and tends to overlook other important influences, like variations in motivation and individual differences in team members.

Shift work

Shift work is any work outside normal daytime hours (i.e. between 7pm and 7am). Biological clocks are not designed for activity outside these times and so are disrupted.

The most disruptive kinds of shift work are those that include night work. There is evidence to suggest that night shift work can be harmful to health, and it has been linked to diabetes, cancer, hypertension and gastric and immune system problems.

Evidence of consequences of shift work – accidents and heart disease

Czeisler et al (1985) – US police officers on night shift had 4 times as many accidents as those on day shift. This was improved hugely by changing shift patterns, i.e. how many night shifts a person worked before moving onto day shifts, and how the day/night hours were allocated.

Knutson et al (1999) – night shift increased the risk of heart attack by 30% in men and women who had been doing night shifts for 16 to 20 years.

Evidence of consequences of shift work – risk of cancer

Research on incidence

Kubo et al (2006) – men in Japan who worked any kind of night shift (either regular or with rotating day/night schedules) were 4 times more likely to develop prostate cancer than other workers.

Shernhammer et al (2001) – for US nurses, the risk of breast cancer increased significantly with the number of years spent working nights.

Schwartzbaum et al (2007) – could find no link between night shift work and cancer, although the study has been criticised on its methodology.

Research on possible causal mechanisms

Swerdlow (2003) – reduced levels of melatonin cause increased levels of hormones associated with breast cancer.

Schernhammer and Hankinson (2003) – blind women who do not have melatonin suppressed by light have lower incidence of breast cancer.

Spiegel and Sephton (2002) – disagree with melatonin being a cause and suggest that cancer is due to disruptions in the release of cortisol.

QUESTION TIME
(a) Outline the nature of sleep. (9 marks)
(b) Assess the consequences of disrupting biological rhythms. (16 marks)

ASK AN EXAMINER
Whilst questions won't ask specifically for jet lag or shift work, knowing about both gives you the kind of depth of knowledge that makes it easier to get high marks.

IDea
Whilst some individual pieces of research could be accused of having a gender bias, overall, research into the consequences of disrupting biological rhythms through shiftwork has avoided this problem. Research has considered the consequences for both men and women across a range of occupations.

QUESTION TIME
(a) Outline the role of endogenous pacemakers in any one biological rhythm. (4 marks)
(b) Outline and evaluate evolutionary explanations of the function of sleep. (21 marks)

QUESTION TIME
(a) Outline and evaluate the restoration theory of the function of sleep. (4 + 8 marks)

SECTION 2: SLEEP STATES

THE NATURE OF SLEEP

Sleep is a behaviour seen in all mammals, with something resembling mammalian sleep occurring in all other species.

The circadian rhythm of sleep

Sleep follows a circadian rhythm. Light signals to the SCN from the retina influence sleep and arousal states whilst also influencing the pineal gland in its production of melatonin.

The ultradian rhythm of sleep

Sleep is traditionally broken down into a series of stages, according to the activity of the brain. Stages 1 to 4 are known as NREM, which are followed by REM sleep. NREM/REM cycle throughout the night, controlled endogenously.

THE NATURE OF SLEEP

Disorders of sleep

The most common sleep problem is insomnia, of which there are two types: primary and secondary. One common cause of insomnia is apnoea, but it has also been related to mental health and brain injury.

Functions of sleep

Evolutionary explanations suggest that we sleep to conserve energy and to avoid predators. Indeed, many of the sleep habits of animals can be understood by considering their ecological niche. However, it may also be that sleep serves to restore the body after the wear and tear of waking activity. Evolution and restoration theories are not necessarily exclusive – even though sleep evolved for survival reasons it could also have evolved restorative functions, since sleep provides an ideal opportunity for them.

Sleep and ageing

There are age-related changes in sleep, including total sleep time and changes in the structure of sleep. After birth, sleep gradually changes to resemble adult sleep by adolescence, with both total sleep and REM sleep declining. A key change in old age is more awakening during the night and increases in daytime naps.

Discuss the nature of sleep. (9 + 16 marks)

Using evidence from research, discuss the consequences of disrupting biological rhythms. (9 + 16 marks)

A question on the nature of sleep is dead easy to answer. Anything which tells us something about sleep is saying something about its nature. Carefully select content from the various topics in this section and form them into an extended response – remember all the rules of writing EWR's – description, evaluation, research and I&D!

QUESTION TIME ?

(a) Outline evolutionary explanations of sleep. (9 marks)
(b) Evaluate evolutionary explanations of sleep. (16 marks)

FUNCTIONS OF SLEEP – RESTORATION THEORIES

Being awake involves wear and tear on the body, and sleep is a time when repair and restoration can best take place.

1. The growth and repair hypothesis

Patterns of brain activity change during sleep to allow restoration.

According to Oswald (1980) REM allows restoration and reorganization of of the nervous system and NREM (especially SWS) allows general body repair through the release of growth hormone (GH).

Horne (1988) claims that repair generally happens during *core sleep* (REM and SWS) but without REM and SWS repair could take place in *optional* sleep (everything else) or even during relaxed wakefulness.

Evaluation

A. *Sleep deprivation studies*. These studies only suggest some kind of physiological function of sleep. They do not tell us what it is.

» Randy Gardner stayed awake for 264 hours, suffering hallucinations and lapses of concentration. His sleep for the following week showed that he made up for lost SWS and REM, suggesting a restorative function of sleep. However, this was a poorly recorded case study.

» Animal studies indicate a restorative function, but it is difficult to separate the effects of sleep loss from the effects of stress caused by the method used to keep them awake. Coren (1996) – older dogs tend to die after 13 days of total sleep deprivation whilst puppies die after about 6 days. Rechtshaffen (1983) – rats die after 13-21 days of total sleep deprivation.

B. *Increased exercise*. The more activity in the day, the more we might expect to need to sleep to restore the body.

» Shapiro et al (1981) – 56 mile ultra-marathon runners slept considerably more for 2 days following the race, with much more (up to 45%) SWS and less REM.

» Adey et al (1968) – paralyzed people should need less sleep to restore their bodies according to the restoration theory but infact had only a small reduction in SWS compared to non-paralyzed sleepers.

» Horne and Horley (1989) – it is not the amount of exercise that increases the amount of sleep needed but the increase in brain temperature caused by exercise. Raising the head temperature of physically relaxed participants by 1% with a hairdryer increased the amount of SWS in the sleep cycle that followed.

ASK AN EXAMINER

As with evolution theory, there is more than one kind of restoration theory of sleep. Learning more than one under the heading of 'restoration theory' will give you more to describe and evaluate, and therefore you'll have a better chance of getting marks. And, like evolutionary explanations, the restoration theories don't need to be written about in exactly the same detail.

2. The cell-repair hypothesis

Sleep allows maintenance of the body at a cellular level. The damage is caused by oxidative stress, a result of the increased metabolic activity when awake.

Evaluation

» Ramanathan et al (2002) – sleep-deprived rats showed cell damage in the hippocampus and brain stem.

» Smaller animals with faster metabolic rates (where there is more cell damage) sleep more than larger animals with slower metabolisms (where there is less cell damage).

3. Neurogenesis theory

Whilst most brain cells do not regenerate, some of those in the hippocampus (part of the brain important for storing memories) do. Sleep is a time for new cell formation.

Evaluation

» Guzmán-Marín et al (2003) – numbers of new cells reduced by 50% in rats deprived of sleep for four days.

» Guzmán-Marín et al (2005) – cells formed during sleep depravation do not mature normally and thus do not function properly.

LIFE SPAN CHANGES IN SLEEP

Pre-natal and infant sleep

» Okai et al (1982) – at 28 weeks gestation, REM in the unborn child is hard to identify but by 32 weeks it is clearly present.

» This correlates with the development of brain structures important in REM and NREM control.

» The newborn sleeps for about 17 hours a day, 50% in REM, in bursts of 3–4 hours. This declines during the first year to about 13 sleep hours.

» At 1 year sleep lasts about 13 hours, with about 4 hours of REM a night.

» From 5 yrs to adolescence sleep continues to fall to about 8 hours a night.

Factors influencing infant sleep

Infant sleep changes because parents try and encourage them into a cycle.

» Armitage et al (2009) – children of depressed mothers have different sleep patterns than those of non-depressed mothers, sleeping more erratically and taking longer to fall asleep.

» Baird et al (2009) – mothers who experienced pre-conceptual depression had children who were 23% more likely to wake between midnight and 6am.

Adolescent Sleep

» Changes that happen to sleep patterns in adolescence are largely due to changing social pressures – staying out later, waking later, less parental influence.

» Crowley et al (2007) – sleep patterns vary according to the school year.

• Sleep during school term is affected by extra-curricular activities, social activities, TV, internet.

• Compensation comes with increased sleep at weekends.

• This has the effect of giving adolescents a weekend 'jet lag', resulting in poor school performance.

ASK AN EXAMINER

It makes sense to learn about lifespan changes in sleep in the order in which they happen. This will give your exam answer a look of being organized, as well giving the impression that you are really covering the lifespan.

QUESTION TIME ?

Discuss research into lifespan changes in sleep. (9 + 16 marks)

Adult sleep

» Sleep does not change much after the age of 60 in healthy people.

» Older adults:

• are more easily woken

• are more sensitive to noise

• wake more often in the night

• nap more often throughout the day (caused by waking more often)

• are more likely to have sleep disturbed by medical problems

	Adults 19–59 years	Older adults 60–102 years
Total sleep time	⇓	⇔
Sleep latency (time from full wakefulness to sleep)	⇔	⇔
WASO (wake after sleep onset)	⇑	⇔
Sleep efficiency (the amount of sleep time actually spent sleeping)	⇓	⇓
Percent stage 1	⇑	⇔
Percent stage 2	⇑	⇔
Percent SWS	⇓	⇔
Percent REM	⇓	⇔
REM latency (amount of time before REM sleep begins)	⇔	⇔

Adapted from Vitello (2006).
Key: ⇔ = remains the same; ⇓ = decreases;
⇑ = increases
Summary of significant findings from Ohayon et al (2004).

SECTION 3: DISORDERS OF SLEEP

INSOMNIA

Insomnia is a reduction in sleep resulting from difficulty getting to sleep, difficulty staying asleep, waking too early, or a combination of these. It is very widespread (Morin et al (2009) found it in 76% of adults in their survey). It may be *acute* (coming and going for 4 weeks to 6 months) or *persistent* (it lasts for over 6 months), and comes in two forms: *primary* and *secondary*.

Primary Insomnia

This is where insomnia is caused by something other than a disease process, i.e. it is not caused by drug, psychiatric or environmental influences.

Hyper-arousal hypothesis

It is usually associated with increased body temperature, heart rate and metabolic rate over a 24-hour period. Insomniacs may sleep less at night and may actually feel more awake than non-insomniacs during the day. It is thought that this 'hyper-arousal hypothesis' explains the sleep disturbance. It may also be influenced by personality and genetic characteristics.

Evidence for the hyper-arousal hypothesis

Vgontzas et al (2001) – higher levels of ACTH (a stress hormone related to arousal) in insomniacs.

Nofzinger et al (2004) – the usual decrease in brain activity in some areas of the brain in sleep is not present in insomniacs so, even when asleep, insomniacs are still aroused.

Winkelman et al (2008) – those with persistent insomnia showed reduced levels of GABA, (a neurotransmitter associated with reduced brain activity). They appear not to be able to 'switch off' at night.

Genetic influences on insomnia

Some researchers believe that insomnia is genetic. Joho et al (2008) for example found mutated genes in mice who slept 50-60% less than normal mice.

Evidence for a genetic influence

Beaulieu-Bonneau et al (2007) – 37% of insomniacs had a close relative with the problem

Watson et al (2006) – monozygotic twin insomnia was highly correlated (0.47) but dizygotic twin insomnia was not.

The influence of personality

Because personality is relatively stable (it doesn't come and go) it is not hugely influenced by medical issues (which come and go), as in secondary insomnia and so it relates better to primary insomnia.

Evidence for the influence of personality

Kales et al (1976) – insomniacs share certain personality characteristics. These include how they handle stress and conflict by internalizing their problems.

Kales et al (1983) – traits such as depression, obsessiveness and inhibition of anger are all shared in insomniacs.

Saint-Hilaire et al (2005) – certain personality traits, such as harm avoidance, are closely related to the type of brain activity associated with insomnia.

Outline and evaluate one or more explanations for insomnia.
(9 + 16 marks)

You may be asked specifically for primary and/or secondary insomnia in the exam, so make sure you know what they both are, and how both can be explained.

Secondary Insomnia

This is where insomnia is caused or made worse by disease processes and interventions, which include drugs and other treatment and physical and psychiatric disorders. For instance, pain (as experienced with arthritis) can influence sleep, so the resulting insomnia is 'secondary' to this medical condition.

Insomnia and drugs

Both medication (such as drugs to help sleeping) and leisure drugs (such as smoking and alcohol) are associated with insomnia.

Evidence for the influence of drugs

Bardage and Isacson (2002) – 20% of those using hypertension medication also suffered with insomnia.

Kales et al (1978) – withdrawing from sedatives that are used to treat insomnia can lead to even heavier use of the drug as the user has become reliant on it for sleep.

Philips and Danner (1995) – smokers are more likely to be insomniacs than non-smokers.

Insomnia and mental health

Kamerow (1989) claims insomnia is ten times more likely as a result of mental health problems (such as depression and anxiety) than physical ones. Weisz et al (1962) say that 72% of psychiatric patients suffer with insomnia.

Evidence for the influence of mental health

Benca and Peterson (2008) – depression and insomnia are so closely related that they may share similar underlying mechanisms; for example, genetic abnormalities in circadian pacemakers, or shared neurochemical imbalances. However, not all people with insomnia have depression and vice versa.

Steiger (2007) – levels of hormones secreted by the HPA (part of the stress system) normally reduce in the first few hours of sleep, but in depressed people they remain elevated. This fits in with hyper-arousal theory.

Insomnia and brain injury

Many people are diagnosed with insomnia after brain injury.

Evidence for insomnia and brain injury

Cohen et al (1992) – found insomnia incidences of up to 72% in patients with a previous brain injury, which is much higher than the general population.

Ayalon et al (2007) – 40–65% of those with a brain injury suffer with insomnia. Many of their patients suffered circadian rhythm sleep disorder (CRSD), which might be the reason for their insomnia. Treatment for insomnia in such cases is not going to help.

Apnoea and Insomnia

Apnoea means 'stopping breathing'. The most common type is obstructive sleep apnoea (OSA), where breathing tubes become blocked. Central sleep apnoea (CSA) is where the airways remain open, but for some reason the nervous system does not drive the body to breathe. Both can cause sleep disturbance through snoring and choking.

QUESTION TIME

(a) Explain what is meant by the term *primary insomnia*. *(4 marks)*
(b) Outline one *factor influencing insomnia*. *(5 marks)*
(c) Evaluate explanations for any one *sleep disorder*. *(16 marks)*

Narcolepsy

This is excessive daytime sleepiness, and narcoleptics often fall asleep during boring tasks. Some suffer with cataplexy, which is suddenly falling asleep as though a switch has been flicked. It is thought to affect between 0.03 and 0.18% of the population.

Neural explanations

Damage to the hypothalamus (where there are hypocretin (Hcrt) cells) has been found to cause narcolepsy. Reduced levels of the brain chemical hypocretin (Hcrt) are related to narcolepsy.

Evidence for neural explanations

Scammell et al (2001) – a case study of a 23-year-old with a damaged hypothalamus who suffered with narcolepsy showed reduced Hcrt.

Arii et al (2001) – a 16 year old girl with a damaged hypothalamus (thus reduced Hcrt cells) as a result of a tumour developed narcolepsy.

Grashchenko et al (2003) – The more cells in a rat's hypothalamus were damaged, the less hypocretin was released.

Genetic explanations

Since dogs can inherit a genetic defect influencing hypocretin and thus display narcolepsy, this might apply to humans.

Evidence for genetic explanations

It is *not* the same genetic defect causing narcolepsy in dogs and humans. There is no evidence that narcolepsy in humans is absolutely genetic.

It's much more likely that narcolepsy is caused by a combination of genetic and environmental issues, such as hormone levels.

NARCOLEPSY

NEURAL	GENETIC
↓	↓
HYPOTHALAMUS (HCRT CELLS)	NARCOLEPSY GENE FOUND IN DOGS = HUMANS?
↓	↓
DAMAGE CAUSES NARCOLEPSY	○ NO EVIDENCE FOR SAME GENE DEFECT
↓	+
○ SCAMMELL et al – CASE STUDY REDUCED Hcrt	○ ~~NO GOOD HUMAN~~ GENE EVIDENCE
+	+
○ ARII et al – TUMOUR IN HYPOTHALAMUS = NARCOLEPSY	○ GENE + ENVIRONMENT INTERACTION?
+	
○ GRASHCHENKO et al – RATS DAMAGED HYPOTHALAMUS = LESS Hcrt	

Sleepwalking

This is also known as somnambulism, and happens during slow-wave sleep (SWS), appearing to result from an abnormal transition from NREM to REM sleep. Elements of one sleep state (muscle tone in NREM) intrude upon another (dreaming in REM). Episodes can last over 30 minutes and there may be partial or complete amnesia of events during and following the sleepwalk.

Psychodynamic explanation of sleepwalking

Sleepwalking is an expression of our unconscious conflicts. SWS, where the recall of harmful memories is minimal, is the ideal place for this to happen.

Evidence for psychodynamic explanation

There is no evidence for the psychodynamic explanation and most researchers now agree that sleepwalking is biologically based, not psychological. In fact, there is no evidence for a purely psychological explanation of this problem.

Genetic explanations of sleepwalking

In a large sample of identical (MZ) and non-identical (DZ) twins, responses to a questionnaire indicated a substantial genetic influence – Hublin et al (1997).

Evidence for genetic explanations

Bakwin (1970) found that sleepwalking in both MZ twins is more likely (a concordance rate of 47%) than in both DZ twins (concordance of 7%).

Bassetti (2002) – 50% of sleepwalkers carry the HLA gene abnormality found in most narcoleptics.

Neural explanations of sleepwalking

Brain scan studies have suggested the brain is in a different state during sleepwalking episodes.

Evidence for neural explanations

Bassetti et al (2000) – some parts of the brain are 'selectively activated', and some are 'inhibited' during sleepwalking, as indicated by cerebral blood flow.

Karayan (2000) – there is abnormal activity in the temporal lobes. Treatments with anti-convulsive drugs completely removed sleepwalking.

Oliviero (2008) – neurotransmitter GABA released during sleep prevents activity in the brain's motor system. Sleepwalkers have under-developed GABA systems so that physical activity is not inhibited.

ASK AN EXAMINER
Other than insomnia, you are required to know about another two disorders. Narcolepsy and sleepwalking are presented here – don't choose between them, learn them both.

IDea
The best explanations available for sleepwalking appear to be biological – genetic and neural. We should, however, be careful not to conclude that these reductionist explanations provide a complete answer. It is likely that psychological factors (such as anxiety) interact with a biological predisposition to make sleepwalking more likely to occur.

QUESTION TIME
Discuss explanations for two sleep disorders. (9 + 16 marks)

QUESTION TIME
(a) Outline explanations for sleepwalking. (4 marks)
(b) Outline explanations for narcolepsy. (5 marks)
(c) Evaluate explanations for either sleepwalking or narcolepsy. (16 marks)

HOW WELL DO I KNOW IT?	NOT AT ALL	MAYBE	OK	WELL	SUPERBLY
SECTION 1: BIOLOGICAL RHYTHMS					
Circadian rhythms					
Infradian rhythms					
Ultradian rhythms					
Role of endogenous pacemakers					
Role of exogenous zeitgebers					
Consequences of disrupting biological rhythms – Jet Lag					
Consequences of disrupting biological rhythms – Shift work					
SECTION 2: SLEEP STATES					
The nature of sleep					
Functions of sleep: Evolutionary explanations					
Functions of sleep: Restoration theory					
Lifespan changes in sleep					
SECTION 3: DISORDERS OF SLEEP					
Explanations of primary and secondary insomnia					
Factors influencing insomnia: Apnoea					
Factors influencing insomnia: Personality					
Explanations for sleepwalking					
Explanations for narcolepsy					

Perception

You are expected in the examination to show both the skills of knowledge and understanding and the skills of analysis and evaluation in relation to the topic Perception.

Where opportunities for their effective use arise, you will need to demonstrate an appreciation of issues and debates. These include the nature/nurture debate, ethical issues in research, free-will/determinism, reductionism, gender and culture bias, and the use of animals in research.

You will also need to demonstrate an understanding of How Science Works. You can do this through the effective use of studies in your answer (as description or evaluation) or where appropriate by evaluating methodology and findings.

WHAT YOU NEED TO KNOW

THEORIES OF PERCEPTUAL ORGANISATION
- Gibson's bottom-up/direct theory of perception and Gregory's top-down/indirect theory of perception

DEVELOPMENT OF PERCEPTION
- The development of perceptual abilities, e.g. depth/distance, visual constancies, face processing
- Infant and cross-cultural studies of the development of perceptual abilities
- The nature-nurture debate in relation to explanations of perceptual development

FACE RECOGNITION AND VISUAL AGNOSIAS
- Bruce and Young's theory of face recognition, including case studies and explanations of prosopagnosia

SECTION 1: THEORIES OF PERCEPTUAL ORGANISATION

Perceptual organisation refers to how we make sense of the world around us – that is, how we convert the masses of sensations we receive into meaningful perceptions.

GIBSON'S BOTTOM-UP (BU) DIRECT THEORY

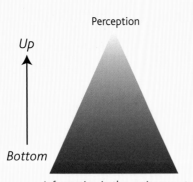

» In order to perceive the world, we need nothing but the information arriving at our senses.
» The **optic array** is the collection of patterns of light entering the eyes, and is basically all of the things we can see at any one time.
» As we move, things which are close to us appear to move faster than those further away. These changes in the optic array make up the **optic flow** and tell us about depth and position.
» Some things always remain the same, even when we move about, such as mountains on the horizon. These are **invariants** and provide us with more information.
» Things nearer to us are larger and take up more of the optic array than things further away. This **texture gradient** provides useful information about depth and distance.
» Many objects 'afford' themselves to a certain task or action: e.g. a knife 'affords' itself to cutting food. Gibson said **affordance** means we need no previous knowledge of forks and knives.

Describe and evaluate Gibson's bottom up/direct theory of perception. (9 + 16 marks)

GREGORY'S TOP-DOWN (TD) INDIRECT THEORY

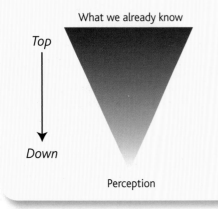

» Sensory information does not always provide us with enough evidence to make sense of things, for example in ambiguous situations.
» In such cases we form **hypotheses** and **test** them against what we know.
» Our stored knowledge then 'guides' our perception.
» We act as 'scientists', forming and testing hypotheses about the world around us.

Describe and evaluate Gregory's top-down/indirect theory of perception. (9 + 16 marks)

ASK AN EXAMINER

If an exam question allows you to write about both theories then do so! It is easier to get detail into your answer this way. However, if you are asked for one theory then it is probably best to choose bottom-up theory, as it has the most detail. Use top-down theory then as evaluation.

A good way of getting evaluation marks is to compare BU and TD theories. Anything else which appears in this section which tells us something about top-down or bottom-up processing (e.g. culture and perception) can also be used as evaluation.

Comparing top-down and bottom-up theories: Evaluation of Gibson and Gregory

THE STUDENT SAYS …	TOP-DOWN THEORY	BOTTOM-UP THEORY	THE EXAMINER SAYS …
'Sometimes different people perceive the same thing differently.'	TD theory says that because people have different experiences they may perceive things differently.	BU theory cannot explain why this happens. If perception was truly 'bottom-up' we should all perceive everything the same.	'BU theory clearly cannot explain this and so this evaluation point supports TD theory and can be used as negative evaluation of BU theory.'
'How am I able to perceive things I have never even seen before?'	TD theory relies heavily on stored knowledge and experience, and so cannot explain how we perceive things we have never experienced.	BU theory can explain this because it does not rely on our past experiences. All items are perceived as if for the first time.	'This is a strong point in favour of BU theory, but the BU claim that everything is new at each perception runs counter to logic and experience.'
'How do you explain this one then? **THE CAT** I can see this as an A or an H'	TD theory would say that this is evidence that we use 'context' in perceiving (i.e. background knowledge).	BU theory says that an identical image (the H) should be perceived the same way each time, but this is not the case here.	'Not only does this evaluation point favour TD theory, it can be used as a negative evaluation of BU theory.'
'Is that the same as this example? **A 13 C**'	TD theory describes this as 'perceptual set' and it is similar to the A/H example. TD theory says that you read a B here (not a 13) because your experience perceptually 'sets' you to read ABC.	BU theory cannot explain this. BU theory would expect the items between A and C to be perceived the same, irrespective of context.	'By using this example in addition to the others you really show you understand this area. Apt examples always help show the examiners that you understand.'
'What about visual illusions and reversible figures like this Necker cube?'	As you stare at the 'cube' it appears to 'flip' or change. This is because we are trying to make sense of what we are seeing based on our experience of the world. Both perspectives are just as likely and therefore both appear.	With just the information provided by the drawing we can conclude two different things – that the 'cube' may be in one 'position' or another. The illusion happens because we experience exactly what we see!	'In this case both the BU and TD theories have equally sensible explanations! There is no explanation that's better, they just explain our perception of the cube differently! This allows you to use this example as evaluation of either theory.'

QUESTION TIME

Discuss one or more theories of perceptual organisation. (9 + 16 marks)

ASK AN EXAMINER

Questions on perceptual development are just that – questions on development. Gibson and Gregory don't really cover that issue very clearly, so questions on development should just include material from section 2. Although we always encourage you to use material from wherever it is relevant, on this occasion ONLY use stuff from section 2 in development questions as it will earn you much better marks.

SECTION 2: THE DEVELOPMENT OF PERCEPTUAL ABILITIES

DEPTH/DISTANCE PERCEPTION
Depth perception relates to how far down something appears to be, whilst distance perception concerns how far away things appear to be.

Infant study: **Perception of depth – the visual cliff (Gibson and Walk, 1960)**

What they did
The apparatus consisted of a sheet of strong glass placed on a chequered pattern surface. Half the glass had a pattern just beneath the surface, after which the pattern dropped away to form a 'cliff'. From above the surface, the pattern looked continuous. Infants were placed on the middle of the glass and the mother called to them either from the 'shallow' or 'deep' side.

What they found
Out of 36 infants between 6 and 14 months, 27 would crawl to their mother over the shallow side. Only 3 would crawl over the deep side. Some infants refused to move at all.

What this means for perceptual development
Infants somehow knew that a drop is dangerous, so must have good depth perception. Such a fear would have clear survival advantages. This means that we must be born with depth perception abilities.

Evaluation of Gibson and Walk
Because the babies had to be mobile to take part in this study (i.e. be at least 6 months old), it could be that they had learned depth perception.

» Campos et al (1970) – studied 2–3 month infants who were too young to crawl, using a visual cliff. They found heart rate actually decreased on the deep side, suggesting that babies *do not* have depth perception. They were more relaxed because the deep side was more visually interesting.

» Nánez (1988) – found that infants as young as 3–6 weeks reacted with avoidance to looming objects that looked as though they were going to 'hit'. This did not happen before 3 weeks, suggesting that avoidance is quickly learned, or is there already but the visual system is not mature.

Infant study: **Perception of distance – interposition (Granrud and Yonas, 1984)**
Objects nearer to us obscure part or all of objects further away. This *interposition* gives clues to distance.

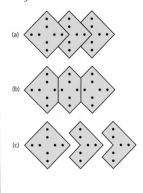

What they did
Children aged between 5 and 7 months were presented with two-dimensional images (see diagram). Some images showed interposition (e.g. the top image, *a*); some did not show interposition but used the same shapes (e.g. the bottom image, *c*); and some did not show interposition (e.g. the middle image, *b*).

What they found
Children aged 7 months reached more often for the image which showed interposition (they perceived one part of the image to be nearer to them).

Children aged 5 months spent the same amount of time reaching for the images showing interposition and those of the same shape without interposition, i.e. *a* and *c*.

What this means for perceptual development
Since 7 month olds could understand interposition but 5 month olds could not, this ability must *develop* between 5 and 7 months. Whilst some aspects of depth and distance perception appear very early on in life, they may not be innate.

The specification requires you to know about studies. You could even get a question asking simply for 'studies', so be sure to learn the details.

VISUAL CONSTANCIES

To have visual constancy means that you know an object remains the same even though what you are seeing seems to change, e.g. the changing shape of a door opening. There are different kind of constancy, e.g. shape and size.

Infant study: Visual constancy – shape (Bower, 1966)

Wooden rectangle at 45 degrees

2 metres

Position of child

What he did
Bower trained very young infants (50 to 60 days old) to expect an exciting 'peek-a-boo' response from the researcher whenever an angled wooden rectangle stimulus was presented. The child was then required to recognise the original stimulus, even when presented in slightly different ways, from similar but different stimuli.

What he found
Children could distinguish the conditioned shape from other similar shapes even when it was presented at different angles.

What this means for perceptual development
Because they understood that the original stimulus was the same despite changes in how it appeared, children of a young age have shape constancy.

Evaluation of Bower
Slater and Morison (1985) found similar results to Bower. Children soon after birth responded not to the shape an object made on the retina, but to the physical properties of the object, showing very early shape constancy. It could be, however, that the skills shown in these two studies are learned quickly at a very young age.

Discuss the development of perceptual abilities. (9 + 16 marks)

Infant study: Visual constancy – size (Bower, 1966)

What he did
6 to 12 week-old babies were rewarded for turning their heads every time they saw a 30 cm cube placed 1 metre away with an enjoyable peek-a-boo game. When they had learned this they were then presented with other cubes, some of which would create the same-size retinal image – for example a 90 cm cube at 3 metres.

What he found
Children demonstrated size constancy by turning their head more times to the 30 cm cube at one metre than to a 90 cm cube at three metres, showing that they were not fooled into thinking that the same retinal image meant the same object.

What this means for perceptual development
Very young children demonstrated size constancy, strongly suggesting that this skill is present at birth.

FACE PROCESSING

Research suggests that face processing may be an innate perceptual skill, with the ability to recognise faces developing gradually over the first year.

Infant study: Face processing – preference for attractiveness (Langlois et al, 1987)

What they did
Infants aged 2–3 months and 6–8 months were shown pairs of colour slides of adult Caucasian women's faces. The faces had previously been rated by adults for attractiveness, and were projected life-size. The amount of time infants spent looking at particular faces was recorded.

What they found
Infants looked longer at attractive than at unattractive faces.

What this means for perceptual development
Very young infants have a built-in preference for attractive faces.

ASK AN EXAMINER

You need to know about the development of at least two perceptual abilities. The three summarised here have plenty of material with which to construct a good detailed answer.

Infant study: Face processing – the looking chamber (Fantz, 1961)

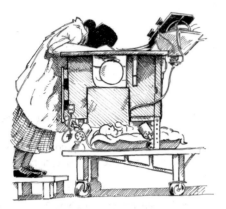

What he did
Fantz placed babies face up on a crib in a chamber, through the top of which he could present visual stimuli. The gaze of the infant was recorded.

What he found
Babies younger than 6 months old showed a clear preference for looking at 'realistic' faces rather than scrambled faces or other patterns.

What this means for perceptual development
At a very young age, infants know what faces are and have a preference for looking at them.

Evaluation of Fantz
The study doesn't prove that babies are born with face processing skills, since the babies tested had at least a few days' visual experience so they might have learned during this time that faces are interesting.

 Outline and evaluate two or more infant studies of the development of perceptual abilities. (9 + 16 marks)

Research has shown that infants exhibit a range of face processing skills which are unlikely to have been learned with so limited experience. Neonates can make sophisticated judgments about faces:

- 2–3 month-old infants seem to have a built-in preference for attractive faces.
- As early as 3 months, infants can distinguish one face from another.
- 6-month-olds can tell between similar faces on the basis of age and sex.
- By 9 months, infants can tell apart facial expressions.

 (a) Outline and evaluate cross-cultural studies of the development of perceptual abilities. (4 + 8 marks)
(b) Use infant studies to discuss the extent to which nature influences the development of perceptual development. (5 + 8 marks)

Cross cultural studies

Cross cultural studies provide us with an additional way of thinking about the nature-nurture debate. Regardless of where we are born, the eyes and related perceptual systems are the same (*nature*). Our experiences, however, (*nurture*) can influence how we perceive things.

THE STUDY	WHO DID WHAT	RESULTS AND CONCLUSIONS
	Gregory and Gombrich (1973) Europeans and East Africans were all shown the same picture and asked to describe it.	East Africans described a woman with a box on her head and children beneath a tree. Europeans saw a family inside a house and the woman sitting beneath a window. Conclusions were that the two groups were using different experiences in their interpretation of the picture. These differences demonstrate top-down processing, and how *nurture* influences perception.
	Hudson (1960) African tribal communities were shown the picture and asked what the hunter was about to shoot.	Because those in the tribal communities had no real experience of seeing 'flat' 2-D images like this, most reported that the hunter was about to shoot the 'baby' elephant. Most westerners would immediately identify the deer as the target because of their understanding of the depth cues in the illustration. This points to a significant role for *nurture* in perception.
	Segall et al (1966) The researchers showed the Müller-Lyer illusion to people from different cultures, and asked them to comment on the 'length' of the vertical central lines.	In the Müller-Lyer illusion the 'open' vertical line appears longer than the enclosed one. This illusion might occur because people in western countries live in 'carpentered' environments with lots of straight edges and angles. When Segall asked non-westerners who did not live in carpentered environments what they saw, the illusion was weakened or absent. This suggests it is our culture (nurture) that influence this particular perceptual experience.
The Müller-Lyer illusion in Zambia and America	**Stewart (1973)** The Müller-Lyer illusion was presented to different groups in Africa. Some were schooled, some not, some from rural areas, some from towns. The results were compared with those for black and white Americans.	Environment rather than race was the important factor in falling for the illusion. Least susceptible were Africans living in very traditional 'uncarpentered' environments, with susceptibility becoming greater with increasing wealth and education (i.e. the people were beginning to live in 'carpentered' towns). Both black and white Americans were more susceptible to the illusion than the Africans.

(a) Outline cross-cultural studies of the development of perceptual abilities. (9 marks)
(b) Consider the extent to which perceptual development can be explained in terms of nurture. (16 marks)

You could get a question on cultural studies, so make sure you know the details of some. This material is also very useful in other areas, for example to support the nurture argument or top-down processing.

THE NATURE-NURTURE DEBATE IN RELATION TO EXPLANATIONS OF PERCEPTUAL DEVELOPMENT

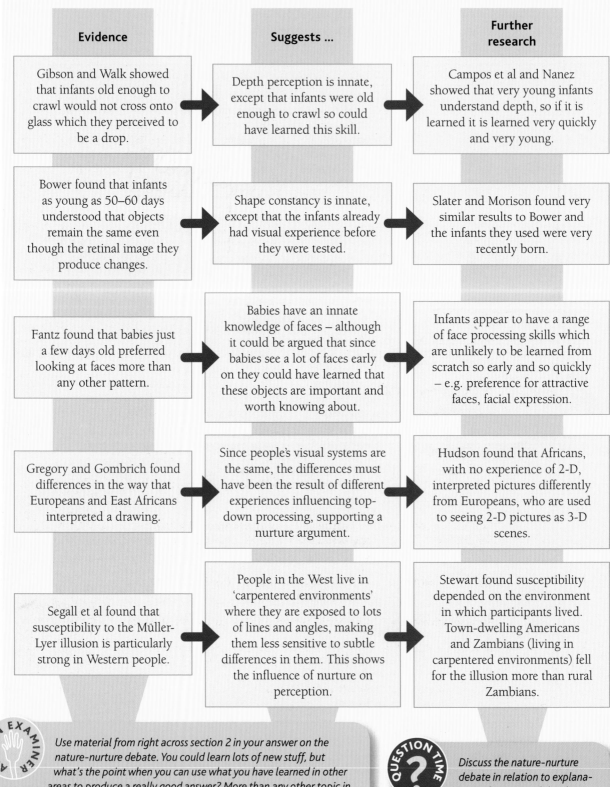

Evidence	Suggests ...	Further research
Gibson and Walk showed that infants old enough to crawl would not cross onto glass which they perceived to be a drop.	Depth perception is innate, except that infants were old enough to crawl so could have learned this skill.	Campos et al and Nanez showed that very young infants understand depth, so if it is learned it is learned very quickly and very young.
Bower found that infants as young as 50–60 days understood that objects remain the same even though the retinal image they produce changes.	Shape constancy is innate, except that the infants already had visual experience before they were tested.	Slater and Morison found very similar results to Bower and the infants they used were very recently born.
Fantz found that babies just a few days old preferred looking at faces more than any other pattern.	Babies have an innate knowledge of faces – although it could be argued that since babies see a lot of faces early on they could have learned that these objects are important and worth knowing about.	Infants appear to have a range of face processing skills which are unlikely to be learned from scratch so early and so quickly – e.g. preference for attractive faces, facial expression.
Gregory and Gombrich found differences in the way that Europeans and East Africans interpreted a drawing.	Since people's visual systems are the same, the differences must have been the result of different experiences influencing top-down processing, supporting a nurture argument.	Hudson found that Africans, with no experience of 2-D, interpreted pictures differently from Europeans, who are used to seeing 2-D pictures as 3-D scenes.
Segall et al found that susceptibility to the Müller-Lyer illusion is particularly strong in Western people.	People in the West live in 'carpentered environments' where they are exposed to lots of lines and angles, making them less sensitive to subtle differences in them. This shows the influence of nurture on perception.	Stewart found susceptibility depended on the environment in which participants lived. Town-dwelling Americans and Zambians (living in carpentered environments) fell for the illusion more than rural Zambians.

ASK AN EXAMINER

Use material from right across section 2 in your answer on the nature-nurture debate. You could learn lots of new stuff, but what's the point when you can use what you have learned in other areas to produce a really good answer? More than any other topic in this exam, perception lends itself to using the same material in different questions. This means you have less to learn – that can't be bad!

QUESTION TIME ?

Discuss the nature-nurture debate in relation to explanations of perceptual development. (9 + 16 marks)

SECTION 3: FACE RECOGNITION AND VISUAL AGNOSIAS

Bruce and Young's theory of face recognition

Face processing is a modular system.

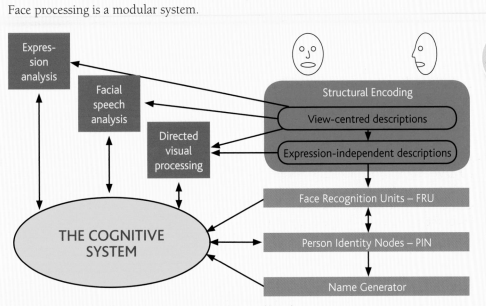

A functional model of face recognition Bruce and Young (1986)

ASK AN EXAMINER

You could have a question specifically on Bruce and Young's theory, so this is a great diagram to learn – it's not that difficult to do! It's colour-coded to help. Briefly describe what is going on in each part and, along with the diagram, you will get good marks.

PROCESSING STAGE	DESCRIPTION
Structural encoding	Face represented as basic pattern and placed into the face processing system.
View-centred descriptions	Part of structural encoding. The image is described providing inputs into modules dealing with expression, facial speech analysis and directed visual processing.
Expression-independent descriptions	Part of structural encoding. Some facial features (e.g. overall size and shapes of the nose and ears) that do not change with expressions are processed here.
Expression analysis	Here we decide how a person is feeling by reading their expression.
Facial speech analysis	Lip reading' is engaged, to help us understand speech.
Direct visual processing	The focus is on particular aspects of a face to aid recognition, e.g. 'Does that person have a beard?'.
Face recognition units (FRU)	Structural descriptions of faces we know are stored here.
Person identity nodes (PIN)	Biographical information about people we know is stored here (their favourite foods, musicians, etc.).
Name generation	Names are stored here.
The cognitive system	All our knowledge of the world is stored here, and such information is vital in face recognition.

QUESTION TIME

(a) Outline one or more case studies of prosopagnosia. (5 marks)

(b) Outline and evaluate one or more explanations of prosopagnosia. (4 + 16 marks)

QUESTION TIME

Outline and evaluate Bruce and Young's theory of face recognition. (9 + 16 marks)

Evaluation of the Bruce and Young model

Support for Bruce and Young's model

» Sometimes we are able to recognise a face but remember nothing more (biographical information etc.) about the person it belongs to. Recognition (FRU) and other systems must, therefore, be separate.

» Once we remember a name we always recall something about the person. This is because biographical information (PIN) must have been accessed before the name was identified, so the two must therefore be separate systems.

» Bruce and Young (1993) found that soldiers with brain damage suffered with different types of face processing problems, suggesting that some stages or modules were damaged and some not.

» An accumulation of evidence from brain damaged and normal face processing studies suggests that face processing is indeed as Bruce and Young describe it – a stage-like, modular process.

Criticism of Bruce and Young's model

» The explanation of the individual stages often lacks detail. The cognitive section in particular is very poorly described. For instance, it is improbable that you will bump into Brad Pitt in Sainsbury's, so even though you may *think* the person you are speaking to looks like him, you are unlikely to make the identification mistake. It is not at all clear how this kind of 'likelihood' calculation is done.

» Sometimes a face can be familiar without us recognising it (covert recognition). Patient WJ could not select famous faces but did better when asked "Which one is…?" The model cannot explain why this happens.

» de Haan et al (1991) describe the case of a person who could recognise famous faces but could not give any biographical information about them. This never happens in everyday experience, and so is contrary to the model.

» Whilst it is likely that we learn many face processing skills as we develop, the model does not explain this, nor what model of face processing exists before this learning takes place.

Prosopagnosia

This is a kind of visual agnosia (meaning 'not knowing'), where a person has difficulty recognizing faces.

Rumiati et al (1994) describe the case of Mr W, who was able to process individual parts of faces but could not identify the faces as a whole. This suggests that early stages of processing were intact but later stages where individual features are combined were affected by brain damage. This case provides good evidence for the Bruce and Young model.

Bornstein et al (1969) describe a farmer who lost not only ability with faces but also the ability to recognise cows in his herd, when he could previously recognise them all individually. They argue this is not because human faces are particularly special but because they are hard to tell apart, just like cows. Prosopagnosia, they suggest, is a loss of fine processing skills.

Face recognition is fine discrimination

Gauthier et al (1999) used face-like objects called 'greebles' to test face recognition skills. They found that the same parts of the brain are active when recognising greebles as when recognising faces. They suggest there is no special face processing system in the brain, but one specialised in telling apart similar objects.

Face recognition is special

Duchaine et al (2004) studied face processing in prosopagnosic patient Edward. He had no problem recognising previously seen objects but struggled specifically with faces.

He knew what a face was, so structural encoding (Bruce and Young model) was intact. He could not retain information about faces, however, suggesting a problem with face recognition units.

Edward performed as well as normal on greeble training, suggesting faces and greebles do not use the same mechanism. His problem was specific to faces and not one with fine discrimination, contradicting Gauthier et al.

Duchaine et al argue that we recognise faces in a different way from other objects and that there is a brain region just for this function.

ASK AN EXAMINER

You could be asked a question on prosopagnosia: if so, you have several case studies here to use. This material would also be what you use if there is a general question on visual agnosia.

HOW WELL DO I KNOW IT?	NOT AT ALL	MAYBE	OK	WELL	SUPERBLY
SECTION 1: THEORIES OF PERCEPTUAL ORGANISATION					
Gregory's top-down/indirect theory of perceptual organisation					
Gibson's bottom-up/direct theory of perceptual organisation					
SECTION 2: THE DEVELOPMENT OF PERCEPTION					
Development of perceptual abilities: depth/distance					
Development of perceptual abilities: visual constancies					
Development of perceptual abilities: face recognition					
Development of perceptual abilities: infant studies					
Development of perceptual abilities: cross-cultural studies					
The nature-nurture debate in explanations of perceptual development					
SECTION 3: FACE RECOGNITION AND VISUAL AGNOSIAS					
Bruce and Young's theory of face recognition					
Case studies of prosopagnosia					
Explanations of prosopagnosia					

Relationships

You are expected in the examination to show both the skills of knowledge and understanding and the skills of analysis and evaluation in relation to the topic Relationships.

Where opportunities for their effective use arise, you will need to demonstrate an appreciation of issues and debates. These include the nature/nurture debate, ethical issues in research, free-will/determinism, reductionism, gender and culture bias and the use of animals in research.

You will also need to demonstrate an understanding of How Science Works. You can do this through the effective use of studies in your answer (as description or evaluation) or where appropriate by evaluating methodology and findings.

WHAT YOU NEED TO KNOW

THE FORMATION, MAINTENANCE AND BREAKDOWN OF ROMANTIC RELATIONSHIPS
- Theories of the formation, maintenance and breakdown of romantic relationships: e.g. reinforcement/affect theory, social exchange theory, sociobiological theory

HUMAN REPRODUCTIVE BEHAVIOUR
- The relationship between sexual selection and human reproductive behaviour
- Evolutionary explanations of parental investment: e.g. sex differences, parent-offspring conflict

EFFECTS OF EARLY EXPERIENCE AND CULTURE ON ADULT RELATIONSHIPS
- The influence of childhood and adolescent experiences on adult relationships, including parent-child relationships and interaction with peers
- The nature of relationships in different cultures

SECTION 1: THE FORMATION, MAINTENANCE AND BREAKDOWN OF ROMANTIC RELATIONSHIPS

Reinforcement/affect theory (Byrne and Clore, 1970)

» Based on learning theory (classical and operant conditioning).

» We make an indirect association between two events (classical conditioning) and either seek to engage in similar (direct) behaviours again if there are pleasurable consequences, or avoid them in future if unpleasant (operant conditioning).

» The theory says that experiences in the relationship may or may not reinforce a positive affect (emotion).

» We are attracted to and will want to be around others whose company is rewarding, but less so when it is not rewarding.

FORMATION	MAINTENANCE	BREAKDOWN
If we experience positive feelings we are more likely to like the people around us at that time and possibly engage in behaviours that may result in our forming a relationship with them. If experiencing negative feelings we are less likely to like the people.	If positive feelings develop we are more likely to stay in the relationship. As relationships develop the needs of partners change. The flexibility of the relationship to meet these changing demands will influence the reinforcement experienced.	If positive feelings (affect) are no longer generated the relationship may begin to break down because of lack of reinforcement. A behaviour may have once provided positive reinforcement, but no longer does. If this is the case the relationship may break down.

ASK AN EXAMINER

You can use reinforcement/ affect theory in questions which ask for either formation, maintenance or breakdown. Describe the theory first then follow that with how it applies to whichever of the three you are asked about!

Research into reinforcement/affect theory

May and Hamilton (1980) – Attraction and music

» Female participants rated the attractiveness of attractive and unattractive males in photographs.

» There were three conditions:

• Condition 1: Positive affect (Listening to rock-music).

• Condition 2: Negative affect (listening to unpleasant music).

• Condition 3: Neutral (Silence).

» The results showed higher attractiveness in condition 1 than in the others.

» The more positive we feel, the more attractive we find others.

Aronson and Linder (1965) – Reciprocal liking

» Participants conducted a conversation with a person then later overheard the person expressing opinions about them to the researcher on seven different occasions.

» There were four conditions:

• Condition 1: The person was entirely positive on all occasions.

• Condition 2: The person was entirely negative on all occasions.

• Condition 3: The person went from negative at first to positive.

• Condition 4: The person went from positive at first to negative.

» Results showed that participants found the other person most attractive in condition 3.

» The idea that someone grew to like them during a conversation increased attraction.

Griffith and Veitch (1971) – Comfort and liking

» Participants were seated in comfortable or uncomfortable surroundings with a 'stranger'.

» Ratings of how much the participants 'liked' the stranger were higher in comfortable surroundings.

» The strangers had become associated with participants' feelings at the time, as predicted by the theory.

Criticisms of reinforcement/affect theory

» Supporting evidence lacks ecological validity – a good deal of it is lab-based using very unrealistic tasks.

» The theory may be culturally biased. Lott (1994) suggests that different behaviours are rewarding in different cultures.

» The theory could be regarded as reductionist. Some would say that the complex behaviours involved in relationships cannot be reduced to simple associations and rewards.

» It could be argued that the theory is too deterministic in that it suggests that we have little or no actual control over our relationships.

Discuss the formation and/or breakdown of romantic relationships. (9 + 16 marks)

ASK AN EXAMINER

You have a choice here: the research can be used either as description or evaluation. As long as you have described the theory well then the research is best used as evaluation. However, if you think you need more description in your answer you can use research descriptively to gain more marks.

Social exchange theory (Homans, 1974)

» We consider the actual and potential past, present and future rewards and costs before deciding whether or not a relationship is likely to be profitable (i.e. worth the effort).

» We are attracted to those who provide us with economic rewards, so relationships are therefore based on rational economic decisions.

» 'Satiation' means that when something is in short supply you appreciate it more, e.g. if you get attention from a partner that you do not get elsewhere it is valued more.

» The more mutually beneficial a relationship is to both partners, the more likely it is to develop.

» The reward (or 'payback') from a relationship can be different for each person, but might include feeling loved, financial safety, status, attention, pleasure etc., whilst the costs are anything unpleasant.

ASK AN EXAMINER

Watch out! Don't get these two theories muddled up. The term 'reward' is used in both, but the theories are different. Make sure you make that clear in the exam.

Thibaut and Kelly's 'minimax' theory

» We attempt to minimise relationship costs whilst maximising benefits.

» People's feelings in a relationship depend on a number of factors:

• Perception of rewards and costs

• Perceptions of the relationship they feel they deserve (the 'comparison level' or cl)

• Perceptions of chances of getting something better (the 'comparison level for alternatives' or cla).

» The formula used to calculate relationship outcome is:

OUTCOME = REWARDS – COSTS

» The cl and cla are crucial since they have a big influence on the outcome.

Relationships progress through a number of stages

Sampling	People consider the potential costs and rewards of a relationship and compare it with others.
Bargaining	There is a giving and receiving of rewards at the beginning of the relationship which tests whether the relationship should continue.
Commitment	Focus is on the relationship and the costs and rewards are stabilised.
Institutionalisation	Norms of rewards and costs are established by the partners as they 'settle down'.

FORMATION	MAINTENANCE	BREAKDOWN
Relationships are formed on the basis of costs and rewards. If perceived or expected rewards are more than costs we may begin to form the relationship. If there is a choice of entering any number of relationships we are more likely to choose the one with the greatest reward-cost balance.	Maintenance requires the rewards to remain beneficial for both parties. If we invest more in a relationship than we get out of it we may think again about staying in that relationship.	When costs are greater then rewards the relationship is more likely to break down. Where effort to maintain reward is too great the benefits of the effort are very small in comparison. The cost-benefit balance changes and the relationship risks breakdown.

ASK AN EXAMINER

You can use social exchange theory in questions which ask for either formation, maintenance or breakdown. Describe the theory first then follow that with how it applies to whichever of the three you are asked about!

Research into social exchange theory

Rusbult (1983) – Satisfaction and alternatives
» College students were given questionnaires every few weeks for seven months.
» Satisfaction, alternatives and investment all predicted commitment to a relationship.
» This finding is supported by other research with married couples and homosexual relationships.

Simpson et al (1990) – Role of available alternatives
» Available alternatives are viewed differently according to the current relationship.
» People who were dating viewed members of the opposite sex as less attractive than did those who were single.

Rusbult and Martz (1995) – Relationship investment and abusive relationships
» Women seeking refuge from abusive relationships were interviewed.
» It was found that those most likely to return to an abusive partner were those who:
  • had poorer alternatives to the relationship
  • were more heavily invested (e.g. married with children)
  • were less dissatisfied (e.g. reported less severe abuse).

QUESTION TIME

(a) Outline and evaluate one theory of the formation of romantic relationships. (4 + 8 marks)
(b) Discuss theories of the maintenance of romantic relationships. (5 + 8 marks)

Criticisms of social exchange theory
» It accounts well for individual differences – why some may stay in a relationship that others would not.
» Costs may not be as important in some stages of a relationship as in others: e.g. at the beginning of a relationship costs are less important than when maintaining a longer term relationship.
» Most research has been done with students and has been based on relatively short term heterosexual relationships, and so the theory may not be applicable to other types of romantic relationships in different groups of people, e.g. gay and lesbian.
» The model lacks the ability to predict at what point the cost/reward balance in a relationship alters to the point that the relationship fails.
» Clark and Mills (1979) point out that in addition to exchange relationships there are also communal ones (where the principal concern is with the needs and welfare of a partner). It appears that social exchange theory applies only to certain types of relationships.

IDea *It has been suggested that the use of concepts such as 'exchange' when talking about relationships is a reflection of the values of the culture from which the theories originated, namely North America. Such cultures are predominantly individualistic and the ideas expressed in theories reflect westernised relationship values: that is, they emphasise individual freedom, happiness, and rights. Exchange theory therefore might have little relevance when applied to relationships which do not share these values.*

Further explanations for relationship breakdown

There are some theories that deal specifically with the breakdown of relationships.

Duck's model of relationship dissolution

Duck says that there are three categories of relationship breakup:

1. *Pre-existing doom:* The couple are incompatible. For instance 85-year-old man marries 17-year-old woman.
2. *Mechanical failure:* The couple just can't live together.
3. *Sudden death:* Something such as infidelity or betrayal is discovered, ending a relationship.

Duck says that breakdown is a process rather than a single event, going through a number of stages.

STAGE	EXPLANATION
Stage 1: Intrapsychic phase	Dissatisfaction is experienced by one or both. This phase begins with the 'I can't stand it anymore' level if dissatisfaction is reached, either in private or in conversation with others
Stage 2: Dyadic phase	Reached when the 'I'd be justified in pulling out' level is expressed. Faults are aired and the commitment of one or both may be questioned. A less formal relationship may end here with a 'See you then' or 'I'll call you'. Discussions to mend or end the relationship are aired here.
Stage 3: Social phase	Reached when the 'I mean it' level is expressed. Unhappiness, dissatisfaction and the possibility of breakup are openly discussed. A counsellor, or friend, may be sought in an attempt to rescue the relationship.
Stage 4: Grave-dressing phase	Reached when the 'It's now inevitable' level is expressed. Acceptable versions are constructed of the life and death of the relationship. Blame is often levied on the other partner: 'She expected me to change', 'He changed me too much'.

ASK AN EXAMINER

If you get a question on breakdown, you can choose just to focus on the theories of Duck and Lee. You can consider them both together using a general evaluation and perhaps use social exchange as an alternative 'evaluative' theory.

QUESTION TIME ?

Discuss theories of the breakdown of romantic relationships. (9 + 16 marks)

Lee's model of relationship dissolution

Surveying the breakdown of 112 premarital romantic relationships, Lee argued that breakdown goes through a series of distinct stages.

Stages 2 and 3 are the most exhausting, and not all relationships pass through all stages, with some skipping stages entirely and going directly from stage 1 to stage 5.

STAGE	EXPLANATION
Stage 1: Dissatisfaction	One partner becomes dissatisfied.
Stage 2: Exposure	The partner reveals their dissatisfaction openly.
Stage 3: Negotiation	Discussions take place about the dissatisfaction.
Stage 4: Resolution	Attempts to resolve the problem are made.
Stage 5: Termination	The relationship breaks down.

Learn both Duck's and Lee's theories in detail if you intend to use them in an answer. Students often confuse the two in exam answers – don't do this: you will lose loads of marks! Learn them both really well so you don't confuse them.

Evaluating Duck's and Lee's models

The emphasis is slightly different in each case. Duck focuses on the beginning and end of the relationship. Lee focuses on the earlier stages where the relationship may be saved.

» Relationships are individual and dynamic and these theories cannot be applied to all of them.

» The models are culturally specific and therefore biased, as they only truly apply to western individualist cultures.

» Breakdowns are usually investigated after they have happened, and such retrospective data is prone to inaccuracies.

» The theories are basically descriptive, i.e. they explain the process of break-up rather than its reasons.

» Femlee's *fatal attraction hypothesis* offers an alternative:
  • The qualities that attract two people also contribute to breakdown.
  • People are 'blinded' to undesirable qualities early in a relationship, and over time it becomes more difficult to overlook these things.

» Argyle and Henderson's *rule violation theory* offers another alternative:
  • Some relationship rules are *prescriptive* (i.e. they say what is expected) and some are *restrictive* (i.e. say what is permissible).
  • Breaking restrictive rules could be interpreted as betrayal and lead to relationship breakdown.

Both Duck's and Lee's models are stage models and so have similar strengths and weaknesses. These evaluative points apply to both, but don't get the theories muddled up!

IDea

Theories of relationship breakdown have been accused of bias because they are based on the experiences of a particular type of person – namely white, middle class heterosexuals. Not only do these theories fail to represent other kinds of relationships, such as cohabiting and dating couples, but they also do not represent relationships such as gay and lesbian ones. It seems that not only do the theories have a bias across larger cultural groups (for example, individualistic and collectivist cultures), but they may also have subcultural biases. Since it is doubtful that all these different kinds of relationship experience the same processes, one should perhaps be cautious about the kind of cultural group to which the theories are applied.

(a) Outline one theory of the formation of romantic relationships. (4 marks)
(b) Outline one theory of the maintenance of romantic relationships. (5 marks)
(c) Evaluate theories of the breakdown of romantic relationships. (16 marks)

SECTION 2: HUMAN REPRODUCTIVE BEHAVIOUR

ASK AN EXAMINER

The specification requires that you know about HUMAN reproductive behaviour. Non-human animals are relevant as explanations, and can support your argument, but don't overdo it!

THE RELATIONSHIP BETWEEN SEXUAL SELECTION AND HUMAN REPRODUCTIVE BEHAVIOUR

Natural selection suggests that successful animals evolve characteristics which enable them to out-perform rivals, increasing reproductive opportunities. Sexual selection is where individuals advertise both their own requirements in a mate and their own attractive characteristics as a mate. There are two basic types of sexual selection: *inter-sexual selection* and *intra-sexual selection*.

Inter-sexual selection

Members of one sex compete for the attention of the opposite sex. Men have evolved to respond to females who are young and attractive (a sign of fertility), and women are sensitive to cues that a male has resources necessary for survival of her and offspring (e.g. socio-economic status).

Study

Buss (1989) – A large cross-cultural study of over 10,000 people from 37 countries showed consistent gender differences in characteristics favoured by men and women.

ASK AN EXAMINER

This study by Buss is a very famous one, which you can also use elsewhere in this topic. A very useful one to learn!

GROUP	FINDINGS	EVOLUTIONARY EXPLANATION
Require-ments of females seeking males	· Able to provide financially	Access to financial resources increases chance of providing for young and can improve reproductive success in females.
	· Tall, physically strong, healthy	The best physical specimens were typically better hunters and providers.
	· Older than themselves	With age comes greater access to resources and so improved reproductive success in females and ability to provide.
	· Facial and physical symmetry	Symmetry is associated with health. A healthy father means healthy offspring.
Require-ments of males seeking females	· Younger than themselves	Fertility decreases with age. Younger women are likely to be more fertile.
	· Healthy and phys-ically symmetrical	Healthy mother means healthy offspring. Symmetrical mother suggests healthy genes.
	· Good waist to hip ratio	A good waist to hip ratio improves the chances of a healthy birth. The higher the waist to hip ratio (if the waist is the same size as the hips) the more likely the woman is to have trouble conceiving.

The biological market place – Noë and Hammerstein (1995)

It's unlikely that we will get exactly what we want and so mate choice is a trade-off between individual demands and those of available potential mates. E.g., the more desirable traits we have, the stronger our bargaining position, therefore the more choosy we can be, and vice-versa.

Research with personal adverts has found that women with youth and beauty and men with resources are most in demand.

Waynforth and Dunbar (1995) claimed that courtship in humans is influenced by the same rules that govern sexual selection in non-human animals. They studied 479 adverts placed by men and 402 placed by women. → Men of 40–49 (maximum personal resources) expressed preferences for physical attractiveness whilst women (especially women in their peak reproductive years 20–39) demanded wealth 4.5 times more often than men did. → Supported by Campos et al (2002) who found as women aged their adverts became less demanding in their mate selection, whilst males became more demanding.

However ...

Strassberg and Holty (2003) placed 'female seeking male' adverts, differing slightly in wording, on personal bulletin boards on the internet. The most popular advert was where the woman described herself as 'financially independent, successful and ambitious', contradicting other research.

Discuss the relationship between sexual selection and human reproductive behaviour (9 + 16 marks)

Intra-sexual selection

This is competition among members of one sex for access to members of the other sex, e.g. males competing against one another for females. This results in *sexual dimorphism*, mostly seen as secondary sexual characteristics (indicators of reproductive fitness) – e.g. human males are on average 15% larger than females, who have widened hips and smoother skin.

Male aggression

Males may be protective of their chosen mates, often behaving aggressively to other males they see as competition.

Research

Daly and Wilson (1988) – 90% of male murders involve men of mate-competition age.

Buss and Dedden (1990) – Female verbal aggression is an attempt to reduce the apparent attractiveness of their competitors in the eyes of the males.

Sperm competition

When sperm from two or more males compete to fertilise an egg, especially in promiscuous species (like humans) where there is sex with multiple partners.

Males protect their investment in females carefully, ensuring that theirs is the only sperm to reach the egg of the female.

It is vital, therefore, for the male to ensure the fidelity of the female.

Male testis size

Large testes evolved due to female infidelity rather than to fertilise widely, since large quantities of sperm would not be needed if females could be trusted.

Evidence

The more sperm competition, the larger the testes relative to body weight.

Humans have less sperm competition than chimpanzees so have evolved smaller testicles, producing fewer sperm.

Sperm allocation

Where there are lots of opportunities to copulate, being economical with sperm increases the chance of reproducing, as the amount of sperm available decreases with each copulation.

Evidence

In species with more females than males, there is less sperm in each ejaculate, and where there are fewer females there is more sperm in each ejaculate.

Packer and Pusey (1983) – a male lion may copulate up to 100 times a day but only ejaculate a limited number of sperm each time.

Female orgasm

Female orgasms are not necessary for conception.

The contractions during orgasm help to pull the sperm nearer to the egg: this improves the chance of conception and ensures that males with best indicators of fitness are favoured.

Thus, the number of times a female copulates and the timing, intensity and frequency of orgasm affects the outcome of sperm competition.

Study
- » Shackleford et al (2000) – The female orgasm is designed for discriminating male quality.
- » 388 US and German heterosexual females in committed relationships responded to a questionnaire about their partner and relationship.
- » They found that those who were with more attractive men were more likely to reach orgasm during copulation.

Study
- » Pollet and Nettle (2009) – using a large representative Chinese survey sample, found that frequency of female orgasm increased with partner's income.
- » This could not be explained by age, happiness, health and educational achievement among other things.
- » Female orgasm is an adaptive response promoting conception with higher quality males.

(a) Outline what is meant by the term sexual selection. (4 marks)
(b) Outline and evaluate the relationship between sexual selection and human reproductive behaviour. (5 + 16 marks)

Your knowledge of research methods should make you question everything you read. For example, Shackleford et al's work relied on a volunteer sample and a very restricted age range of respondents. This limits how well the findings can be applied elsewhere as well as the reliability of the findings.

Explanations of female mate choice

Two theories have been proposed to explain why females are choosier than males.

'Sexy sons' hypothesis (Fisher, 1930)
- » Populations could develop preferences for certain characteristics (tallness, muscular physique).
- » Mating with these individuals means that the characteristics are passed on to the next generation.
- » Eventually these characteristics become the norm.
- » By creating these 'sexy sons', who will be desired by others, the female ensures her genetic material is passed on to those with whom her sons mate.
- » Over generations of mate selection the characteristics will become more pronounced – the 'runaway' process, which only stops when the characteristic becomes too costly or females change preference.

Handicap process (Zahavi, 1975)
- » Males who survive in spite of having a handicap are genetically superior to other males (e.g. the expense of driving a Ferrari handicaps the man economically, but he still manages to survive and so is more attractive to women).
- » Such 'handicaps' could be seen as a 'badge' of healthiness and be attractive to females.

Parasite-mediated sexual selection
- » Maintaining a healthy immune system is very costly for the body, but essential for survival, e.g. a defence against effects of parasites.
- » However, immune functioning is worsened by the effects of testosterone (needed for development of secondary sexual characteristics).
- » Males with the best secondary sexual characteristics are showing high levels of reproductive fitness since they are maintaining these features whilst remaining strong and healthy.
- » Females therefore select males because of the male handicap of superior secondary sexual characteristics.

Your focus when thinking about sexual selection should be on what it tells us about human reproductive behaviour.

 'It is argued that certain physical features and behaviours evolved specifically to help make animals attractive to the opposite sex'.
Discuss explanations of human reproductive behaviour. (9 + 16 marks)

General criticisms of evolutionary explanations of human behaviour

STATEMENT	CRITICISM
Men are more fertile than women and higher status men are preferred by females.	This is a gross over-generalisation. Not all men are more fertile than women and not all women prefer high status males. These are behavioural *trends* only
Evolutionary principles are the same for all animals.	While this is indeed true, evolutionary principles often ignore or underestimate social and cultural factors.
The principal drive is to procreate.	It is not for homosexuals. How does evolution explain the increase in, and indeed increased acceptance of, homosexuality? Also, many women *choose* not to have children.
Evolution just makes perfect sense.	True. However, it is largely un-falsifiable. Often the theory is adjusted to fit any findings that do not agree with it, making it extremely difficult or impossible to falsify.
Females choose male mates on the basis of their economic resources.	Not necessarily. Weiderman and Allgeier (1992) say that this is a perfectly rational choice. Men tend to be richer than women! Evolution is very hard to test in controlled conditions and so we can never be sure whether alternative explanations like this are any better than the evolutionary explanation.
Infertile people should be disinclined to have sex. There is no point in doing so in terms of adaptation.	Not true at all. Infertile people enjoy sex as much as, or more than, fertile people. In many cases they do not have the concern about whether their actions may result in unwanted pregnancies.
Women are more likely to be monogamous, certainly after reproducing, and they will choose older, more resource-rich males as partners.	Not necessarily true. Women are often unfaithful, and often choose younger men than themselves. Men often choose older women even though they know they cannot provide them with young.

 There are some general points you can make about evolutionary explanations for human behaviour, regardless of the actual question being asked. You can select from the points in this table to help you get those evaluative marks.

EVOLUTIONARY EXPLANATIONS OF PARENTAL INVESTMENT
Evolutionary explanations can be applied to parental behaviour.

Sex differences in parental investment
Male investment in offspring is more variable than female, since females can be 100% certain that the child is theirs whilst men can never be sure.

Birkhead (2000) – reports 17 women waiting for fertility treatment falling pregnant before treatment even though the husband produced no sperm.

Apicella and Marlowe (2004) – If men think their children resemble them and feel the woman is loyal, they increase parental investment.

Anderson (2007) – The less confident men are of paternity, the less time they spend with their offspring.

 Parental investment is closely linked to sexual selection – after all, the ultimate goal of sexual selection is to choose the right mate, including the one that will satisfy parental needs of the offspring. You MUST however make sure that you don't confuse the two things.

Trivers' theory of parental investment (1972)

» When the amount of energy that each sex must devote to reproduction and parental care is different, the sex with the greater burden will be the choosier.

» Human females invest much more than males, including egg production, gestation, possibly dangerous childbirth and then long term child care. Also, female fertility reduces significantly after 35 years of age, but males produce sperm from puberty to death.

» Mistakes in mate choice can be very costly for females so they need to be selective.

Problems for Trivers' theory from observations of non-human animals

» Werner and Lotem (2003) – Just because males invest less does not necessarily mean they are less choosy than females. When given a choice, cichlid fish males choose the largest female, who is likely to produce the most eggs.

» Bel-Venner et al (2008) – The higher the competition, the more choosy male orb-weaving spiders are, choosing larger females.

» Trivers' theory assumes that choosiness is the opposite to competition – if one sex is choosy, the other is competitive. This is not always so. Many species, including humans, exhibit bi-parental care, where the male and female invest equally in young.

 ASK AN EXAMINER

You MUST make sexual selection really relevant to the issue of parental investment if you are going to include it in your answer. As examiners, we like things simple and organised – why not keep sexual selection and parental investment separate? It's not as though there is a shortage of things to write about each!

Parent–offspring conflict

This happens when the needs of the parent are at odds with those of the child.

Pre-natal conflict

» Mother needs to maintain own health while foetus makes demands on her body.

» Morning sickness may be due to foetus attempting to avoid food-based toxins.

» High blood pressure due to foetus demanding more blood from the placenta.

Offspring mate choice

» Parents would prefer their children to choose certain mates to ensure 'fit' grandchildren: they therefore attempt to impose their own mating choices on offspring, e.g. long-term rather than short term mating.

» The 'grandmother hypothesis' suggests that the menopause evolved to allow older females to care for grandchildren: they therefore want to maximise this investment by ensuring their offspring mate with partners who can produce healthy offspring.

» Buunk et al (2008) – In a cross-cultural study, parents tended to reject offspring mate choice based on poor parental investment traits, whilst their children found more undesirable those traits which indicated lack of heritable fitness.

Infanticide

Sexual selection theory says that infanticide occurs as a result of reproductive competition between males, since for a male this behaviour may have advantages:

• The female is available to reproduce if she is not caring for young.
• The male stands a greater chance of being the father of the next infant.

This is supported by the observation that males rarely kill their own offspring. Hardy (1979) suggests that females can use promiscuity to guard against infanticide, since this confuses the issue of paternity.

 QUESTION TIME

Discuss evolutionary explanations of parental investment. (9 + 16 marks)

 ASK AN EXAMINER

Remember! This section is about HUMAN reproductive behaviour. Examples of animal behaviour can be used very effectively but use them carefully.

SECTION 3: EFFECTS OF EARLY EXPERIENCE AND CULTURE ON ADULT RELATIONSHIPS

Experiences in childhood and adolescence may well shape our experiences of adult relationships.

INFLUENCE OF CHILDHOOD EXPERIENCES ON LATER ADULT RELATIONSHIPS

Parent–child relationships

The years after birth are a time of rapid social and emotional development, and what happens now can leave impressions which last into adulthood. Attachment theory suggests that the attachment styles we learn as children become an *internal working model* for what we believe relationships are like.

ATTACHMENT STYLE	CAREGIVER AND INFANT BEHAVIOUR.	ADULT BEHAVIOUR
Secure attachment style (Type B)	Caregivers are responsive to the infant's needs. Infants trust their caregivers and are not afraid of being abandoned.	Develop mature trusting and long lasting adult relationships.
Anxious/avoidant insecure attachment style (Type A)	Caregivers are distant and do not want intimacy with the infant. Infants want to be close to the caregiver but learn that they are likely to be rejected.	Difficulty with trusting others and developing trusting intimate relationships.
Anxious/resistant insecure attachment style (Type C)	Caregivers are inconsistent and overbearing in their affection. Infants are anxious because they never know when and how caregivers will respond.	Want to be close to partners but worry that their partners will not return their affections.
Disorganised/disorientated insecure attachment style (Type D)	The child does not know whether to approach or avoid the caregiver when they have been absent. A mixture of type A and C.	Chaotic; insensitive; explosive; abusive; untrusting even while craving security.

ASK AN EXAMINER

This is quite a complicated section because of the number of questions that could be asked. You need to know about childhood AND adolescence for both parent–child relationships AND interaction with peers. We've got it covered here – don't cut corners in your learning!

Attachment stability

Waters (2000) – 72% of adults retested 20 years after their attachment style was identified in childhood were given the same classification. Where there was a change it was related to negative events such as bereavement or parental divorce.

but →

Lewis et al (2000) – found only a 42% stability when 18 year olds were retested 17 years after initial classification. But, changed classifications were also linked to negative personal events, particularly parental divorce.

Hazan and Shaver (1987) – assessed attitudes to love expressed by newspaper readers. The readers chose statements (relating to different attachment styles) that best reflected their attitudes to relationships. The results showed a similar distribution of attachment types as was found in infancy.

but →

There are concerns about methodology – it is self report, correlational and used a self-selected sample.

Attachment type and adult romantic relationships

ANXIOUS/RESISTANT (Type C)

» As adults these have the most short-term romantic relationships, and are more likely to have shorter courtship prior to marriage (Senchak and Leonard, 1992).

» They are likely to be particularly upset by and ultimately to reject unsupportive partners (Collins and Fenney, 2004).

ANXIOUS/AVOIDANT (Type A)

» As adults these are least likely to enter into a romantic relationship and most likely to say they have never been in love (Campbell et al, 2005).

» They are likely to be particularly upset by unsupportive partners, labelling them unreliable (Collins and Fenney, 2004).

» Kirkpatrick and Davis (1994) found that these types (who expect lower commitment) can be attracted to anxious/resistant types (who expect to invest highly in a relationship).

» A stable relationship is most likely with a resistant-type female and an avoidant-type male the partner (Morgan and Shaver, 1999).

SECURE (Type B)

» Banse (2004) found that a marriage is happiest if both partners are type B.

» Unlikely to be affected when their partners appeared unsupportive.

QUESTION TIME

Discuss the influence of childhood experience on adult relationships. (9 + 16 marks)

Childhood interaction with peers

As children mature their peers become more important in healthy social and emotional development. According to Parker and Asher (1987) friendships between peers are 'training grounds' for adult relationships.

» Hartup (1989) – Lonely children are more likely to become adults with lower self-esteem who are less capable of maintaining intimate relationships.

» Ostrov and Collins (2007) – The kind of problems experienced during middle childhood predict the kind of problems experienced as adults.

Some children have unavoidable life experiences (e.g. chronic illness) which prevent them developing relationships with peers, e.g. due to hospitalisation and extended school absences.

» Thompson et al (2008) – Childhood cancer survivors tend to report fewer adult relationships and greater distress with relationship breakdown.

» Dolgin et al (1999) – Report lower rates of marriage and cohabitation and older age at first romantic relationship and marriage.

The strength and quality of childhood friendships, and when they form, make a big difference to early romantic relationships.

Zimmer-Gembeck et al (2004) – Those forming early, strong relationships at age 11 were more likely to enter into earlier romantic relationships.

The type of behaviour experienced as children and the behaviour used in relationships, in particular bullying and teasing, influence later relationships.

» Connolly et al (2000) – Children who are bullies are more likely to use aggressive behaviour in adult relationships.

» Ledley et al (2006) – Those teased or bullied as children found it harder to engage in intimacy and closeness as adults and had trust problems in their relationships.

ADOLESCENT EXPERIENCES AND LATER ADULT RELATIONSHIPS

Parent-child relationships

Adolescence can be seen as a period during which young people reshape the internal working models of childhood relationships into new models that will shape adult relationships.

Relationships within the family may act as a 'training ground' for later adult relationships.	Crockett and Randall (2006) – Longitudinal research shows a relationship between family relationships at this time and the quality of adult romantic relationships.
The quality of parent-adolescent conflict resolution is related to style of conflict resolution in romantic relationships.	Reese-Weber and Bartle-Haring (1998) – If adolescents adopted an attacking style of conflict resolution with their parents, this was more likely to be adopted in later romantic relationships.
Research suggests that the quality of relationships with parents during adolescence is related to the quality of later romantic relationships. Feldman et al (1998) for example found that adolescent reports of family interaction patterns predicted happiness and distress in romantic relationships in early adulthood.	» Conger et al (2000) – Having the experience of supportive, involved parents during adolescence was associated with greater commitment and satisfaction at age 20. » Linder and Collins (2005) – Individuals with a history of hostile interactions with parents during adolescence were more likely to experience romantic relationship violence as young adults.

You could be asked separately about the influence of parents and the influence of peers on later adult relationships. Remember to focus on the question – emphasise the effect on adult relationships rather than just describing the experience with parents and peers.

Discuss the influence of adolescent experiences on adult relationships. (9 + 16 marks)

Adolescent interaction with peers

Peer groups assume greater importance during adolescence.	Kirchler et al (1991) – Not developing peer relationships and staying very close to family can mean problems in establishing independence and in forming relationships when adults.
Relationship skills learned in the 'best friend' relationship during adolescence can be transferred to later romantic relationships.	» Meeus et al (2007) – Their longitudinal study suggests that commitment to a best friend is a predictor of commitment to an intimate partner later in life. » Crockett and Randall (2006) – Peer relationships appear to have little impact on adult romantic relationships, with family relationships having a greater influence.
Experiences with peers appear to be able both to increase the likelihood and to moderate the likelihood of later violent behaviour.	» Connolly et al (2000) – suggest that adolescents identified as bullies are more likely to report using physical violence with a partner later in life. » Linder and Collins (2005) – Individuals who had higher quality relationships at 16 reported lower levels of violence in subsequent romantic relationships at 21.

THE NATURE OF RELATIONSHIPS IN DIFFERENT CULTURES

Relationships in Western cultures tend to be individualistic, voluntary and temporary while those in non-Western cultures tend to be collectivist, involuntary and permanent (Moghaddam et al, 1993). Research has consistently found that these cultures differ greatly in terms of mate selection.

Love and Marriage

» Janovick (1995) identifies aspects of romantic love in over 88% of cultures studied: however, what constitutes romantic love is culturally specific and is not necessarily a condition of marriage.

» What is ideal in a spouse in one culture may not be in another. DePaulo and Morros (2005) say that in American relationships the social role of the partner may take in multiple roles, including, adviser, best-friend and lover.

» Marriage is not universal. For the Na people of the Himalayas, marriage does not exist. Brothers and sisters live together and care for the sisters' children together. Men 'visit' other women at night, since incest is prohibited (Tapp, 2002)

» In some cases, such as in Sri Lanka, there is a *cooperative traditional pattern* where the partners choose one another and encourage the parents to arrange the marriage for them.

Collectivist cultures	Individualist cultures
49% would consider marrying a person they were not in love with if they had everything else they desired (LeVine et al, 1993).	7.3% would consider marrying someone they did not love if they possessed everything else they desired (LeVine et al, 1993).
Arranged marriages often organised by families on the basis of alliances and economic considerations.	Arranged marriages are rare: the individual has the power to choose.
Husbands and wives in arranged Indian marriages were 'satisfied' with their choices (Yelsma and Arthappily, 1988).	Husbands and wives in 'love' American marriages were less satisfied with their choice (Yelsma and Arthappily, 1988).
Marital satisfaction in Indian arranged marriages was similar to US free-choice ones, but love was a less important factor in marriage decision (Myers et al, 2005).	In US free-choice marriages, high priority was given to love and loyalty as a requirement for marriage (Myers et al, 2005).
Finances and shared values most important to Indian and American Asians in arranged marriages (Madathil and Benshoff, 2008).	Love is most important for American couples in free-choice marriages (Madathil and Benshoff, 2008).

ASK AN EXAMINER

Should you have to answer a question on the influence of culture, then it will help if you organise your learning as we have organised this section. This will enable you to demonstrate breadth and depth – something which examiners like and give lots of marks for!

QUESTION TIME

Discuss the nature of relationships in different cultures. (9 + 16 marks)

Divorce

Failed relationships occur in all cultures, although rates of divorce vary. E.g., in India the divorce rate is 1% compared to 55% in the US.

This difference is due to cultural factors:

- The status of women is higher in individualist cultures and they have more economic freedom to survive alone out of marriage.
- The stigma of divorce is lower in individualist cultures.
- Cultural differences in motivation to marry may also be a factor – love, sex and beauty for instance change over time and, when they are gone, so too may be the reason for the marriage in the first place.

Reasons for divorce vary widely – factors like adultery, sterility and cruelty are common to all cultures, whilst culturally specific factors include witchcraft, bad dreams and omens.

Cultural differences in opinions of physical attractiveness

» Physical attractiveness is important in attraction and relationship formation across cultures.

» Cunningham et al (1995) found that Asian, Hispanic and Caucasian participants consistently rated highly large neonate eyes, facial symmetry, small noses, dilated pupils, larger smiles and well-groomed hair.

» From an evolutionary point of view humans should be sensitive to visual clues to reproductive fitness, although there are anomalies. E.g., Fessler (2005) found a general preference for small foot size in males across nine cultures.

Waist to Hip Ratio (WHR)

WHR is an evolutionary indicator of reproductive fitness.

Marlowe and Wetsman (1984) – A desirable WHR amongst American males was different from that sought by the Hadza of Tanzania, who preferred heavier women regardless of the WHR.

Yu and Shepard (1998) – The more westernised of the Matsigenka Indians of Peru preferred a more western idea of WHR than the less westernised members of the same ethnic group.

Body mass index (BMI)

BMI may be more important than WHR as a predictor of attraction.

Swami et al (2006) – British and Japanese males both identified BMI as most important when judging the attractiveness of females, irrespective of WHR. Japanese preferred a lower BMI than Britons.

Socioeconomic development

Cultural preference for a particular shape is influenced by living in harsh conditions, which makes finding a healthy partner difficult.

Stone et al (2008) – People in more developed countries placed greater importance on 'mutual attraction/love' whilst those physical characteristics indicating good health were more important in less economically developed countries.

IDea

Whilst culture clearly has a strong influence, cross-cultural studies consistently indicate general agreement on the issue of what is considered physically attractive. It appears that ideas of attractiveness are to some extent inborn and part of human nature. This is supported by studies of newborn infants who show a preference for the same kind of faces as are considered attractive by adults.

QUESTION TIME **?**

(a) Outline the influence of parent-child relationships and interaction with peers on later adult relationships. (9 marks)
(b) Consider the effects of culture on adult relationships. (16 marks)

SECTION 1: SOCIAL PSYCHOLOGICAL APPROACHES TO EXPLAINING AGGRESSION

SOCIAL LEARNING THEORY

According to SLT (proposed by Bandura), aggression can be learned by *modelling*, i.e. observing and imitating the aggressive behaviour of other people.

Aggression is learned through **direct experience** (i.e. direct reinforcement for aggressive behaviour) or by **vicarious experience** (we learn to be aggressive ourselves by observing others being rewarded for their aggressive behaviour).

Individuals interact reciprocally with their environment, i.e. individuals influence their environment, which in turn influences them (**reciprocal determinism**).

A number of factors make imitation more or less likely:

» **Self efficacy**
  • The belief that a behaviour is within an observer's ability to perform.
  • The person will only act aggressively in situations where they are more likely to be successful.

» **Characteristics of the model**
A model is more likely to be imitated if it has:
  • Status
  • Power
  • Similarity (increasing self efficacy)

Four essential conditions for an individual to model the behaviour of someone else:

Attention	A person has to pay some attention to the behaviour of the model in order for it to be imitated. A number of factors influence the attention given to the model, including as already mentioned the status, similarity and attractiveness of the model.
Retention	The behaviour has to be remembered if it is going to be imitated.
Reproduction	The observer has to be able to replicate (i.e. copy) the behaviour.
Motivation	The observer must want to imitate the behaviour.

Evaluation of social learning theory

Johnny and Rocky study – Bandura et al (1961) looked at the effects of observing a model being punished or rewarded. They found that children who had seen a character in a film (Rocky) being rewarded for aggressive behaviour used more aggressive behaviour whilst playing than those who had not witnessed this.

Practical application – Patterson et al (1982) studied the origins of children with problem behaviour including aggression and found that parents had both modelled aggressive behaviour and rewarded problem behaviour. Training parents to model more appropriate behaviour helped the children.

Support from biology – mirror neurons are active not only when we perform an action but also when we observe it. This might be a biological basis for social learning.

Bobo doll study

Children saw an adult behave aggressively towards a bobo doll; a second group were exposed to a non-aggressive model; and a third saw no model. The children were then allowed to play in a room full of toys, including a bobo doll. When frustrated by being prevented from playing with the toys, those who had seen the aggressive model were more likely to imitate by hitting the doll. A later study that included film footage of an aggressive model also produced more aggression in children. This is evidence of learning by observation.

Criticisms of bobo doll studies
» Creating aggression like this is unethical.
» The setting is artificial so findings may not apply to real life.
» Is play or aggression being measured? Bobo dolls are toys.
» It is not clear if changes in behaviour are long term.

You need to know social learning theory in detail: the concepts here will help you demonstrate understanding.

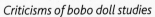

DEINDIVIDUATION THEORY

Being deindividuated means losing one's sense of individuality and identity. When individuals feel less identifiable (e.g. by being hidden by a uniform or being in a large group) they engage in less inhibited behaviour (i.e. their behaviour is not constrained by normal acceptable standards).

Factors that enhance deindividuation:
» Shared responsibility, which reduces the sense of guilt if the action results in violent behaviour and harm to others or property
» Alcohol and drugs create an altered state of consciousness that can contribute to the lack of inhibition.
» Uniforms, where individuals identify with roles created by the uniform and lose their sense of individuality.

Le Bon's theory

In 1896, Le Bon pointed out that when part of a large anonymous group, individuals are more likely to behave anti-socially because crowds create a 'collective mindset'.
» Individuals in large anonymous groups are more likely to behave in an anti-social and aggressive manner.
» In crowds a 'collective mindset' is created and the group acts as one; Le Bon termed this 'a mob'.
» The individual becomes submerged in the group and feels less identifiable, leading to less inhibited behaviour.
» Loss of inhibition means that individuals are not so constrained by internal standards of acceptable behaviour. Less identifiable = less risk of social disapproval for actions.

Diener's theory

» Deindividuation occurs when self-awareness is blocked by environmental factors, such as increased arousal, strong group feelings, feelings of anonymity, and a focus on external rather than internal events.
» Thus, rational thinking and planning is affected.
» A focus on external events means that individuals are more impulsive and prone to aggressive behaviours.
» Prentice-Dunn and Rogers (1982) modified this theory to distinguish between two types of self awareness. Reductions if *public* and *private* self-awareness can result in aggression, but only reductions in private self-awareness lead to genuine deindividuation.

increased arousal → external focus → strong group feelings → sense of anonymity

reduced self-awareness

DEINDIVIDUATION

Diener's theory of deindividuation.

ASK AN EXAMINER

Use both these theories and you will have a thorough description of deindividuation. And don't be afraid to use the diagram!

Evaluation of deindividuation theory

» Ellison et al (1995) found that Participants (P's) in a driving simulator who imagined they were in a top-up convertible car drove more aggressively than P's imagining they were in a top-down convertible car. Top-up drivers had greater anonymity, leading to deindividuation.
» Zimbardo used deindividuation to explain the rapid increase of aggressive behaviour in his Stanford Prison Experiment. The clothes of prisoners and guards increased anonymity and gave a strong sense of role.
» Zimbardo (1969) found that hooded and anonymous (hence deindividuated) P's were more likely to shock other P's than those who were identifiable (with name tags and without hoods).
» In cross-cultural research, Watson found that in conflict situations warriors who wore face and body paint (so had anonymity) were more aggressive than those who were identifiable. Similarly, Silke (2003) found that the greatest aggression shown in violent assault was by those wearing masks. Both studies suggest anonymity contributes to deindividuation, resulting in higher levels of aggression.
» Many crowds gather peacefully and induce a sense of belonging rather than aggression, e.g. religious and music festivals.

QUESTION TIME **?**

Outline and evaluate two social psychological theories of aggression. (9 + 16 marks)

EXPLANATIONS OF INSTITUTIONAL AGGRESSION

Aggression can occur within institutions, such as educational and prison settings. This can often be explained by factors within the institutions.

Deindividuation

Institutions that reduce individuality, e.g. by using uniforms, increase likelihood of deindividuation and therefore aggression. E.g. police in riot gear are hard to identify and this anonymity reduces the likelihood of being caught and might encourage aggression in addition to loss of personal values and morals.

Research

In prisons Zimbardo's Stanford Prison Experiment showed that a loss of personal identity in guards and prisoners can result in aggression. The clothing of guards and prisoners contributed to this.	*In educational settings* Hazing, the illegal ritualistic abuse of an individual or group among United States undergraduates, has a long history. Hazing rituals are shrouded in secrecy and perpetrators and/or victims are usually unidentifiable because of masks or costumes.	*In healthcare settings* Research has found increased aggression by staff in psychiatric units, and this may be because of loss of individual patient identity and the clothing worn by patients and staff.

Identification with a role

A person's behaviour can change according to the expectations of the role in an institution they have adopted. Clothing such as uniforms, or something denoting membership of a group, encourages this.

Research

In prisons In Zimbardo's Stanford Prison Experiment P's were given very powerful roles – prisoners and guards. Conforming to these roles contributed to aggressive behaviour.	*In educational settings* It is tradition that American under-graduates prove they are worthy of joining a high status fraternity or sorority. To do this they take part in hazing – aggressive behaviour such as kidnapping or sexual abuse.	*In healthcare settings* Staff and patients occupy very strong roles, especially in psychiatric units: e.g. staff have power over patients who may have lost certain rights such as the entitlement to privacy.

Situational variables

Characteristics of the institution's environment can contribute to aggressive behaviour. These can be physical or to do with rules and norms. Clothing and hierarchies of power contribute (e.g. people who wear suits are seen to have more power than those who do not).

Research

In prisons Research has suggested a relationship between crowding in prisons and higher levels of aggression.	*In educational settings* Some sororities and fraternities have high status and memberships can have life-long implications. Strong expectations for admission to such 'elitist' groups can contribute to maintenance of hazing rituals.	*In healthcare settings* Research has found increased aggression by staff in psychiatric units, and this may be due to the strong environmental cues such as the hierarchy of power.

Discuss explanations for institutional aggression. (9+16 marks)

Three explanations of institutional aggression are offered here, which will be sufficient for an exam answer. Zimbardo's Stanford Prison study is really useful here as research evidence, but use it wisely – don't over describe the procedures and findings.

SECTION 2: BIOLOGICAL EXPLANATIONS OF AGGRESSION

THE ROLE OF NEURAL AND HORMONAL MECHANISMS

Research in the 1930s suggested the involvement of the limbic system (a set of structures deep in the brain), but most recent research has focused on the amygdala and the prefrontal cortex.

Neural mechanisms

Amygdala

» Electrical stimulation produces aggression in humans and animals.
» Wong et al (1997) found reduced amygdala size and activity in violent criminals.
» Contradiction:
  • Müller et al (2003)
    – Positive and negative pictures were presented to six male psychopaths and six normal male controls.
    – At the same time, brain activity was measured using fMRI.
    – They found increased activity in several brain areas, including the amygdala.
» The exact role of the amygdala is unclear, but it seems it is part of a circuit of structures responsible for aggression, which is controlled in a top-down fashion by the prefrontal cortex.

Prefrontal cortex

» Thought to regulate amygdala-driven emotional responses, and damage here can result in a loss of control, impulsivity, immaturity, altered emotionality.
» Anderson et al (1999)
  • Damage to prefrontal cortex in infancy increases the risk of aggressive behaviour as adults.
  • The risk is greater than in people with adult-onset damage.
  • This may be because of a negative influence of brain damage on social development.
» Raine et al (1997) found reduced brain activity in the prefrontal cortex of 41 murderers. This is supported by other research, e.g. Volkow et al (1995) found reduced prefrontal cortex activity in the brains of 8 violent psychiatric prisoners.

Hormonal mechanisms

Aggression more often occurs in males than females, which is usually attributed to the male sex hormone testosterone.

 ASK AN EXAMINER

You could get a question on either neural or hormonal factors, or one requiring both.

Research with animals

» Vom Saal (1983) found that female rats who had occupied spaces in the womb closest to males were the most aggressive females in the litter. This is because they were exposed to more testosterone.
» Vom Saal's Organisation/activation model – prenatal exposure to androgen organises neural networks involved in aggression. These networks are later activated by exposure to testosterone. If there is no later burst of this hormone (e.g. due to castration), the networks are not activated, resulting in less aggression.
» Castration before puberty has long been used to make domestic animals more manageable. Beeman (1947) reduced aggression in male mice through castration and re-established normal aggression with testosterone injections.

Research with humans

» Dabbs et al (1995) investigated the relationship between testosterone, crime and prison behaviour and found those who had committed sexual and violent crimes had the highest levels of testosterone. They were also more likely to be the most confrontational prisoners.
» Dabbs et al (1988) measured testosterone in female inmates and found it positively related to unprovoked violence. Other research has not found this, which highlights problems that researchers have with operationalising aggression.
» There are issues with human ressearch – it is correlational, measuring aggression is problematic and unreliable, and many factors other than hormones influence aggression.

THE ROLE OF GENETIC FACTORS IN AGGRESSIVE BEHAVIOUR

Genes do not directly cause aggression but influence elements of our biology that contribute to it. A combination of *structural* (e.g. bone and muscle development) and *functional* (e.g. neurochemical and hormonal) genetic effects contributes to aggressive behaviour.

Selective breeding

This involves choosing animals with aggressive characteristics and mating them with others to enhance this trait. This has a long history, e.g. Spanish fighting bulls and fighting cocks.

Research

» Lagerspetz (1979) selectively bred mice to be 50% more aggressive than normal mice within 19 generations. They had heavier testes and forebrains and altered levels of neurochemicals serotonin and noradrenaline.

» Lagerspetz (1981) points out that genetic factors do not absolutely determine aggression since selectively bred aggressive mice can be conditioned to be less aggressive, and also aggressive wild animals can be tamed.

Twin studies

As selective breeding in humans is not possible, the next best thing is to study people with known genetic factors – i.e. twin studies, especially twins reared apart.

As humans are much more biologically complex and also live in more complex environments, discriminating between genetic and environmental influences on human aggression is very difficult.

Research

» A meta-analysis by Miles and Carey (1997) suggested heritability of 50% for aggression, but Plomin et al (1990) estimated a much smaller heritability.

» Canter (1973) found a small correlation of 0.14 for MZs reared together, but O'Connor (1980) found a correlation of 0.72 for the same population.

• This variability may be due to differences in methods of assessing aggression:

    – e.g. Rhee and Waldman (2002) found heritability estimate was 39% for self-reported aggression but 53% when reported by others.

• However, studies consistently show greater similarity of aggressiveness in MZs than DZs, indicating a genetic contribution.

Identical (MZ) twins		Non-identical (DZ) twins	
Reared together	Reared apart	Reared together	Reared apart
0.72	0.64	0.42	0.34
0.39	0.46	0.42	0.06
0.14	0.53	0.30	0.39

Table summarising correlations for MZ and DZ twins reared apart and together. Adapted from Miles and Carey (1997).

XYY syndrome

Some men have an extra male Y chromosome, and since males are more aggressive than females anyway, this might suggest further aggression in XYY males.

Research

» Jacobs et al (1965) found the incidence of XYY syndrome was 3% in a prison population compared to 0.1% of the normal population. These men were taller, had higher levels of testosterone and lower intelligence levels.

» Witkin et al (1976) could find no link between XYY syndrome and increased aggression in prison inmates, but did find lower levels of intelligence. Inspection of crimes showed that they were not more violent in nature but they were poorly planned. The researchers suggest that lower IQs in XYYs make them more likely to be caught, hence more of them in the prison population.

ASK AN EXAMINER

A question specifically on genetic factors could appear in the exam. Four kinds of evidence are presented here, which will give you loads of depth. Don't be afraid of the terminology – learn it and use it; it shows how well you understand things.

QUESTION TIME **?**

Describe and evaluate the role of genetic factors in aggressive behaviour. (9 + 16 marks)

MAOA gene and aggression

A number of studies have linked aggression to the monoamine oxidase A (MAOA) gene, which regulates the enzyme monoamine oxidase A. This enzyme breaks down several important neurotransmitters (e.g. serotonin, dopamine) which are associated with mood. A build up of these chemicals can cause people to respond to stressful situations aggressively. Removing excess amounts of neurotransmitter might thus reduce likelihood of aggression.

Research

» Brunner et al (1993) discovered a defective MAOA gene in Dutch family with a history of male violence which meant they had a deficiency in MAOA. The gene was passed on to men from the X chromosome of their mothers. Only men were affected because they have only one X chromosome, whilst women have two.

» Cases et al (1995) disabled the MAOA gene in the X chromosome of mice and found that without the mono-amine oxidase A enzyme, levels of dopamine and serotonin increased and males became highly aggressive. Females were unaffected. Restoring the function of the gene returned male mice to a normal state.

» Different forms of defective MAOA gene have been identified:
  • MAOA-L is a low activity form that produces less of the monoamine oxidase A enzyme.
  • MAOA-H is a high activity form that produces more of monoamine oxidase A enzyme.

  Research shows that the MAOA-L gene in particular is related to aggression.

» In an fMRI study Meyer-Lindberg et al (2006) found reductions in volume of amygdala and prefrontal cortex in MAOA-L compared to MAOA-H participants. These brain areas are often found to be impaired in anti-social individuals.

ASK AN EXAMINER

Whilst you could get questions which specifically ask for a combination of neural, hormonal and genetic explanations, you could get a very general one on biological explanations. The question is straightforward enough, but you are going to have to plan really carefully for this one since you can't write about everything.

QUESTION TIME ?

(a) Outline the role of neural mechanisms in aggression. (4 marks)
(b) Outline the role of hormonal mechanisms in aggression. (5 marks)
(c) Evaluate biological explanations of aggressive behaviour. (16 marks)

GENETICS AND AGGRESSION

SELECTIVE BREEDING

e.g. bulls

↓

LAGERSPETZ - BRED AGGRESSIVE MICE

↓

NOT ABSOLUTELY GENETIC - CAN BE TAMED WITH CONDITIONING

↓

DIFF's DUE TO METHODS OF MEASURING AGGRESSION

TWIN STUDIES

Alternative to selective breeding

↓

SEPARATING NATURE AND NURTURE?

↓

CANTER - 0.14
O'CONNOR - 0.72

↓

TREND - MZ's ARE MORE SIMILAR IN AGGRESSION THAN DZ's

MAOA GENE

Regulates enzymes without which neurotransmitters increase to make aggression more likely

↓

BRUNNER et al - DEFECTIVE MAOA GENE IN AGGRESSIVE MALES WITHIN A DUTCH FAMILY

↓

CASES et al - DISABLED AND RESTORED MAOA GENE IN MICE INFLUENCING AGGRESSIVE BEHAVIOUR

SECTION 3: AGGRESSION AS AN ADAPTIVE RESPONSE

Remember, you must focus on human aggressive behaviour here: use animal research carefully.

EVOLUTIONARY EXPLANATIONS OF HUMAN AGGRESSION

From an evolutionary perspective, humans are most likely to survive if they have access to resources; if they can defend their resources and protect their families; and if they can attract and gain access to mates. Aggressive behaviour may have evolved to support the human race in achieving these goals.

Aggression in males

» Males are motivated to acquire status since high status males have access to mates and resources for survival.
» High status males are more likely to be selected by females since such males will be better able to guarantee the survival of her and her offspring.
» NOT engaging in conflict with other males can therefore be costly.
» Low status males have to engage in high risk strategies to enhance their chances of reproduction.

> *Research evidence*
> Daly and Wilson (1985) – a review of murders found that the motive behind most conflicts was status. The victims and offenders were most likely to be men of low status and without a mate (unemployed and unmarried). Most victims/offenders knew each other so understood the status of their rival. Those of equal status were more likely to resort to aggression to a bid to move their status above their opponent.

Aggression in females

» Females are generally viewed as less aggressive since the costs of such behaviour outweigh the benefits.
» It is more important for the mother to survive because her presence is more critical to the survival of offspring than the father.
» A woman has nothing to gain by exhibiting aggression since her aim is not to gain high status but to secure a valuable male.
» To this end females have evolved low risk and indirect strategies in disputes and conflicts: e.g. they are more likely to use gossip and ostracism, aimed at reducing the attractiveness of competing females.

> *Research evidence*
> Hill and Hurtado (1996) – among the Ache of Paraguay, children are 5 times more likely to die if the mother dies, and 100% likely if this happens before the child is one year old.
>
> Griskevicius et al (2009) have shown that sex differences in aggression exist for both direct physical aggression (men exhibit more) and for indirect, verbal and psychological aggression (which females make more use of).

Infidelity and jealousy

» A woman can be 100% certain that the child she carries is hers, but a man has no such certainty. Sexual jealousy therefore has evolved to help males protect their investment. Daly and Wilson (1985) – found that sexual jealousy was the underlying factor in 58 out of 214 cases of murder.
» Male aggression against females is designed to deter females from indulging in behaviour which is not in the interests of the male. Bellis and Baker (1990) estimate that 7 to 14% of children are not fathered by the mother's husband or partner. Miller (1980) – of 44 battered wives living in a women's hostel in Canada, 55% cited jealousy as the reason for their husband's behaviour.
» Male aggression may also occur in response to a threat from a rival suitor. Young (1978) – asked to describe their likely reactions to a jealousy-inducing situation in a film, men predicted anger, drunkenness and threatening behaviour. Women however predicted crying, pretending not to care and increasing their own attractiveness.

Explanations of group display

Group display in animals is a specialised patterns of behaviour used for courtship or intimidation. It is linked to survival: males fight for access to females and to warn off rivals for their territory. The same factors are said to apply to human group display, e.g. sport and war.

Group display and war

From an evolutionary perspective, war is the formation of a coalition to attack others within the same species. Although there is risk to individuals it is reduced by aggressive *group* display. War allows one group status over another, giving them access to their land, resources and their women.

Chagnon (1968)

» Warfare exists among many modern-day tribal societies, e.g. Yanomamo of the Amazon rainforest.
» The only advantage one group can have over another is manpower, so they are obsessed with the size of their villages.
» The most frequent cause of conflict is abduction of women to increase their size.
» Battle can also give a warrior status and increase his chances of attracting females – successful warriors have more wives and children.

Pinker (1997)

» Points out that in WWII the Germans invading Eastern Europe carried out systematic rape and abuse of women.
» In Bosnia during the Yugoslavian conflict more than 20,000 Muslim women were raped as part of an organised attempt by Serbs to impregnate women who would then raise Serbian children; and also to terrorise others into fleeing their land.

Lehmann and Feldman (2008)

» Men who are stronger and more aggressive will win wars and survive to pass on their genes, leading to an increasingly aggressive species.
» Two traits have evolved in humans that determine the likelihood of conflict:

1. *Belligerence* (which increases the probability that one group will attack another).
2. *Bravery* (which increases the chances of winning).

Groups with males high in both qualities are most likely to go to war and win.

 Describe and evaluate one or more evolutionary explanations of human aggression. (9 + 16 marks)

Group display and sport

It has been argued that tribal warfare has been replaced by sporting events.

The New Zealand All Black rugby team does the 'Haka' before a game: this was originally performed by Maori warriors before going into battle.

These are ritualised forms of aggression where the benefits of success (e.g. high status and access to desirable mates) are available to competitors, but also felt by fans who belong to the wider 'tribe' ('basking in reflected glory').

Fans display their connection with winners (e.g. flags, clothes) to enhance their own image.

Marsh (1978)

Hooliganism is the equivalent of ceremonial conflict seen in some animal species.

» e.g. they are exclusively male and involve trials of strength over territory, and risk of physical harm and death are minimised.

This is a way of gaining power and status and therefore access to resources without threatening the survival of group members, thus preserving the species.

 Make sure that you know about two examples of group display in humans: one may not be enough.

(a) Outline and evaluate institutional explanations of human aggression. (4 + 8 marks)
(b) Outline and evaluate evolutionary explanations of human aggression. (5 + 8 marks)

HOW WELL DO I KNOW IT?	NOT AT ALL	MAYBE	OK	WELL	SUPERBLY
SECTION 1: SOCIAL PSYCHOLOGICAL APPROACHES TO EXPLAINING AGGRESSION					
Social psychological theories of aggression – Social leaning theory					
Social psychological theories of aggression – Deindividuation					
Explanations of institutional aggression					
SECTION 2: BIOLOGICAL EXPLANATIONS OF AGGRESSION					
The role of neural mechanisms in aggression					
The role of hormonal mechanisms in aggression					
The role of genetic factors in aggressive behaviour					
SECTION 3: AGGRESSION AS AN ADAPTIVE RESPONSE					
Evolutionary explanations of human aggression: infidelity and jealousy					
Explanations of group display in humans					

Eating behaviour

You are expected in the examination to show both the skills of knowledge and understanding and the skills of analysis and evaluation in relation to the topic Eating behaviour.

Where opportunities for their effective use arise, you will need to demonstrate an appreciation of issues and debates. These include the nature/nurture debate, ethical issues in research, free-will/determinism, reductionism, gender and culture bias, and the use of animals in research.

You will also need to demonstrate an understanding of How Science Works. You can do this through the effective use of studies in your answer (as description or evaluation) or where appropriate by evaluating methodology and findings.

WHAT YOU NEED TO KNOW

EATING BEHAVIOUR

- Factors influencing attitudes to food and eating behaviour, e.g. cultural influences, health concerns, mood and stress
- Explanations for the success or failure of dieting

BIOLOGICAL EXPLANATIONS OF EATING BEHAVIOUR

- The role of neural mechanisms involved in controlling eating and satiation
- Evolutionary explanations of food preference

EATING DISORDERS

- Psychological explanations of one eating disorder: e.g. anorexia nervosa and obesity
- Biological explanations, including neural and evolutionary explanations, for one eating disorder: e.g. anorexia nervosa and obesity

EXPLANATIONS FOR THE SUCCESS OR FAILURE OF DIETING

There are many reasons why people diet. Two important ones concern health (e.g., greater risks of type 2 diabetes when overweight) and body dissatisfaction (e.g., due to stigmatisation and prejudice).

ASK AN EXAMINER

There's a plural here – explanations. You are expected to know more than one!

Genetics

» The potential success or failure of dieting needs to be viewed in the context of genetic predispositions.

» Research suggests some people are genetically pre-disposed to being overweight (e.g., influencing things such as appetite regulation, metabolic rate, fat cell quantities etc.).

» From twin and adoption studies, Stroebe (2000) estimates that heredity can account for between 40% and 70% of weight.

Individual differences in responses to portion size

People who diet may be more prone to over-eating than people who do not diet. Herman et al (2005) suggest three reasons for this:

1. Distress

» Dieters are more likely to eat when distressed than non-dieters.

» Over-eating is more likely to occur when distress is 'personal' and related to negative or low moods.

2. Craving

» Dieters seem prone to experience cravings.

» Reasons for this are unclear, but cravings in dieters may be heightened due to:
Internal factors (being deprived of certain foods)
External factors (exposure to food cues)

3. Pre-loading

» 'Pre-loading' refers to the food someone is given to eat before free access to other foods.

» Pre-loading suppresses appetite in non-dieters, but does not have this same effect in dieters.

» This may be due to a 'what the heck' response – having eaten, dieters may take the view that there is no point maintaining a diet, and eat when there is an opportunity to do so.

The boundary model (Herman and Polivy, 1984)

» Eating is controlled by biological pressures to keep food intake within a set range between hunger and satiety.

» Between the satiety and hunger boundaries (a 'zone of biological indifference'), eating is largely regulated by social and environmental influences.

» Dieters have this physiological control of food undermined in two ways:

First:
• Because dieters impose a cognitively determined diet boundary within their zone of indifference, food intake is no longer solely regulated by biological cues.
• If this cognitive boundary is breached then dieters will overeat.

Second:
• Alternations between dieting and overeating widen the zone of biological indifference.
• As a result, dieters become less sensitive to hunger and satiation cues.
• This means that when their diet boundary is crossed, they are likely to eat more than non-dieters.

» The ability of dieters to prevent breaches of the 'dietary boundary' is lessened by things like distress and cravings.

SECTION 2: BIOLOGICAL EXPLANATIONS OF EATING BEHAVIOUR

THE ROLE OF NEURAL MECHANISMS INVOLVED IN CONTROLLING EATING AND SATIATION

We eat in order to function and survive. When and how much we eat is largely determined by our metabolism (the rate at which the body uses energy). Several physiological mechanisms try to maintain this energy homeostasis (balance).

The specification is very clear on this point. Both eating and satiation are required. Don't make the mistake of only learning one in the hope that the other will not come up.

Set point theory of homeostasis
» Our body weight is regulated to a biologically determined 'target'.
» If we eat too little or too much, homeostatic mechanisms alter our metabolism and appetite accordingly, in order to return us to our original weight.
» It becomes difficult for homeostatic mechanisms to do this if we persistently over-eat or under-eat and so we may settle on a new weight.

Don't worry too much if on the day of the exam you can't remember the biological terms: you can get away with using abbreviations like VMH and NPY.

Neural mechanisms controlling eating

The main area of the brain involved in the regulation of appetite is the hypothalamus.

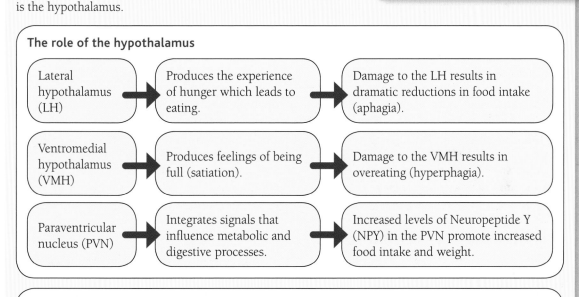

The role of the hypothalamus

Lateral hypothalamus (LH)	Produces the experience of hunger which leads to eating.	Damage to the LH results in dramatic reductions in food intake (aphagia).
Ventromedial hypothalamus (VMH)	Produces feelings of being full (satiation).	Damage to the VMH results in overeating (hyperphagia).
Paraventricular nucleus (PVN)	Integrates signals that influence metabolic and digestive processes.	Increased levels of Neuropeptide Y (NPY) in the PVN promote increased food intake and weight.

The role of ghrelin
» Ghrelin is a hormone secreted from the mucous membrane of an empty stomach.
» Contributes to eating behaviour by inhibiting signals to the brain that indicate satiety.
» When food is eaten the secretion of ghrelin stops.
» Lutter et al (2008) found that, in mice, hunger, stress and anxiety are associated with ghrelin.

IDea
Biological explanations of eating behaviour could be accused of being too deterministic. For example, whilst biology certainly plays an important part in eating behaviour, social and psychological factors also have a role. Timing of meals and types of food eaten are influenced by things like culture and convenience. Simply thinking about food has also been found to influence activity of brain areas involved in appetite, causing for example the release of saliva.

(a) Outline research into neural mechanisms involved in controlling eating. (4 marks)
(b) Outline research into neural mechanisms involved in controlling satiation. (5 marks)
(c) Assess biological explanations of eating behaviour. (16 marks)

The role of glucose (glucostatic theory)

» Blood glucose (sugar) levels are monitored by sensors in the liver and hypothalamus.

» The body consumes energy in the form of glucose.

» A decline in blood glucose levels triggers a drive to eat in order to replenish these glucose levels and maintain energy homeostasis.

» Whilst a drop in glucose concentrations increases feelings of hunger, increases in glucose are related to feelings of satiety.

Problems with glucostatic theory

» Blood glucose levels decline slightly a few minutes before eating but reverse just prior to eating. This happens even if no food is then eaten. This suggests that it is the brain initiating a dip in blood sugar levels prior to eating.

» A number of physiological changes are associated with eating, not just glucose levels. E.g. Woods et al (2000) found, in experiments on rats, that body temperature also fluctuates.

» Fats are also used for energy homeostasis, so it is likely that consumption of food is influenced by a number of factors, including glucose levels.

You need to know biological explanations for one eating disorder, so lots of the material here on the biology of eating behaviour can be used again in that section! Whilst it is good to organise your learning, it is not good to separate things strictly – be aware that there is a lot of cross-over and stuff from one place can often be used again in another.

Neural mechanisms controlling eating – evaluation

» Meal times and food types are more likely to be determined by social factors than by biology.

» Hunger is not the only thing to initiate eating – just *thinking* about food generates activity in the food-related parts of the brain and therefore changes eating behaviour.

» Pleasure centres in the brain also influence eating, with both the anticipation and onset of eating associated with increased dopamine activity (a neurotransmitter associated with mood).

» Learning is a very important factor – animals can learn to produce neurotransmitters and hormones that help regulate food intake at times of day when food is expected.

Neural mechanisms controlling satiation

When we eat, this eventually generates several body signals that cause us to feel full and stop eating.

The role of leptin (lipostatic theory)

Leptin is a hormone secreted by fat cells (adipocytes) which causes a decrease in appetite and energy expenditure. It is released in direct proportion to the amount of fat stored in fats cells and as such is an adipose (fat) signal to the brain. Leptin does not directly affect satiety but moderates other satiety signals:

Increase in adipocytes leads to secretion of more leptin, influencing satiety signals and thus making us feel full sooner.	**+**	A loss of adipocytes (e.g. because of dieting) results in a decline in leptin levels, reducing satiety signals and increasing our interest in food.

Research evidence

Mice with genetic mutations in the leptin gene (ob/ob mice) or leptin receptors (db/db mice) do not readily reach satiety, consume excessive amounts of food and become extremely obese (Zhang et al, 1994).

The VMH (considered a satiety centre) is particularly sensitive to leptin. Damage to the VMH can cause hyperphagia and obesity (Mayer and Thomas, 1967).

Discuss biological explanations of eating behaviour. (9 + 16 marks)

Material on neural explanations of eating disorders is also relevant here – after all, eating disorder is one aspect of eating behaviour!

The role of other mechanisms involved in satiation

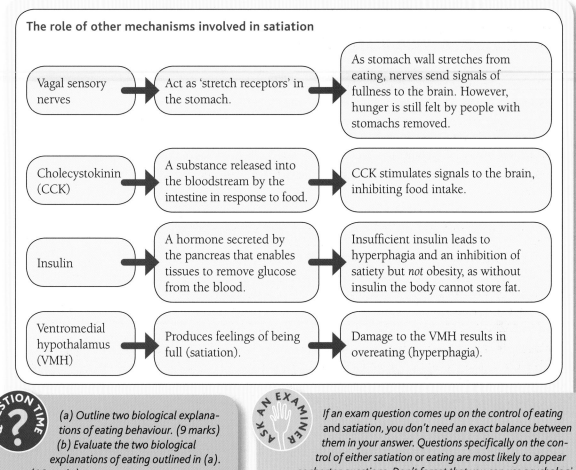

Vagal sensory nerves	Act as 'stretch receptors' in the stomach.	As stomach wall stretches from eating, nerves send signals of fullness to the brain. However, hunger is still felt by people with stomachs removed.
Cholecystokinin (CCK)	A substance released into the bloodstream by the intestine in response to food.	CCK stimulates signals to the brain, inhibiting food intake.
Insulin	A hormone secreted by the pancreas that enables tissues to remove glucose from the blood.	Insufficient insulin leads to hyperphagia and an inhibition of satiety but *not* obesity, as without insulin the body cannot store fat.
Ventromedial hypothalamus (VMH)	Produces feelings of being full (satiation).	Damage to the VMH results in overeating (hyperphagia).

QUESTION TIME

(a) Outline two biological explanations of eating behaviour. (9 marks)
(b) Evaluate the two biological explanations of eating outlined in (a). (16 marks)

ASK AN EXAMINER

If an exam question comes up on the control of eating and satiation, you don't need an exact balance between them in your answer. Questions specifically on the control of either satiation or eating are most likely to appear as shorter questions. Don't forget that you can use psychological explanations as evaluations of biological ones!

NEURAL MECHANISMS - SATIATION

LEPTIN - 'FAT' SIGNAL TO BRAIN
= LESS EATING & ENERGY USE

— MODERATES SATIETY SIGNALS

MICE WITH MUTANT LEPTIN GENE / RECEPTORS
— DO NOT FEEL FULL
— EAT LOADS
— BECOME OBESE.

VMH (SATIETY CENTRE) - SENSITIVE TO LEPTIN
DAMAGE = HYPERPHAGIA & OBESITY

TOO REDUCTIONIST - CULTURE? PSYCHOLOGY?

OTHERS

• VAGAL NERVES - STRETCH RECEPTORS

• CCK = ↓ EATING

• DAMAGED VMH = HYPERPHAGIA

EVOLUTIONARY EXPLANATIONS OF FOOD PREFERENCE

Evolutionary explanations focus on the role of food preference in survival and reproductive fitness. We have evolved favourable attitudes towards particular foods, and these influence food preference.

We are predisposed to learn to associate foods with contexts and consequences:
- Prevents us eating harmful things, thus increasing survival chances.
- Reduces the likelihood of eating life-threatening foods again.

Neophobia (fear of new things)

» Children (especially young ones) tend to reject new foods in favour of those that are familiar.

» Sweet and salty foods are preferred to those that are bitter and sour.

» Predispositions towards food change as we grow older, hence neophobia reduces:
  - Initially, access to food is controlled by adults so neophobia is less useful.
  - Neophobia heightens with increasing independence, serving a protective function.
  - Neophobia reduces in adulthood since rules of food sourcing and preparation have been learned and can be applied.

Preference for nutritious foods

» Food preference changes, with age, to flavours associated with high energy.

» This would have been adaptive in environments where high energy foods are in short supply.

» It is also adaptive to know which foods are most nutritious.

» Nowadays, where there is often ample food, this is no longer adaptive and leads to unhealthy weight gain.

» Animals and humans can learn very quickly to prefer high calorie foods (Booth, 1982).

Preference for sweet foods

» Sugar (glucose) is an extremely valuable substance that helps us survive.

» It provides fast effective energy and is essential for brain and body functioning, giving a survival advantage.

» Excess glucose is stored as fat by the body for use in the future when sweet foods may be harder to come by.

» Sweet foods are preferred over non-sweet foods.

» This is instinctive:
  - Grill and Norgren (1973) found that laboratory rats immediately accept sweet foods.
  - Desor et al (1973) found that infants as young as 1–3 days prefer sweet flavours.
  - Bell et al (1973) found that Inuit people of Alaska lack sweet foods in their diet and have little or no experience of them but are quick to accept them when available.

» We are biologically sensitive to sugar – e.g. areas of the tongue sensitive to sweet things carry more fibres linked to the brain.

You will find material on evolution in the section on eating disorders too. You can use some of that in an essay on food preference; just be sure to shape the material to the question.

'From an evolutionary point of view, food preference is related to survival and the propagation of one's genes'.
Discuss evolutionary explanations of food preference. (9 + 16 marks)

IDea *Evolutionary explanations of human behaviour are deterministic. Whilst biological inheritance no doubt plays a role in food preference, evolutionary explanations largely ignore or at least underestimate the importance of social and cultural influences on eating behaviour.*

SECTION 3: EATING DISORDERS

Don't get too involved with describing anorexia. Unless you are asked to describe the features of your chosen eating disorder, doing so will gain you few if any marks.

ANOREXIA NERVOSA

What is it?

» Refusal to maintain minimum normal weight and fear of weight gain.

» Deliberate weight-loss and a weight of 15% or more below normal.

» Disturbance in perception of own body shape, leading to an insistence that the person is overweight.

» It is often co-morbid with obsessive compulsive disorder (OCD) and/or depression.

» There are two kinds: 'restricted' type – associated with self-starvation, but not purging; and 'binge-eating/purging' type.

» There are many medical side effects, with about 5% dying of the disorder.

Psychological explanations of anorexia nervosa

Remember – only ONE disorder, so anorexia OR obesity, not both!

Experiential factors

» Trauma, abuse, bullying, teasing about appearance, and bereavement are linked to eating disorder development.

Research

• Rastam and Gillberg (1991) found that 14% of anorexics had experienced a negative life event in the three months prior to the disorder onset whereas none of the controls had.

• Other research supports this, but such research is correlational and retrospective so hard to interpret.

» Childhood sexual abuse is a risk factor, but not every abused child grows to develop an eating disorder, nor is it clear why there should be a link.

Research

• Casper and Lyubomirsky (1997) suggest that adverse early experiences lead to other psychopathologies underlying eating disorders.

• Polivy and Herman (2002) suggested that where a person feels their life is 'out of control' in some way, controlling themselves and their body and weight provides them with a sense of control. Individuals therefore derive emotional gratification from anorexia.

Cognitive factors

» Anorexia is associated with obsessive thoughts and rigid thinking patterns.

» Socio-cultural pressures can be converted into behaviours through cognitive processes.

» Once established, negative schemata about weight distort perceptions and experience.

» Consequently, self worth becomes dependent on weight control.

Research

Cooper (2005) says anorexics:

• Experience disturbances in information processing about food and eating, weight and body shape.

• Have attentional biases to food, weight and body shape, as revealed by a modified Stroop procedure.

• Have a memory bias for words related to food, weight and body shape.

Personality and dispositional factors

Stress and low mood may precede the onset of anorexia, and mood disorders often co-occur. It is not clear whether such things are a cause or consequence however.

Low self-esteem
» Prominent among those with eating disorders.
» May be due to distorted body perception.
» Anorexia may be a coping strategy, a means of establishing control and combating low self-esteem.
» Perfectionism may be a predisposing factor.
» Perfectionists set very high standards for themselves and are very self-critical, possibly leading to damaged self-esteem.

Research
Bardone-Cone et al (2007) found that anorexics score highly on measures of perfectionism, also correlated highly with body dissatisfaction and the pursuit of thinness.

Body dissatisfaction
» Negative feelings about the self are often expressed as negative feelings about the body.
» Body dissatisfaction is associated with dieting, which in turn is associated with anorexia.
» The influence of media is thought to operate through body dissatisfaction. May be exaggerated, or developed through media images of thinness.

Research
Polivy and Herman (2002) say body dissatisfaction is a 'necessary' factor in the development of anorexia but does not wholly explain it. Unhappiness with one's body is possible without dieting.

(a) Outline and evaluate psychological explanations of one eating disorder. (4 + 8 marks)
(b) Discuss biological explanations of one eating disorder. (5 + 8 marks)

Sociocultural factors

» Preoccupation with thinness is only found in cultures where food is abundant.
» The more thinness is prized the more prevalent it is.
» Such preoccupation can both cause and maintain the disorder.
» There is however huge variation in the desire to be thin within every culture.

Family systems theory

Anorexia has been thought to be a symptom of dysfunctional family relationships and structures.

Disturbed families
Minuchin et al (1978) suggest a family may exhibit at least one of the following:

Enmeshment: Parents are intrusive and over-involved, dismissive of child's emotional needs.
Over-protection: Family members are over-concerned about parenting.
Rigidity: Tendency to avoid change and maintain status quo.
Conflict avoidance: Conflicts remain unresolved.

Bennett (2005) suggests that anorexia helps to direct attention away from other problems in the family. Weight loss might also be used as a way of gaining acceptance, of punishing parents and avoiding responsibilities.

Family reinforcement
» Families reinforce anorexia by praising slenderness and self-control.

Evaluation
Polivy and Herman (2005) – A problem is that family research of this kind is correlational and retrospective and so the cause of the disorder is impossible to determine clearly.

You could well get an exam question asking for a specific number of psychological explanations – one, one or more, two, two or more. It is good to know about a variety of explanations as it gives you more to evaluate.

Biological explanations of anorexia nervosa

Describe and evaluate biological explanations of one eating disorder. (9 + 16 marks)

Genetics

Family studies

» Studies have found higher rates of anorexia in people who have relatives with the disorder.

» Lilenfield et al (1998) looked at the family history of 26 anorexics and found a family vulnerability.

» Vulnerability does not necessarily mean full-blown anorexia. Relatives were seven to twelve times more likely to have 'sub-threshold' forms (not quite anorexia).

Twin studies

» Identical (MZ) twins share 100% of their genes, so shared eating disorders might be due to genes.

» Holland et al (1988) found that 56% of MZ twins in their study both had anorexia but only 5% of DZ twins both suffered with it. This clearly indicates a genetic component (since MZ/DZ twins share environments, the difference must be due to genes).

» However, not 100%, so it is not possible to discount environmental influence completely.

Genes

» Grice et al (2002) compared DNA samples from families with two or more members with restricted-type anorexia and found susceptibility for anorexia on chromosome 1.

They concluded that the cause is unlikely to be a single gene, but more likely to be a number of genes each contributing to the onset of the disorder.

Evaluation of genetic explanations

Recent increases in anorexia cannot be wholly explained by genetics.

Genetic evidence is inconclusive – separating genetic and environmental influences is extremely difficult.

It is not clear how a genetic predisposition would lead to anorexia – e.g. would it make self-starvation more likely, or increase vulnerability to risk factors such as low self-esteem?

Neural mechanisms

> ASK AN EXAMINER
>
> *You could be asked specifically about neural mechanisms, so make sure you know that well. Genetics is really useful to know about for questions about general biological explanations.*

Hypothalamus

» Involved in the regulation of appetite.

» Damage to the lateral hypothalamus (LH) causes a loss of appetite.

Evaluation

Unlikely to be a central cause of anorexia since animal studies show damage results in lack of hunger. By contrast, anorexics often report intense hunger.

Serotonin

» Thought to be involved because of anorexia/OCD similarities, and serotonin levels influence OCD.

» Kaye et al (2005) found lower levels of serotonin during starvation and recovery in anorexics than in controls.

Evaluation

There is a problem of cause and effect – are changes in serotonin levels a cause or consequence of anorexia?

Insula

» Nunn et al (2008) suggest problems with the insula are linked to the condition, since this brain area integrates functions of other centres relevant to features of anorexia.

» A failure to complete this integration properly may result in the disorder.

Evaluation

It is difficult to test this hypothesis since doing anything to the insula would affect all the areas of the brain to which it is connected.

> ASK AN EXAMINER
>
> *Look back the section 'Biological mechanisms controlling eating behaviour' – lots of that material is relevant here too!*

Evolutionary explanations of anorexia nervosa

Discuss evolutionary explanations of one eating disorder. (9 + 16 marks)

Pseudopathology (Crawford, 1998)

» A pseudopathology is an illness brought about by an entirely intact adaptive mechanism responding in a modern environment it was not designed for.

» In terms of evolution, women strive to be attractive to men. In the past this will have meant being able to provide and carry children; now it means being thin.

» The result is that there is an adaptive advantage to being thin.

» The adaptation mechanism is in place and is working, but under the socio-cultural pressures of the media of today the result may be anorexia.

Adapted to Flee Famine Hypothesis (AFFH) (Guisinger, 2003)

» Features of anorexia helped early humans to migrate to more plentiful environments in response to local famine.

» Efficient migration meant switching off the usual adaptations to hunger (lethargy, energy conservation and hunger).

» Therefore, restricting food intake, denial of starvation and hyperactivity could help migration.

» Whilst no longer an adaptive response, a very low body weight (e.g. through dieting) may make the body respond as if threatened by famine, and result in anorexia.

Controlled infertility (Wasser and Barach, 1983)

» Whilst on the face of it an evolutionary disadvantage, stopping menstruation may actually be adaptive.

» Women invest a lot in the relatively few children they can have in their lifetime, so that having one in a time of famine is very risky indeed.

» Infertility brought about by controlled food intake might have allowed our ancestors to control when they produced children.

» This protects the mother, frees up food for others that need it, and existing children would be more likely to survive to the next generation.

Delayed reproduction (Sturbe, 1987)

» Delaying reproduction to later in life allows a woman to seek and achieve security and provide better for a child.

» E.g., instead of becoming pregnant, teenagers may go to university and afterwards get a better job.

» This allows the woman to be more choosy and attract a better quality mate.

Caring-for-kin hypothesis (Voland and Voland, 1989)

» Anorexics are often very caring and protective of their own families.

» Anorexic women often come from extremely protective (even over-protective) families.

Being anorexic and therefore infertile produces an additional family helper, providing for advancement of the genetic line vicariously through other children in her family.

Evaluation of evolutionary explanations

Given the importance of survival and reproduction in evolutionary theory, eating disorders are puzzling conditions since both are threatened by these disorders.

Evolutionary explanations are difficult to prove or disprove scientifically.

It is not clear whether one evolutionary explanation is correct or whether they all are; and eating disorders could occur for a number of evolutionary reasons – this is a weakness of the approach.

OBESITY

Don't get too involved with describing obesity. Unless you are asked to describe the features of your chosen eating disorder, doing so will gain you few if any marks.

What is it?

Obesity can be identified by looking at Body Mass Index (BMI), population averages, waist circumference, or percentage of body fat measured with calipers at various points on the body, but there are difficulties with all of these.

Prentice (1999) argues that, for obesity to occur, energy intake must remain higher than energy expenditure over a prolonged period. According to Kopelman (1999) obesity is better seen as group of varied disorders rather than as a single one, with causes ranging from purely biological to purely psychological.

Remember – only ONE disorder so anorexia OR obesity, not both!

Psychological explanations of obesity

Emotional and restrained eating

» There is a greater risk of over-eating in emotional eaters.

» Herman and Mack (1975) – emotional arousal reduces eating restraint.

» Heatherton et al (1993) – over-eating is an escape from self awareness caused by emotional pain.

Evaluation

Not all research agrees that emotional eating results in weight gain.

The theory explains why people might fail to maintain diet weight loss over time.

Emotional problems

» Some studies show the incidence of anxiety and depression is higher than usual among obese binge-eaters.

Evaluation

Studies have failed to consistently show higher incidence of emotional problems amongst the obese than in the general population.

Wardle (1999) – emotional disorders in obese people are better thought of as an effect rather than a cause of the eating disorder.

Binge-eating disorder

» Defined as eating an objectively large amount of food while feeling a lack of control on at least two occasions a week.

» Usually develops in later adolescence/early adulthood and is associated with depression, low self-esteem and body dissatisfaction.

Evaluation

Although it occurs in 1 to 3% of the population, up to 30% of people seeking weight loss complain of it.

Not present in all obese people: therefore does not explain all cases of obesity.

'Eating disorders are complex and highly distressing phenomena, but have a great deal in common in terms of underlying psychological processes'. Discuss psychological explanations of one eating disorder. (9 + 16 marks)

Food addiction

» Obesity may be due to carbohydrate craving (an overwhelming desire to consume high carb food).

Evaluation

Obese people do not always eat more carbs, tending to prefer sweet, fatty foods. Rather than addiction, it might be a control difficulty due to palatability of modern foods.

Night-eating syndrome (NES)

» More common in obese people, it involves consumption of over 25% of daily calories after evening meal, insomnia and little/no breakfast. Sometimes there is nocturnal eating/drinking syndrome (NEDS), where a person wakes up and must eat/drink before sleeping again.

Evaluation

Little evidence of a positive relationship between NES or NEDS and degree of obesity.

Environmental uncertainty

» The environment was much more unpredictable for our ancestors, leading to uncertainties about food supply.

» They would cycle through periods of famine and plenty.

» A useful strategy would be to eat as much as possible whenever they could so that if famine arrived then they would have stored fat to see them through.

» What results in obesity now might have provided an evolutionary advantage in the past.

QUESTION TIME

Outline and evaluate neural and evolutionary explanations of one eating disorder. (9 + 16 marks)

Pima Indians – Chamala et al (2008)

» Modern Pima Indians show unusually high levels of obesity.

» Researchers found that their metabolic efficiency was being genetically influenced.

» They suggested that this provided an evolutionary advantage for their ancestors:

   The Pima would have lived in harsh barren desert-like conditions.
   Their genes provided them with the maximum advantage from any food they found.

ASK AN EXAMINER

You can apply the general criticisms of evolution theory presented earlier on page 41 to obesity, here.

IDea

Evolutionary explanations tend to ignore or at least underestimate the crucial role played by social and cultural influences in obesity. Because of this, evolutionary explanations of obesity could be accused of being too deterministic.

EVOLUTIONARY EXPLANATIONS OF OBESITY

SURVIVAL — MISMATCH – BODIES & MODERN LIVING → ADAPTIVE FAT STORAGE → NOT ADAPTIVE NOW – LOTS FATS/SUGARS

PREFERENCE — SUGAR → GOOD BUT RARE SO EATEN SPARINGLY → NOW ABUNDANT = OVEREATING

UNCERTAINTY — DODGY FOOD SUPPLIES → EAT LOTS WHEN AVAILABLE → ADVANTAGE DURING FAMINE

CHAMALA et al – PIMA INDIAN METABOLIC EFFICIENCY IN MODERN ENVIRONMENT = OBESITY

- SURVIVAL & REPRODUCTION THREATENED – MAKES NO SENSE
- DIFFICULT TO SCIENTIFICALLY PROVE / DISPROVE
- MORE THAN ONE EXPLANATION – ALL CORRECT OR ONE?
- TOO REDUCTIONIST?

HOW WELL DO I KNOW IT?	NOT AT ALL	MAYBE	OK	WELL	SUPERBLY
SECTION 1: EATING BEHAVIOUR					
Factors influencing attitudes to food and eating behaviour: cultural influences					
Factors influencing attitudes to food and eating behaviour: mood					
Factors influencing attitudes to food and eating behaviour: health concerns					
Explanations for the success or failure of dieting					
SECTION 2: BIOLOGICAL EXPLANATIONS OF EATING BEHAVIOUR					
The role of neural mechanisms involved in controlling eating and satiation					
Evolutionary explanations of food preference					
SECTION 3: EATING DISORDERS					
Psychological explanations of one eating disorder: anorexia nervosa					
Biological explanations, including neural and evolutionary explanations, for one eating disorder: anorexia nervosa					
Psychological explanations of one eating disorder: obesity					
Biological explanations, including neural and evolutionary explanations, for one eating disorder: obesity					

Gender

You are expected in the examination to show both the skills of knowledge and understanding and the skills of analysis and evaluation in relation to the topic Gender.

Where opportunities for their effective use arise, you will need to demonstrate an appreciation of issues and debates. These include the nature/nurture debate, ethical issues in research, free-will/determinism, reductionism, gender and culture bias and the use of animals in research.

You will also need to demonstrate an understanding of How Science Works. You can do this through the effective use of studies in your answer (as description or evaluation) or where appropriate by evaluating methodology and findings.

WHAT YOU NEED TO KNOW

PSYCHOLOGICAL EXPLANATIONS OF GENDER DEVELOPMENT
- Cognitive developmental theory, including Kohlberg, and gender schema theory
- Explanations for psychological androgyny and gender dysphoria including relevant research

BIOLOGICAL INFLUENCES ON GENDER
- The role of hormones and genes in gender development
- Evolutionary explanations of gender roles
- The biosocial approach to gender development

SOCIAL CONTEXTS OF GENDER ROLE
- Social influences on gender role: e.g. the influence of schools and the media
- Cross-cultural studies of gender role

SECTION 1: PSYCHOLOGICAL EXPLANATIONS OF GENDER DEVELOPMENT

COGNITIVE DEVELOPMENTAL THEORY

These theories emphasise the importance of internal thought processes in the development of gender.

Kohlberg's theory

» His stage theory says that as a child's cognition matures so does their understanding of gender. They can only acquire concepts of gender when they are 'ready' to acquire this knowledge.
» Children will be affected in different ways by male and female models as they pass through the stages.
» Once they identify themselves as male or female they pay more attention to same sex models and imitate them more (*self-socialisation*).
» Whilst society plays an important role, its influence is limited by the child's level of cognitive development.

Stage 1 – Gender identity: children 2–3 years...
Can label their own sex correctly and can categorise other individuals.
Judgments are based upon the external features from as young as 15 months.
Age 2 – can label categories as male and female.
Age 3 – can describe themselves as boy or girl.
Don't understand what it means to be male or female or that gender is a fixed trait.

Stage 2 – Gender stability: children 3–7 years...
Understand that gender remains stable for life.
Realise that they have always been male or female.
Can correctly answer questions such as "When you grow up will you be a mummy or daddy?"
Understand gender as a fixed trait within themselves.

Stage 3 – Gender consistency: children 7–12 years...
Are confused about gender of others until they acquire gender consistency.
Develop understanding of stability of gender in others.
No longer use external features to judge gender.
Show Piaget's conservation skills – i.e. even if an object changes externally it fundamentally remains the same.

Evaluation of Kohlberg's theory

Thompson (1975) tested 2 and 3 year-olds' ability to apply gender labels. Consistent with Kohlberg, he found the youngest could identify genders correctly but struggled to label their own gender. The oldest could apply labels correctly and recognise their own gender.

Slaby and Frey (1975) support the idea of sequential development, but question the age at which children reach consistency. They found that children as young as 5 may have reached this stage.

It is difficult to separate the relative influence of developing cognition from the influence of society in gender development, since both influences occur simultaneously.

The way that Kohlberg tested his theory may have underestimated children's understanding. Martin and Halverson (1983) found that children show a 'pretend response bias' when asked questions about gender change, suggesting more complex thinking.

Describe and evaluate Kohlberg's cognitive developmental theory of gender. (9 + 16 marks)

When evaluating a theory you can also use another to illustrate differences or shortcomings. E.g., gender schema theory could be used with Kohlberg's, as could biological theories.

Describe and evaluate gender schema theory. (9 + 16 marks)

Gender schema theory

» Challenges Kohlberg – understanding of gender need only be basic to learn sex stereotypes

» Bem (1981) and Martin and Halverson (1981) say child begins to form a gender schema as soon as they notice that people are organised into categories of male and female.

» May be able to make this distinction from 18 months old.

» According to Martin and Halverson (1981) there are two types of sex-related schema:

1. In-group, out-group' schema contains general information about male and female categories.

2. The 'own-sex' schema is a more specific and personalised version: e.g. a child can move the schema on from 'a doll is for a girl' to 'a doll is for a girl, I am a girl, a doll is for me.'

Why do schemas develop?

» Children group information and form rules to make sense of the complex world around them.

» This process helps them to understand where they fit in.

» Important step towards establishing a self-identity.

How do schemas develop?

» Gender schemas become more complex once child categorises self as 'in-group' (same sex) not 'out-group' (opposite sex).

» Evaluate 'in-group' members and their actions and activities as positive.

» Evaluate 'out-group' members and their actions and activities as negative.

» Once the child has established their own group they are motivated to learn more about both groups.

» They establish behaviour consistent with own sex, and behaviour inconsistent and appropriate to opposite sex.

» Own-sex schema becomes increasingly more elaborate.

How schemas guide behaviour

» 'Sex-appropriate plans of action' direct children's behaviour.

» A girl acts consistently with her own sex by playing with dolls but avoiding the train or fire engine.

» A boy knows that boys like football; to remain consistent with this schema he will need to learn to play football.

How schemas influence memory

» Information consistent with a gender schema is remembered better than information that is not.

» Schemas can be responsible for inaccuracies in recall: e.g. an observation of a woman mending a car may be recalled as the woman cleaning the car – a woman mending a car is not consistent with their gender schema.

(a) Outline two cognitive developmental theories of gender. (9 marks)
(b) Evaluate one of the theories outlined in (a). (16 marks)

Evaluation of gender schema theory

Children only need basic gender knowledge prior to an understanding of sex stereotypes.
Martin and Little (1990) looked at the toy preference of 2 to 5 year-old children and found that applying simple labels to toys (e.g. 'something boys like') was enough to encourage strong sex-typed preferences.

Children apply negative evaluations to the opposite sex and positive evaluations to their own sex once they have established an 'in-group, out-group schema'.
Kuhn (1978) found that, as children come to recognise their gender as permanent, they tend to describe their own gender positively and the opposite as bad.

Information that is not consistent with gender schema will be subject to distortion and reconstruction.
Carter and Levy (1988) showed children pictures: half for each sex were consistent with gender stereotypes and the other half inconsistent. They found that gender schema distorted recall, (e.g. a female mending a car would be recalled as a male).

Established gender schema leads to a better memory for gender consistent stereotypes.
Liben and Signorella (1993) showed children line drawings of people engaged in various activities and found that recall was better for images showing men in traditional masculine pursuits than for images of men in feminine roles.

EXPLANATIONS OF PSYCHOLOGICAL ANDROGYNY AND GENDER DYSPHORIA

Psychological androgyny

» Androgyny refers to having a mixture of masculine and feminine traits.
» Young children's sex-role ideas are still very rigid, and no signs of androgyny are seen in children younger than 10 years.
» Martin and Halverson (1981) argue that children learn appropriate behaviour for both sexes but only display behaviour that is reinforced; and since the environment does not reinforce inappropriate behaviour, it is not performed.

Importance of schemas in development of androgyny

» This explains why only older children show androgynous behaviour.
» Schemas become more complex as used to make sense of new situations and become more flexible as individuals widen their experiences.
» As children develop cognitive maturity they become involved with more social groups; they add information to self schemas to define selves as a good musician, student etc.
» These traits cut across gender groups.
» Children learn that rules regarding gender become more blurred.
» Older children lose the 'in-group', 'out-group' aspect of stereotyping and gain a flexible view of sex-typing only possible once a certain level of cognitive development is reached.

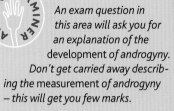

An exam question in this area will ask you for an explanation of the development of androgyny. Don't get carried away describing the measurement of androgyny – this will get you few marks.

Key elements in the development of androgyny

> 1. The child must be at a stage of cognitive development that allows flexibility of thinking.

> 2. The appropriate reinforcement must be available in the environment.

Evaluation

» Bem (1983) claims that parents could create a gender aschematic child by eliminating sex stereotyping in the flow of cultural information that forms the child's gender schema. The concept of gender should be based upon biology and not culture.

» For Sedney (1987), whilst androgynous parents do not produce androgynous children, the children often grow up to be androgynous adults.

» A longitudinal study by Block et al (1973) supports the idea that androgyny is a long-term consequence of non-sex-typed parenting. Two key factors they identified which encouraged the development of androgyny were:
  1. A warm and supportive family atmosphere with psychological healthy and satisfied parents.
  2. Flexibility in defining gender roles, with parents demonstrating androgynous personality styles.

» Guastello and Guastello (2003) found that daughters showed a decline in androgyny and an increase in masculine gender-typing compared to their mothers, challenging the idea of parental influence on psychological androgyny in adulthood.

» Guastello and Guastello (2003) also challenge the claim that androgyny is a sign of mental health, instead finding only masculine traits positively associated with mental health and high self-esteem.

(a) Outline what is meant by psychological androgyny. (4 marks)
(b) Outline one explanation for psychological androgyny. (5 marks)
(c) Evaluate explanations for psychological androgyny. Use research in your answer. (16 marks)

Describe and evaluate explanations for psychological androgyny and/or gender dysphoria. (9 + 16 marks)

Gender dysphoria

» Gender dysphoria is also known as *gender identity disorder* and is characterised by a mismatch between a person's external appearance and the way they feel with regard to their gender.

» Outward appearance is unambiguous – a 'normal' male or female – but the individual feels uncomfortable with their external appearance.

» They feel as though they have been born the wrong sex.

» In the past this was known as transsexualism. However, although the individual may cross-dress to feel more comfortable, the condition is distinct from transvestism as the person achieves no sexual arousal from dressing as the opposite sex.

» The rate of gender identity disorder, although relatively rare, is five times greater in males than in females.

Gender identity disorder is five times greater in males

» Zucker and Green (1992) suggest that this may be due to greater biological vulnerability in boys during the early stage of foetal development – partial secretion or partial response to secretion of androgen could lead to incomplete male development.

» They also note that rates relate only to those who have been diagnosed. As society is less tolerant of cross-gender behaviour in boys, they are more likely to be referred. Girls may need to show more extreme opposite sex behaviour than boys before being referred, so maybe there are as many gender dysphoric females.

Explanations of gender dysphoria: Separation anxiety

Coates and Person (1985) claim that extreme anxiety caused by maternal separation results in feminine behaviour, which they say is an attempt to 'restore a fantasy tie to the physically or emotionally absent mother.'

In an attempt to soothe the anxiety, a boy demonstrates cross-gender behaviour – but in imitating his mother he confuses being her with having the comfort of her presence.

Evaluation

In their study, 60% of 25 boys with gender identity disorder also met the criteria for separation anxiety disorder. This is supported by Lowry and Zucker (1991) who found, from a sample of 29 boys with gender identity disorder, 16 (55%) were diagnosed with separation anxiety.

This is correlational research so we cannot claim that separation anxiety *causes* gender identity disorder, only that there is a possible *relationship* between the two disorders.

Whilst there may be attachment difficulties, Bailey and Zucker (1995) noted other behavioural problems in childhood including depression. This could be due to the stigma and stress associated with gender identity.

Explanations of gender dysphoria: Parental influences

Case histories of boys with gender identity disorder reveal details of reinforcement of traditionally feminine behaviour – for example mothers giving young boys attention for dressing in girls' clothes and declaring them 'cute'.

E.g., Green (1974) found that in a sample of 'feminine' boys, 15% had been dressed by parents in girls' clothes during infancy and as toddlers.

Evaluation

Stoller (1975) found that mothers typically adopted terms used to describe feminine beauty when asked to describe their sons' facial features. He suggested that the attractiveness of the boys acted as a trigger for parental feminisation, particularly from the mother.

Whilst signs of the disorder are evident in very young children, it is not clear if these are shaped by parental behaviour or whether parents are responding to differences that already exist.

The distinct opposie sex behaviour would need extreme environmental responses from parents to explain, e.g. actively and consistently promoting it.

Outline and evaluate explanations for gender dysphoria. (9 + 16 marks)

SECTION 2: BIOLOGICAL INFLUENCES ON GENDER

Discuss the role of hormones and genes in gender development. (9 + 16 marks)

THE ROLE OF HORMONES AND GENES IN GENDER DEVELOPMENT

The role of genes

» Biological sex is determined chromosomally – females have XX chromosomes and males XY chromosomes.
» The ovum (egg) contains the X chromosome, whilst half of the male sperm contain X and half contain Y chromosomes.
» Whether the foetus is male or female is determined by which sperm fertilises the ovum.
» The Y chromosome controls the development of glands that produce male sex hormones.
» Until the sixth week of development in the womb, all foetuses have identical gonads (sex glands) that have the potential to develop into ovaries or testes.
» In the sixth week Y chromosomes produce a protein which causes the undifferentiated gonads to become testes, and if the protein is not present the gonads become ovaries.

The role of hormones

» Once gonads are developed, further sexual development is triggered by the release of sex hormones.
» There are two parts to the undifferentiated gonads:
» The Mullerian system has the potential to develop into female sex organs and the Wolffian system male.
» If testes are present androgens are released and Wolffian system develops; and if androgens are not present Mullerian system develops.
» Androgens are male hormones and two androgens are responsible for masculinisation: testosterone and dihydrotestosterone .
» They prenatally influence the development of the male sex organs and masculinise the brain; postnatally they are responsible for activating the sex organs during puberty.

Research evidence

Milton Diamond (1950s)
» Gender behaviour innate and instinctive.
» Experiments with animals showed the influence of testosterone on gender.
» Pregnant rats injected with testosterone.
» Female offspring had genitals that were male-like in appearance and caused the females to attempt to mate with other female rats.

Money and Ehrhardt (1972)
» Studied children with androgenital syndrome.
» Female foetuses exposed to androgens in utero later showed masculine behaviour.
» But the effects of socialisation cannot be ruled out.
» Children with androgenital syndrome are often born with genital abnormalities, which affects how people behave towards them.

Imperato-McGinley et al (1974)
» Described a rare genetic disorder where males were being born with ambiguous external genitalia resulting in some being raised as girls until puberty when voices broke, testes descended and clitoris-like phallus enlarged into a penis.
» Despite being raised as girls for the first 12 years they had male sexual orientation, showing that they could change their gender identity.

Gorski (1980)
» Found an area in the hypothalamus of rats called the sexually dimorphic nucleus (sdn), which was twice as big in males as it is in females.
» Female pregnant rats injected with testosterone – the offspring exhibited male-like behaviour and on autopsy had male-sized sdn's.
» This shows the influence of testosterone on the rat brain.

Swaab (1997)
» Post-mortems of human brains revealed male sdn's twice the size of female ones.
» This only shows male and female brains are structurally different: it does not explain differences in gender identity.

EVOLUTIONARY EXPLANATIONS OF GENDER ROLES

» Gender differences exist because they have evolved and therefore must be advantageous to each sex.
» Buss (1995) argues that men and women differ in the psychological domains where they have faced different problems of adaption. Where the sexes have been presented with the same problem the evolutionary solution has been the same and there are no gender differences.

Cognitive ability (male) →
» Men's visuo-spatial skills superior to women's since in the EEA men were the providers and spent a significant amount of time hunting.
» This developed coordination for aiming and throwing and improved spatial abilities through building a cognitive map of the terrain.
Support: Masters and Sanders (1993) found men adept at mentally rotating three-dimensional figures.

Physical ability (male) →
» Men able to throw a greater distance and with more speed and accuracy than women.
» In EEA skilled hunters made best providers and therefore were more sexually attractive to women.
Support: Still seen in current traditional tribal societies (Hill and Hurtado, 1989).

Cognitive ability (female) →
» Spent a lot of time in large social groups of women working together to raise children and tend camp.
» This has resulted in better communication skills.
Support: Halpern (1992) found women show more skill on measures of verbal fluency.

Problem solving ability →
» Males and females tend to solve problems in different ways – e.g. boys often use physical force whilst girls use verbal negotiation.
» Both methods are equally successful, but the legacy of communal living has resulted in better female team problem-solving.
Support: Charlesworth and Dzur (1987) found that in same sex groups given problems to solve, girls demonstrated more cooperative behaviour.

Attitudes to sex →
» Men are traditionally regarded as more permissive than the more choosy female.
» This is dictated by female parental investment.
Support: Oliver and Hyde (1993) did a meta-analysis of 177 studies of gender differences and found differences in attitudes towards sexual relationships.

Are gender roles are defined by biology or culture?
» Oliver and Hyde (1993) found that from the 1960s to the 1980s gender differences had narrowed – there was little difference in the number of sexual partners accrued over a life time by each sex.
» Changes may in part be explained by the invention of the contraceptive pill – with no risk of reproduction (therefore investment removed) females can have as many partners as the males.
» However, this behaviour assumes a cognitive approach to decision making not accounted for by evolution theory.
» Nurturing role of the father has increased (e.g. new fathers now take paternity leave); in the past this was discouraged through socialisation. It is no longer necessary for men to hunt, which impacts on the male and female gender roles: e.g. female soldiers. These changes reflect the importance of culture.

QUESTION TIME
Discuss evolutionary explanations of gender roles. (9 + 16 marks)

QUESTION TIME
(a) Outline one psychological explanation for gender development.
(b) Consider the role of hormones and genes in gender development. (16 marks)

THE BIOSOCIAL APPROACH TO GENDER DEVELOPMENT

» Focuses on the interaction of biological and social factors in explaining the development of gender.
» Biology – inborn traits and physical characteristics of a newborn baby affect the way carers behave towards them.
» Social – carers behave in different ways towards their new-born babies, depending on the infant's gender.
» Biosocial theory also emphasises the importance of the influence of the new-born's behaviour on the carer's response to them.
» Moss (1967) found that at 3 weeks old, boys were more irritable and were harder to pacify than girls.

According to biosocial theory the carer responds by applying the social expectation that 'boys don't cry' and therefore does not respond so readily to the infant boy's cries.

This expectation then reinforces the temperament of the baby, as a slow response from the carer will provoke further irritability.

Therefore the biological cues provided by the male infant prompt a reaction from the carer that is consistent with the expectations of society.

Research: Money and Ehrhardt (1972)

» 'Anatomy is destiny': how an infant is labelled at birth (i.e. boy or a girl) determines how it is socialised.
» Also, social factors have a greater influence on gender identity than biological factors but there is a period when a child's gender is still flexible.
» They claim it is possible to change the sex and thus the gender identity of a child without causing psychological damage as long as the child is under 3 years old.

Case study of Mr Blackwell – support for Money and Ehrhardt

» At birth, was taken to be a boy and raised to form a male gender identity. At puberty he began to develop female genitalia and breasts. This is known as hermaphroditism.
» Mr Blackwell's brain was not fully masculinised, yet he thought of himself as masculine and elected to remain male.
» Supports Money and Ehrhardt by showing that early socialisation was the most powerful influence on his gender identity.
» Supports the biosocial theory as it shows that biology alone cannot determine gender development. The anatomical and behavioural cues generated at birth, and the subsequent labelling and socialisation, prompted the future gender identity.

Research – Wood and Eagly (2002)

» Physical differences between men and women cause psychological differences.
» Roles are assigned to males based upon their physical strength, size and speed: thus they are seen as more efficient hunters and providers.
» Women's roles are based upon their physical ability to give birth and feed their young: hence the raising of the offspring can be more efficiently accomplished by the woman.
» Each sex must therefore develop psychological characteristics that equip them for the tasks their sex typically performs.

Cross cultural research – support for Wood and Eagly

» Wood and Eagly state that gender behaviour is constrained by the physical attributes of males and females but is still flexible to a degree and can respond to cultural influences and this is why a biosocial theory is the best explanation for both the consistencies and differences in gender roles and behaviour across cultures.
» In traditional cultures there is a clear division of labour between men and women, and women do not hold positions of power.
» In industrialised societies modern developments such as contraception and bottle feeding make the woman's role more flexible and her status has changed. Women can hold positions of power.
» The attributes women value have also changed in parallel with the physical changes. Women value leadership and power which are attributes more common to men.

Luxen (2007) – criticism of Wood and Eagly

» Wood and Eagly claim that evolution is responsible for physical development only and not brain development.

» Luxen says that psychological development is just as important to survival and claims that there is no reason why evolution cannot design different psychological mechanisms in males and females to respond to the different adaptive problems they have encountered.

This theory is actually named in the specification and so a question could appear on it. Make sure you emphasise the bio and social aspects of the theory when you describe it.

(a) Outline and evaluate one social influence on gender role. (4 + 8 marks)
(b) Discuss the biosocial approach to gender development. (5 + 8 marks)

Evaluation of biosocial theory

Does not explain the role of hormones in prenatal development or the impact of hormone cycles in causing differences in behaviour between the sexes (e.g. the menstrual cycle in women).
Hines et al (2002) found a positive correlation between levels of testosterone during pregnancy and masculine behaviour of the resulting female offspring at 3–4 years of age.

Fails to explain the overlap in human sex differences and findings from studies of animal behaviour and the behaviour of young children.
Luxen (2007) claims that children from as early as 18 months show strong preferences for sex-typed toys – at a point in their development when exposure to social influence is limited.

Fails to explain the excellent fit between partner choice in males and females and potential reproductive success.
Men are highly specialised in detecting fertility cues in females (e.g. a waist-to-hip ratio of 0.7). This can be seen across many cultures, along with a preference for symmetry which indicates good genes.

The advantages of biosocial theory over the evolutionary approach are that it intuitively seems to make sense and has ethical appeal, as sex roles are perceived as products of the interaction between biology and society: as such they are more flexible than if they were just biological.

The social component of the biosocial theory may also be useful in explaining differences in gender behaviour across cultures by referring to the powerful influence of society.

There is every chance that your exam question won't be on just one topic. As you can see from the range of questions here, some can be parted and test your knowledge on more than one topic. Because of this you have to learn thoroughly and be prepared to be flexible when answering questions.

(a) Outline the biosocial approach to gender development. (4 marks)
(b) Discuss social influences on gender role. (21 marks)

SECTION 3: SOCIAL CONTEXTS OF GENDER ROLE

SOCIAL INFLUENCES ON GENDER ROLE

Considering social influences will help us understand how gender roles have changed over time and across cultures and why gender roles have persisted.

The influence of schools

» Children may find themselves treated differently according to their sex.
» Gender stereotypes may be confirmed by teachers in the way they praise and punish pupils.
» Sex-typed behaviour may be supported by the way classes and curriculum are organised and through the use of teaching resources.

Research

Huston (1983) – Although their behaviour was equally disruptive, primary school girls received less disapproval than boys.

Schools reward conformity and non-disruptive behaviour – qualities typically female.

Huston (1983) – Teachers reinforce academic behaviour and punish disruptive behaviour regardless of the behaviour being atypical of the sex.

Serbin et al (1979) observed teachers confirming gender stereotypes by being more likely to ask pupils to demonstrate sex-stereotyped toys to the class – e.g. boys fishing set and girls sewing machine.

When trucks and dolls were introduced to the class children played with them according to the introductions of the teacher, showing the powerful influence of the teacher.

BenTsvi-Mayer et al (1989) asked 300 teachers to nominate their most prominent pupils based on ability, achievement, behaviour and the amount of time they were thought about. Boys were more prominent than girls in most categories, with their need for more discipline not detracting.

Whilst boys were described as 'best' students and as having the most potential, it was considered 'natural' for their sex when girls were in possession of outstanding social skills.

You need to know about at least two social influences – don't choose between these two!

Outline and evaluate two or more social influences on gender role. (9 + 16 marks)

The influence of media
» Books, magazines, television etc. are now an accepted part of daily life: e.g. Eysenck (1996) claimed that children watch an average of 3 hours' TV a day.
» Media contain messages which may have significant impacts on how people see gender roles.

Research

A study looking at the impact of the introduction of TV to a town ('Notel') found that gender role stereotyping had increased particularly amongst the boys, who it would seem had more readily absorbed the gender stereotypical messages generated by the television. It is not clear, however, what programmes the children were watching over the two year period of the study.

Manstead and McCulloch (1981) found that in TV advertisements, men were often the authoritative source of information about products, with women presented as users. Children exposed to this kind of information may demonstrate stronger gender stereotypes than children whose viewing mainly consists of educational programmes.

Thompson and Zerbinos (1997) asked children about the cartoons they watched and about the kinds of jobs they would like to do as adults. Most cartoon characters were perceived in stereotypical ways and children who noticed more gender stereotypical behaviour in the cartoon characters were more likely to report more stereotypical career aspirations.

Levy (1989) found that explicit attempts by educational television to convey messages of equality had more of an impact on girls than boys. This suggests that perhaps TV is not the cause of gender stereotypes but that children who have already developed gender-role stereotypes turn to the type of TV that confirms their views.

Attempts to use media to improve gender-role attitudes (e.g. 'Freestyle') have shown that children's perception of male and female roles can become less stereotyped. It is difficult to assess the long term impact of such projects, especially when media are just one of many influences.

CROSS-CULTURAL STUDIES OF GENDER ROLE
Culture refers to the shared knowledge beliefs and values of a society that are passed down through generations.

Biological differences in gender are those that are universal and persistent, whereas differences between societies represent those that are culturally determined.

It is not always easy to separate biological and cultural influences but one method has been to study traditional cultures and compare them with modern industrialised societies.

Pre-industrialised societies in New Guinea (Margaret Mead, 1930s)
» Three pre-industrialised societies were studied – the Arapesh, Mundugumor and Tchambuli.
Arapesh – Gender roles similar for men and women (e.g. child care shared responsibility).
Mundugumor – Both sexes adopted a masculine role.
Tchambuli – Gender roles were reversed with men displaying sensitivity and child-caring and women assertive and handling business affairs.
» Mead concluded from this that gender roles were neither universal nor biological.

The Ache of Paraguay (Hill and Hurtado, 1989)

» Until recently lived a basic hunting and foraging lifestyle where both men and women had to play a role.

» Men lead the foraging trips with weapons whilst women and children follow behind with family possessions. They eventually split, with men moving off to hunt game whilst women forage for fruit and insects.

» Division of labour reflects traditional roles, with men hunting and women caring, although both sexes do less of this when needs arise: e.g. men spend less time hunting when there are more children to care for.

» Sharing is highly valued by men and women which, with no designated leader, includes decision-making.

» With the loss of traditional lifestyle the Ache have changed: e.g. on reservations they have elected male chiefs. This might reflect Western influence.

Japan (Sugihara et al, 1999)

» Tested 265 Japanese college students using a Japanese version of the Bem Sex Role Inventory (BSRI) and found that whilst men scored higher on things like assertiveness athleticism and ambition, there were no gender differences on leadership, aggression and love of children.

» This did not reflect traditional Japanese gender roles – high masculinity and femininity.

» This and further research suggests diminishing gender role differences, perhaps attributable to developments in equal access to education and workforce.

Evaluation of cross-cultural research into gender differences

Mead's research has been accused of having flawed methodology. Her own cultural interpretation influenced her observations; evidence which did not fit with expectations was excluded; and there are many contradictions in her work.

Support for gender-role reversal as suggested by Mead comes from Margarita where women exhibit high levels of physical aggression (Cook, 1992). This helps women to survive since they and their children are often left to themselves in a harsh environment.

Whilst research highlights cultural differences, it also indicates underlying similarities. This might suggest that culture is influencing biological predispositions rather than directly controlling gender roles.

There are problems using ideas and concepts from one culture and applying them to another. E.g. Kaschak and Sharratt (1983) tried to apply the US version of the BSRI to gender roles in Costa Rica and found that half the items did not represent Costa Rican conceptions of masculinity and femininity.

Watch for plurality in exam questions – if you overlook subtleties in questions it can cost you dearly. For example, a question might ask for 'cross-cultural studies' – this is plural, so you clearly need more than one study, otherwise you will lose lots of marks!

(a) Outline cross-cultural studies of gender role. (9 marks)
(b) Evaluate cross-cultural studies of gender role. (16 marks)

SECTION 1: THEORIES OF INTELLIGENCE

Intelligence can be considered as the ability to acquire knowledge, to think and reason effectively, and to deal adaptively with the environment.

PSYCHOMETRIC THEORIES

These theories attempt to identify how mental ability is constructed and how we might measure intelligence.

Spearman's Theory

Description

» g is the overall general level of a person's intelligence and the factor that determines performance on intellectual tasks.

» g provides your 'core level' intelligence and does not rely on any kind of training.

» Ability in something is due in part to g and in part to ability to learn that subject – referred to as s and the ability to learn the subject – 's' – is added. These determine your performance.

Evaluation

» Schmidt and Hunter (2004) – The higher their g the more likely a person is to succeed in a job regardless of specific job skills.

» Kuncel et al (2004) – g level is highly correlated with success in work and education.

» Jensen (1998) – g is closely related to our ability to process information and may, as Spearman suggests, have a physiological basis and be inherited.

» The theory is based on observation and correlation. High correlation does not mean a perfect correlation however; and factors other than a single level of intelligence may be involved.

» Some say that intelligence is far too complex to be reduced to one factor like this. Cattell and Horn argue that g may be too simplistic, and that it can be split up into at least two sub-levels, crystallised and fluid.

ASK AN EXAMINER

You won't be asked about a particular psychometric theory. Several theories are presented here, providing a good depth of knowledge. It will give you plenty to write about, with lots of description and evaluation.

Thurstone's Theory

Description

» Intelligence can be thought of as seven primary abilities, not as a single factor.

Ability	Definition
SPACE – S	Ability to visualise items and mentally manipulate them
VERBAL COMPREHENSION – V	Ability to define and understand words
WORD FLUENCY – W	Ability to produce words quickly
NUMBER – N	Ability to solve mathematical problems
PERCEPTION – P	Ability to see similarities and differences between things
MEMORY – M	The ability to remember and recall things
REASONING – R	The ability to use rules to deal with problems

Evaluation

» Mayer (2000) – The 7 abilities are very useful when targeting areas for improvement. They allow us to organise teaching and training accurately.

» Carroll (1993) – A meta-analysis of the results of many intelligence tests supports the idea that intelligence has several mental abilities – *general mental abilities* (Spearman's g), *broad abilities* (including Thurstone's abilities), and *narrow abilities* (specific skills).

» Guilford (1982) – Suggests that Thurstone's theory is too simplistic, indicating that there are actually up to 120 subdivisions of intelligence.

» Thurstone's theory can be criticised for relying on correlational analysis to identify associated mental abilities.

Cattell and Horn's theory

This theory splits Spearman's '*g*' in two parts: *chrystallised intelligence (gC)* is the abilty to apply existing knowledge to new problems whilst *fluid intelligence (gF)* is the ability to solve new problems without any past experience or stored knowledge.

Evaluation

» Weinart and Hany (2003) – As we age, *gC* stabilises and improves and then remains stable; *gF* declines in later adulthood. The fact that they behave differently with age is evidence for the two different components.
» Kline (1998) – Some tasks correlate with measures of *gC* and some with measures of *gF*, indicating two different parts of the intelligence system.
» Geary (2005) – Suggests that the two parts of intelligence actually use different parts of the brain, which is more evidence for the distinctive intelligences.
» Brody (2000) – Sometimes *gC* and *gF* correlate very highly with one another, suggesting that far from being distinct they may not be completely separate after all.
» Jaeggi et al (2008) – *gF* is closely related to the well-established concept of working memory. Exercising working memory can help improve *gF*.

QUESTION TIME?

(a) Outline and evaluate information processing theories of intelligence. (4 + 8 marks)
(b) Discuss psychometric theories of intelligence. (5 + 8 marks)

Several criteria must be satisfied for an ability to be included as an 'intelligence'.

Criteria	Explanation
1. Potential for brain damage to affect this ability and not others.	Language, for instance, can be selectively damaged by a stroke.
2. Existence of individuals with exceptional skill in the area.	A 'savant' has exceptional ability in a single skill (drawing, maths etc.).
3. The ability should exist in experimental tasks.	Tasks can be used that isolate the ability and test it separately.
4. The ability should be measurable.	We can test to see which abilities have common underlying factors and which do not.
5. The ability should be different from others, having a distinct developmental course and an end 'expert' performance standard.	An athlete, for instance, takes steps to develop their skill. These steps can be examined.
6. Ability should be plausible in terms of evolution.	*Why* the ability exists must be plausible in terms of evolution. E.g. great spatial skills in birds.
7. The ability should be able to use a symbol system.	Language and maths use symbolic systems.
8. Must have at least one identifiable core operation.	A core operation is a basic information processing mechanism. Examples include *linguistic, musical, spatial* and *logical-mathematical*.

Evaluation of Gardner's theory

Brain damage – Specific abilities can be lost with brain damage, supporting Gardner's idea of multiple intelligences, but the abilities lost do not closely correspond with Gardner's proposed intelligences.

Autism – Some autistics are Savants, which means they have extraordinary abilities in specific areas, supporting Gardner's theory of different types of intelligence.

Project Spectrum – A practical application of the theory, which is claimed to have some success. A long term alternative approach to primary education based on Gardner's theory, where multiple intelligences are addressed with things like singing and dance as well as more traditional subjects.

Lacks adequate research – Waterhouse (2006) says the theory lacks research support, and so should not, yet, be adopted in schools.

Natural Strengths – Applying the theory in schools is controversial. Just because something is not a 'natural strength' does not mean it should not be encouraged. Reading, for instance, is an important skill that we all need, to a certain level, regardless of whether it is something we have an aptitude for.

(a) Outline the psychometric theory of intelligence. (4 marks)
(b) Outline the information processing theory of intelligence. (5 marks)
(c) Evaluate one or more theories of intelligence. (16 marks)

Gardner's theory is named in the specification and you may very well get a question on it. You can include other theories of intelligence as evaluation of Gardner. For example, you might argue that, unlike Gardner's, Spearman's theory only has one intelligence. Indeed, Gardner's theory is unique in having so many different kinds of intelligence.

SECTION 2: ANIMAL LEARNING AND INTELLIGENCE

You need to know about classical AND operant conditioning in a fair bit of detail, since questions can specify one or the other. If you are asked to write about both, you will need to reduce the detail to avoid going over the limited time available.

THE NATURE OF SIMPLE LEARNING
Learning and adaptation to its environment is essential to an animal's survival.

Classical Conditioning
Developed originally by Ivan Pavlov, the theory describes how a natural reflex (*an unconditioned response – UR*) can be caused by something in the environment (*an unconditioned stimulus – US*). E.g. a dog 'salivates' (*UR*) to the 'smell of food' (*US*).

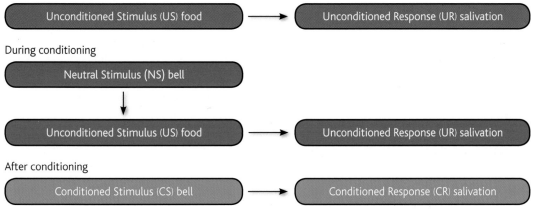

Pavlov's paradigm

During 'conditioning' a *neutral stimulus (NS)* is paired with the US. Eventually the dog learns to salivate to the sound of the bell. When this happens we can say that the Bell is now a *conditioned stimulus (CS)* and the salivation is a *conditioned response (CR)*.

Some key ideas in classical conditioning

Extinction – The CR will fade if the NS and US are never again paired.

Spontaneous recovery – After extinction new learning appears to be lost but it can suddenly reappear at some later date.

Inhibition – The relationship between the NS and US is suppressed, as shown by it suddenly reappearing.

Generalisation – Stimuli similar but not identical to the CS also bring about a CR.

Discrimination – This is where animals can tell the difference between the CS and a similar but different stimulus.

The law of temporal contiguity
Timing is vital in the conditioning process, with the US having to be presented very close to the CS:

» *Forward conditioning* – Bell presented just before and during food, producing very strong learning.

» *Backward conditioning* – Bell presented during and just after food, producing weak learning.

» *Simultaneous conditioning* – Bell and food presented at same time, producing very strong learning.

» *Trace conditioning* – Bell rung and stopped before food is presented, producing weak learning.

Role of Classical conditioning in behaviour of non-human animals

CC can readily be observed in foraging behaviour. E.g., food and illness is a vital link: food determines their physical fitness, and can kill them, or if not, leave them weakened and open to predation. If an animal eats food and then feels unwell it quickly learns to associate the two events.

Cows – A very flimsy electric fence can stop a cow passing from one half of a field to another. The fence is associated with unpleasant feelings following the experience of a mild shock.

Rabbits – Electric fences can help stop rabbits running onto and digging up greens on golf courses.

Squirrels – Pepper-covered bird feed will not be eaten by squirrels after a short learning experience, but birds, who cannot detect the pepper, will eat it.

Discuss the nature of simple learning in non-human animals. (9 + 16 marks)

Remember that the focus MUST be on non-human animals. You will have come across conditioning in humans from your AS studies – DO NOT use it here!

Evaluation of classical conditioning

Positive Evaluation

Hollis (1984) – showed how CC can influence wild animal behaviour. Male gourami fish are aggressive to one another. Pairing a red light with a male eventually made the other male aggressive to the red light. Also, pairing a red light with a female fish resulted in a reduction of aggressive behaviour.

Negative evaluation

» Lab based research lacks the ecological variety and richness of the wild natural environment and therefore might be accused of lacking validity. Just because some animals can be classically conditioned in the lab does not mean all animals can, or that animals respond in this way in the wild.

» Garcia and Koelling (1966) – Rats were given sweetened water. Half were made sick with x-rays; the other half were given a mild electric shock. Pavlov would say that both would become averse to the flavour of the sweetened water, but in fact only the x-rayed rats avoided it. They concluded that this was because the taste/sickness pairing was biologically relevant whilst the taste/shock pairing was not.

» This 'Garcian conditioning' contradicts Pavlov's theory:
  • *One trial learning* – Pavlov would say that many paired presentations must happen for learning. However, taste aversion learning can happen in a single trial.
  • *Extinction* – Taste aversion pairings are hard and sometimes almost impossible to extinguish.
  • *Temporal contiguity* – In taste aversion, the timing of the learning is not nearly as important as classical Pavlovian theory suggests.

In addition to the evaluation points here make sure you also use material on cognitive learning presented later on. They also can be used in evaluating classical conditioning.

Operant Conditioning

An animal's own behaviour determines its learning. The theory was proposed by B.F. Skinner (1940) and was based on an earlier idea by Thorndike (1911) called the 'Law of effect'. This says that if an action has positive consequences it will be more likely to be repeated in the future. This action can be pushing a lever in response to a sound or a light to receive a food reward (as in the famous Skinner Box). The animal did something first – learning was a consequence of this behaviour.

Skinner box.

Some key ideas in operant conditioning

Reinforcement – Something which increases the likelihood of a behaviour being repeated.

Punishment – Behaviours that are met by unpleasant consequences or go unrewarded.

Negative reinforcement – A behaviour is encouraged that makes an unpleasant consequence less likely.

Primary reinforcer – Naturally occurring things such as food, water, warmth, comfort.

Secondary reinforcers – Not-naturally occurring but are associated with primary reinforcers.

Generalisation – When an animal makes a response that resembles the original reinforced response.

Discrimination – When the animal can distinguish a behaviour that will bring about a reward from another which won't.

Extinction – When a response is no longer reinforced, it will fade and eventually disappear.

IDea
Conditioning theory has been accused of being environmentally deterministic. What this means is that it tends to overlook important biological influences on behaviour in favour of overestimating learning. The discovery of biological constraints on operant conditioning, such as instinctive drift, reminds us that an animal is bound at least to some extent by its biology.

QUESTION TIME?
(a) Outline and evaluate classical conditioning as an explanation of animal learning. (4 + 8 marks)
(b) Discuss the role of operant conditioning in the behaviour of non-human animals. (5 + 8 marks)

Some more key ideas in operant conditioning

Behaviour shaping
Complex behaviours can be developed by combining simpler ones. Animals gradually learn the complex behaviour by being reinforced for behaviours that are closer and closer to the desired behaviour.

Schedules of reinforcement
The way that reinforcement is applied can influence the speed and strength of learning. Reinforcement may be *partial* where the animal is only reinforced occasionally or *continuous* where reinforcement always occurs. Partial reinforcement provides better and stronger learning.

Fixed ratio	Reinforcer presented after fixed number of responses. E.g. animal is reinforced after every 10 lever pushes.
Variable ratio	Reinforcer presented e.g. 10 lever pushes on average. E.g. 10 reinforcers every 100 responses: an average of 1 per 10.
Fixed interval	Reinforcer presented e.g. every 30 seconds.
Variable interval	Reinforcer presented after an average amount of time. E.g. 10 reinforcers in 300 seconds: average of 1 per 30 seconds.

Role of operant conditioning in behaviour of non-human animals

» Animals that can learn through operant conditioning have the ability to adapt to changing environments so giving them an evolutionary advantage.

» West and King (1988) – Female cowbirds influence the song of male cowbirds. They are brood-parasites, laying eggs in the nests of another species of bird. The infant is then brought up by the unsuspecting mother, as her own. Consequently the young cowbird does not hear the song of the adult and has to learn to adjust its song to that preferred by females. This occurs by females rewarding particular male song sequences with a 'dance' of appreciation. The more the male bird adjusts its song in response to such reinforcement, the more likely it is to mate.

Evaluation of operant conditioning

Positive evaluation

» There is lots of evidence that OC is an important part of wild animal behaviour. E.g., Fuji (2002) showed that pigeons could be conditioned in just the same way as lab-animals with Skinner boxes places in the wild.

» Morrison (1998) – The US navy have conditioned dolphins to guard for attackers who may approach nuclear submarines from under the sea.

» Holden et al (2003) – Rhinoceros at Whipsnade zoo have been trained using behaviour shaping to respond calmly to medical inspections such as mouth and eye inspections. This relieves their stress and makes life for them and their keepers much easier. One Rhino has been trained to place its foot on a block to have its nails filed.

Negative evaluation

» Mackintosh (1981) – Pigeons taught to peck at an illuminated disk for food will do so even if food is not given. The consequence of their behaviour seems irrelevant to them. This is actually more consistent with classical conditioning, so it has been suggested that perhaps much of what is thought to be operant conditioning is actually classical conditioning.

» An animal's behaviour places limits on what can be learned. E.g., *escape learning* can be taught faster if a pigeon is allowed to flap its wings rather than peck at something as this is a more natural response when escaping. Similarly, in *reward learning* a pigeon learns more quickly if it is allowed to peck for food rather than flap its wings.

» *Instinctive drift* – Sometimes an animal will seem to misbehave in training and will exhibit a behaviour closer to an 'instinctive' one than the one being reinforced. Breland and Breland (1961) had trouble training raccoons to pick up coins and place them in a piggy bank for an advert. Instead the animals reverted to rubbing the coins together when they picked them up, a natural reflection of food washing behaviour seen in the wild.

Evaluation does not have to be negative. You can achieve a sense of balance and understanding in your answers by including evaluation that is both negative and positive.

Describe and evaluate the role of operant conditioning in the behaviour of non-human animals. (9 + 16 marks)

Some problems for both classical AND operant conditioning

Insight and latent learning pose problems for both operant and classical conditioning because learning should be observable and measurable (e.g. trial-and-error learning) and not hidden and cognitive. Ethologists argue that animals should be studied in their natural environments, not laboratories.

Insight learning

This is spontaneous skill learning and expression of cognitive abilities in problem solving beyond those taught.

» *Sultan the chimpanzee* – Kohler (1925) reported that Sultan (and other chimps) could spontaneously solve problems without any training or conditioning.

» *Betty the Caledonian crow* – Weir et al (2002) showed that Betty retrieved food by bending a piece of wire into a hook. Caledonian crows use sticks as tools in the wild, but never a bendable material like wire.

Latent learning

Some animals appear to use cognition in their learning, contradicting basic principles of operant and classical conditioning.

» Tolman and Honzik (1930) – showed that rats could learn to run a maze in the absence of any observable reinforcement.

Ethology

Ethologists argue that to truly understand an animal's behaviour the animal has to be studied in its natural environment. The behaviours of animals in laboratory-based conditioning studies do not arise naturally so ultimately tell us very little. Also, a very limited range of animals is studied (typically rats and pigeons) so a distorted view of animal behaviour has emerged.

(a) Outline operant conditioning in non-human animals. (4 marks)
(b) Outline classical conditioning in non-human animals. (5 marks)
(c) Consider the role of classical and operant conditioning in the behaviour of non-human animals. (16 marks)

Insight and latent learning can be used as a criticism of both classical AND operant conditioning, since neither operant nor classical conditioning accounts for the role of cognition in animal learning. Ethology also offers a criticism of both.

INTELLIGENCE IN NON-HUMAN ANIMALS

As with human intelligence, the difficulty here is deciding what intelligence actually is. This has been resolved by deciding what constitutes intelligence in humans and looking for evidence of this in non-humans. Three possibilities are summarised below.

Discuss evidence for intelligence in non-human animals. (9 + 16 marks)

SELF-RECOGNITION	SOCIAL LEARNING	THEORY OF MIND
The ability to recognise own reflection shows possession of an idea of 'self'.	*This involves understanding that outcomes for others are related to outcomes for themselves.*	*Understanding that others have thoughts and emotions different from one's own: a key example is deceptive behaviour.*

Gallup (1970) – A red mark was placed on the forehead of lightly anaesthetised chimps. When placed in front of a mirror afterwards, many touched their head where the red dot was. This showed that each animal that responded in this way must be self-aware and know the image was its own reflection.

Swartz and Evans (1991) – replicated Gallup, but found fewer responded with self-recognition, suggesting large individual differences. Other research shows higher failure rates in the very young and old.

Hayes (1998) – Red spot research is flawed (there is an order effect) and results are not consistent. It is not clear whether chimps really were touching the red spot. Even if they were, it is a huge leap to claim this as self-recognition.

Plotnik (2006) – Elephants respond similarly to chimps, becoming familiar with their reflections and then, when marked, showing great interest in the reflection of the mark on themselves. Like chimps, elephants live in socially complex groups and this may underlie self-recognition. Whilst not all elephants respond to the mirror test, this is because elephants are not very concerned about appearance and don't spend much time grooming.

Prior et al (2008) – Self recognition may not be unique to mammals and has been shown in magpies. Two birds attempted to remove a yellow mark below their beak (which they could only see in a mirror), but not a black mark (against black feathers). Self-recognition may not after involve higher cortical centres, since these brain regions are not highly developed in birds.

Toda et al (2008) – Pigeons were able to distinguish between a live video image of themselves and a recorded delayed 'reflection'. They seem to be able to tell when the reflected image showed their own current movements. The researchers argue this is a higher cognitive skill than shown by 3-month-old human infants.

Whiten et al (1999) – Troops of chimpanzees on the west bank of a river in Africa used stones to open nuts, while those on the east coast did not. Similarly, different chimpanzees around Africa use different tools to do the same jobs. This variability can be attributed to learning, not genetics. Since the animals were genetically the same, the variability must be attributed to social learning.

Lorenz (1935) – Whether social learning occurs depends on the situation (local enhancement). Ducks could only learn to use a hole to escape from a pen when very close to another duck using the hole. This local enhancement effect can also be seen in the rapid spread across the country of blue tits pecking the silver top off doorstep bottles to get at milk.

Boesch (1991) – Adult chimps observed to teach young *how* to crack nuts with stones. Teaching like this is evidence of higher level social learning, since it involves one animal modifying the behaviour of another.

Rapaport and Ruiz-Miranda (2002) – Wild golden lion Tamarinds have been observed helping their young learn to find hidden food, by using food calls that only their young responded to. The researchers argue that the adults were drawing the attention of young to learning opportunities.

Kawai (1965) – observed a Japanese snow monkey spontaneously use the sea to wash sand from food. This behaviour quickly spread through the troop so that 80% of 2 to 7 year-olds did it. Far fewer older monkeys behaved in this way due to younger monkeys interacting more and having greater opportunities for social learning to take place. Suzuki (1963) observed similar social learning in the use of hot springs by snow monkeys to keep warm during winter.

Kummer (1982) – A female baboon was observed to shift her position carefully so that she could groom a sub-dominant male baboon (an unacceptable activity in the eyes of the dominant male) without his seeing what she was doing. This could be evidence that she knew her action would have been badly received and so acted deceitfully.

Ristau (1991) – Plover birds distract predators by pretending to be injured, thereby allowing others to escape predation. The more closely a predator looked towards their nest (where the young were) the more they engaged in the distraction behaviour, suggesting an understanding of the predator's thinking.

Woodruff and Premack (1979) – describe a chimp who was able to discriminate between two keepers. To get food from one keeper the chimpanzee needed to point to a box containing food. With the other trainer, in order to avoid the food being taken away the animal needed to 'deceive' the keeper by pointing to the empty box. The chimp was very good at this, suggesting that she knew how the keepers would react to her behaviour and could deceive appropriately. However, the findings may just reflect operant conditioning during the training stage.

Linden (2000) – reports intentional deception in wild chimps. A remote controlled feeding station opened when a non-dominant male was nearby. When a dominant male approached, the first male closed the box and pretended it was not open. Another dominant male was watching, waiting patiently in hiding until the first dominant male left the scene. He then moved in and took the food. Evidence of deception, and theory of mind. Whilst many studies appear to show animals with conscious intent to deceive, the fact that this behaviour can be explained in non-mentalist conditioning terms means that no firm conclusion can be reached about theory of mind.

ASK AN EXAMINER — *Three indicators of animal intelligence are presented here, which if you use them should give your answers breadth and depth. The research can be used to gain descriptive or evaluative marks – it depends on how you use it. Remember, it is how you write as well as what you write which will gain you marks.*

QUESTION TIME

(a) Outline one example of intelligence in non-human animals. (4 marks)
(b) Outline one evolutionary factor in the development of human intelligence. (5 marks)
(c) Assess the role of genetic factors associated with intelligence test performance. (16 marks)

SECTION 3: EVOLUTION OF INTELLIGENCE

Humans are by far the most intelligent creatures on the planet, and this superiority can be explained in terms of evolutionary theory.

Brain size

» The human brain is highly evolved, using more energy to sustain it than any other animal, and being three times the size expected for a primate our size.

» Expansion in human brain size occurred about 2 million years ago with the introduction of meat into our diet, providing extra nutrition.

» Since large brain size incurs cost (e.g. more energy needed and more difficult birth), a bigger brain with greater intelligence must have an evolutionary advantage.

» Frontal lobes (which make up 30% of our brain) are regarded as the areas which most distinguish humans from the rest. Krasner et al (1997) argue that human evolution can be thought of as the era of the frontal lobes.

Evaluation

» McDaniel (2005) found that brain size from MRI scans correlated positively with measures of intelligence.

» It is not clear whether brain size allowed us to evolve intelligence or whether evolution provided the bigger brains.

» There is not a perfect positive correlation between brain size and where we are in evolution. E.g., neanderthal man actually had a larger brain than we do, even with much less intelligence.

» Men and women have almost identical IQs, but males have larger brains. The brain size/intelligence relationship is clearly not straightforward.

» The density of the brain may be what matters, not the size. Einstein had a relatively small brain, but it was incredibly densely packed in places.

» Haier et al (1993) suggest that it may be the efficiency of the brain that matters. They used PET scans to show that intelligent people's brains use up less energy when solving problems.

Ecological theory

» This suggests that an animal's environment demands intelligent behaviour.

» Intelligence would help achieve a varied nutritional diet.

» The more intelligent of our ancestors would have been more successful hunters and more likely to survive and raise families.

» Intelligence then allows us to adapt to our environment, but a key breakthrough was the ability to invent and use tools, since this gave a significant survival advantage.

» This allowed more efficient hunting and farming, providing more nutritious food with less energy.

Evaluation

» Smaller-brained species are also good at hunting (e.g. lions).

» Other animals have shown tool use (e.g. chimpanzee, crow) but they are nowhere near as intelligent as humans, so tool use/intelligence relationship cannot be straightforward.

» Tool use did not signify an obvious increase in intelligence. Archeological evidence shows tool use from 2.5 million years ago, but it took 2 million years for it to become sophisticated and varied. It may be that evolved intelligence allowed greater use and development of tools.

Discuss evolutionary factors in the development of human intelligence. (9 + 16 marks)

Social theory

» There are evolutionary advantages to being part of a social group, e.g. shared resources, defence and safety, sharing information, care for young.
» The need to belong to a group is so great that individuals must be careful to avoid rejection.
» Living co-operatively however is difficult, e.g. there is a need for dealing with conflict, co-operation, negotiation, relationship management.
» Individuals who can solve these complex social problems most successfully are those most likely to survive.
» One intellectual skill that would have aided successful social living is *Machiavellian intelligence*, which is where deception is used to obtain goals.
» It would also be advantageous to develop the skills of detecting deception. This cycle of deception and counter-deception brought about growth in human intelligence.

Evaluation

» The *'social brain hypothesis'* says the number of people in a group we can engage in constructive social relationships with is about 150.
» A positive correlation has been found between the size of neocortex (where higher functions like thinking and problem solving occur) and prevalence of deception in primates. Humans have the largest neocortex.
» Cosmides and Tooby (1992) found that humans are much better at solving social problems than abstract mental ones
» Ridley (1993) argues that sexual selection theory is a better explanation than ecological or social theory alone. More intelligent humans were better at presenting themselves in more attractive ways and therefore more successful at mating. This intelligence is then passed on in genes to the offspring.

THE ROLE OF GENETIC AND ENVIRONMENTAL FACTORS ASSOCIATED WITH INTELLIGENCE TEST PERFORMANCE

Evidence suggests that our performance on intelligence tests (such as Spearman's *g*) is to some extent inherited.
» Some chromosomal disorders (e.g. Down's syndrome and PKU) are also associated with lowered intelligence.
» The human genome project has identified a range of genes that may influence intelligence, not a solitary one, and so the genetic component of intelligence can be thought of as an interaction of these genes.
» As the table opposite shows, the more closely related people are, the more similar their intelligence test performance.

Debate in psychology is now focused on the relative contribution of genes and environment in test performance. The problem lies with separating the effects of nature (genes) and nurture (environment).

Relationship	IQ test correlation
Identical twins reared together	0.86
Identical twins reared apart	0.72
Non-identical twins reared together	0.60
Parent with child reared at home	0.50
Siblings reared together	0.47
Siblings reared apart	0.24
Unrelated persons reared together	0.20
Adoptive parent and adopted child	0.19
Cousins	0.15

IQ test correlations of related individuals. Adapted from Bouchard and McGue (1981).

Evidence from twin studies

The main difference between identical (MZ) and non-identical (DZ) twins is genetic so any difference in intelligence would indicate a genetic contribution.

Strong MZ correlation of 0.86 is good evidence for genetics, but the correlation is not perfect, suggesting some environmental contribution. Correlation only slightly dips when reared apart indicating that genetic component is strong.

Wilson (1986) points out that whilst IQ correlation becomes stronger with increasing age in MZ's, it declines in DZ's. This is because of 'niche picking' in MZ's, meaning that as they grow older they make similar gene-compatible choices about their environments.

Evidence from adoption studies

Intelligence of adopted MZ children is closer to that of their natural parents than of their adoptive ones, indicating an important role for genes. However, there are still environmental influences since twins often go to similar families.

Strong environmental influences are suggested by Capron and Duyme (1989) who showed that enriched environments can improve intelligence in adopted children by up to 25 IQ points.

Skodak and Skeels (1949) found that children born to impoverished 'retarded' mothers but adopted by wealthier, more intelligent families showed above normal intelligence as children and adolescents, substantially higher than their biological parents. This indicates the importance of an enriching environment.

The influence of the environment

Home environments have an important influence. Bradley and Caldwell (1984) found that the amount of time children spend with their children, and the amount of toys and books available, are factors positively correlated with the intelligence of the child. Laosa (1982) found that a mother's reading and problem solving with the child plays a very important role in developing intelligence.

IQ is increased by schooling, so that those that attend have higher IQ's.

The higher the socioeconomic status (better food, more money, more books etc.), the higher the IQ.

Children who attend early intervention programmes (e.g. Head Start) show greater short-term improvements in IQ than those who don't.

The effect of environment may even be *transgenerational*, meaning that it may even influence our intelligence before we are conceived. For instance, our grandmother's environment may influence our mother's health and pregnancy, and so may well affect our intelligence once born.

Influence of culture on intelligence test performance

This is a very sensitive subject since suggestions of cultural difference are open to political abuse.

Cultural specificity

IQ tests are often described as *culturally specific*, being designed administered and scored in western countries by (more often than not) white middle class males.

In some cultures, certain skills are highly developed (e.g. by schooling); in other cultures they are not. If the test used requires great skills in areas specific to particular cultures it will be biased towards that culture.

Vernon (1979) suggests a number of problems testing cross-culturally; see table.

PROBLEM	EXPLANATION
Lack of familiarity with testing	No history of testing may mean a lack of motivation to succeed, or an excitement about being tested by an often foreign scientist.
The tests may not make sense	What makes sense in a test in one culture may not in another. Waddington (1951) described Gurkhas who did not understand the concept of right shaped peg in right hole, instead preferring to fit pegs into any hole they could. Also, different cultures may perceive the world differently.
Poor nutrition and medical care	Poor nutrition and medical care may 'handicap' the performance of the test.
Different environmental factors	Education, availability of books, social and medical care etc. all influence intelligence. Not having these things is bound to influence test performance.

Cognition and development

You are expected in the examination to show both the skills of knowledge and understanding and the skills of analysis and evaluation in relation to the topic Cognition and development.

Where opportunities for their effective use arise, you will need to demonstrate an appreciation of issues and debates. These include the nature/nurture debate, ethical issues in research, free-will/determinism, reductionism, gender and culture bias, and the use of animals in research.

You will also need to demonstrate an understanding of How Science Works. You can do this through the effective use of studies in your answer (as description or evaluation) or where appropriate by evaluating methodology and findings.

WHAT YOU NEED TO KNOW

DEVELOPMENT OF THINKING
- Theories of cognitive development, including Piaget, Vygotsky and Bruner
- The applications of these theories to education

DEVELOPMENT OF MORAL UNDERSTANDING
- Theories of moral understanding (Kohlberg) and/or prosocial reasoning (Eisenberg)

DEVELOPMENT OF SOCIAL COGNITION
- Development of the child's sense of self, including theory of mind (Baron-Cohen)
- Development of children's understanding of others, including perspective-taking (Selman)
- Biological explanations of social cognition, including the role of the mirror neuron system

SECTION 1: DEVELOPMENT OF THINKING

The specification requires you to know all three theories of cognitive development outlined in the next few pages. You can't pick and choose: learn all three. Questions could ask you for more than two theories, so you are not simply 'taking a gamble' if you do only one or two!

THEORIES OF COGNITIVE DEVELOPMENT (1): PIAGET'S THEORY

There is a difference in the quality of thinking between adults and children. We are born with the basic skills to allow cognitive development, with thinking becoming more complex as we grow older.

Some key ideas

CONCEPT	WHAT IT MEANS
Constructed knowledge	With less experience of the world than adults, children think in a less sophisticated way. Children construct their knowledge of the world by interacting with it.
Schemata	A vast collection of actions and ideas that represent everything we know about a concept.
Assimilation	When new information is fitted into an existing schema it is said to have been *assimilated*.
Accommodation	When a schema is altered to fit in the new information. E.g. a schema for 'bird' (a small flying animal) must change to accommodate large animals that don't fly and thus don't match our existing schema (e.g. ostrich).
Equilibrium	When assimilating, a child is in balance or 'equilibrium'. When the schema must change through accommodation, the child is said to be out of balance, or in 'disequilibrium'. This uncomfortable mental state is made better by 'equilibration' (moving back into balance). This is a constant process and is how cognition develops.
Stages of cognitive development	We all pass through stages of intellectual development in the same order, i.e. they are 'universal' and 'invariant'.

Stages of cognitive development

STAGE	EXPLANATION
Sensorimotor Birth to 10 months	Child's investigation of the world involves sensing and doing (hearing, touching, smelling, tasting and touching). Up to about 8 months, things out of sight are not believed to exist: children lack an understanding of *object permanence*.
Pre-operational 18 months to 6 years	Language is acquired, allowing the child to think through actions. This thinking process is called performing an *operation*. Children are *egocentric* – they only see the world from their own perspective. They also lack the ability to *conserve*.
Concrete operational 6 years to 12 years	Child develops logical rules (*what is*), understanding *reversibility*, meaning that what they have just done can be reversed and that 2x4 is the same as 4x2. They can use *inductive logic* meaning that what they already know can be applied to different situations – eating too many sweets makes them feel sick, so eating too much of anything would also make them feel sick, a general principle of eating too much.
Formal operational 12 years onwards	Here the *what is* thinking is developed into a *what might be* approach. Situations can be imagined: they do not need to be experienced. Numbers can be replaced by symbols to allow access to algebra, and several problems can be solved simultaneously.

It is very easy to get bogged down in the facts and figures of Piaget's theory. We've provided more than enough detail here to get you maximum descriptive marks. Just go through the key concepts and describe the stages (but be sure to get the details right!).

(a) Outline Piaget's theory of cognitive development. (9 marks)
(b) Evaluate Piaget's theory of cognitive development. (16 marks)

Evaluation of Piaget's theory

1. Egocentrism *(Piaget and Inhelder, 1952)*

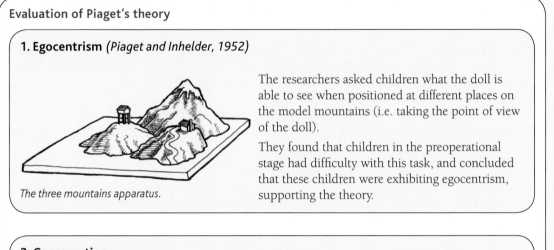

The three mountains apparatus.

The researchers asked children what the doll is able to see when positioned at different places on the model mountains (i.e. taking the point of view of the doll).

They found that children in the preoperational stage had difficulty with this task, and concluded that these children were exhibiting egocentrism, supporting the theory.

2. Conservation

Piaget said that children in the pre-operational stage are unable to conserve things like volume, mass and number. For example:

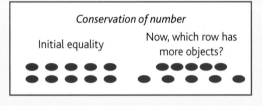

Conservation of number

Initial equality

Now, which row has more objects?

When asked "Which row has more counters, or are they both the same?" a child confirms, in the initial condition, that they are the same. But when one row is spread out and the question is repeated, the child now answers that the spread row has more counters.

However, McGarrigle and Donaldson (1974) changed the way the task is presented so that children could better understand what is being asked of them by using 'Naughty Teddy' to transform the row of counters. They showed that much younger children (below the age of 6 and within the pre-operational stage) showed conservation, contradicting Piaget.

3. Object Permanence *(Baillargeon and DeVos, 1991)*

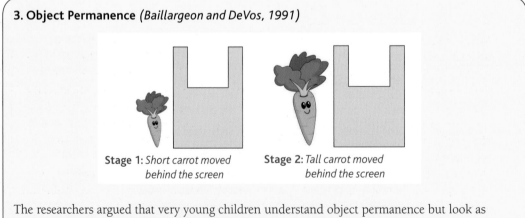

Stage 1: *Short carrot moved behind the screen*

Stage 2: *Tall carrot moved behind the screen*

The researchers argued that very young children understand object permanence but look as though they don't because they are unable to maintain attention.

There are predictable outcomes when the carrots are moved behind the yellow screen, but in a third 'impossible' stage a tall carrot does not appear in the notch as expected. Children as young as 3.5 months (much younger than Piaget's predicted 8 months), looked for much longer at the apparatus (as if confused) when the carrot 'magically' reappeared, suggesting that they understood that it should have appeared in the notch.

4. Further evaluation of Piaget's theory

» Dasen (1994) – We do not necessarily move through all the stages, estimating that only 1 in 3 adults ever reach formal operations. This figure applies only to Western industrialised nations: elsewhere it is lower, suggesting a cultural bias in the theory.

» Matsumoto and Hull (1994) – Piaget's work was sample and culture-biased (ethnocentric). Much of his research was done with his own children and with those from wealthy Western cultures. He was also looking for certain intellectual skills which might not be favoured by other cultures.

» Karmillof-Smith (1992) – It is an oversimplification to say that all children pass through the same stages in the same order. Some children develop concepts and understanding in one way and at one point in a stage and some develop completely differently.

» Piaget argued that maturation dictated stage development, but research has shown that much younger children are capable of the intellectual skills predicted by Piaget in older children (e.g. McGarrigle and Donaldson, Baillargeon and DeVos).

ASK AN EXAMINER

Three well known studies are presented here which are quite easy to remember and will gain you lots of marks with a bit of detail. Along with some of the further evaluative points, and some issues/debates/approaches, you will have the basis of a very effective evaluation!

QUESTION TIME ?

Discuss Piaget's theory of cognitive development. (9 + 16 marks)

Applying Piaget's theory to Education

Stage specific instruction – readiness

» We should only teach children material that they are able or *ready* to learn, and this depends on the stage of cognitive development they are in.

» Educators *facilitate* by recognising where children are in their development and providing activities and resources to encourage further development: toys/props, problem solving requiring stage-appropriate logic.

evaluation →

Burns and Silbey (2000) – Support stage-specific instruction: children learn best when activities match their stage of development.

Brainerd (1983) – Piaget underestimated the readiness of children to learn. Even 4 year olds trained on tasks related to the concrete operational stage could do them, even though they should not be able to until 7.

Egan and Kauchak (2000) – Stage-specific instruction may be good for some children and not others, so teachers must be careful to alter tasks accordingly.

Being able to describe and evaluate theories of cognitive development is not enough for the exam. You are also expected to know specifically how each of Piaget's, Vygotsky's and Bruner's theories can be applied to education.

Discovery learning

» In Piaget's theory children are not passive learners but are active explorers, developing their cognitive abilities through self-discovery.
» The role of the teacher is to encourage self-discovery.
» Teachers must challenge children, placing them in a state of *disequilibrium* so that the child develops intellectually.

evaluation →

Stigler et al (1987) – Some criticise discovery learning as not being universally appropriate: e.g. Asian children usually do very well with traditional school instruction. Stigler supports Piaget, saying that cross cultural comparisons like these can be misleading. E.g., in Taiwan twice as much time is spent on Maths than in American schools.

Meadows (1994) – Discovery learning underestimates the added benefits of more direct teaching. Brainerd (1983) argues that the more traditional lecture/tutorial style found in Asian countries is more effective than discovery learning.

DeJong and VanJoolinen (1998) – Discovery learning is very effective in computer-based environments. However, instruction is still important where assistance is needed with difficult problems. This method may also be valuable in helping learners into a state of disequilibrium.

QUESTION TIME

(a) Describe Piaget's theory of cognitive development. (9 marks)
(b) Consider the application of Piaget's theory to education. (16 marks)

THEORIES OF COGNITIVE DEVELOPMENT (2): VYGOTSKY'S THEORY

Vygotsky's stage theory is often referred to as *sociocultural*, since he says that it is cultural knowledge which prescribes what children learn. Social activity is key to developing natural abilities available from birth.

The role of language in development

STAGE	EXPLANATION
Pre-intellectual speech 0 to 3 years	Before 2, language and thinking are completely separate. Learning is through conditioning. Speech is eventually learned but is only used to express basic feelings (e.g. hunger), and in attempts to control those around the child (e.g. mummy). It is regarded as social speech.
Egocentric speech 3 to 7 years	Language used in problem solving for the first time. Child often speaks to themselves out loud, as an expression of their thought process in a *monologue*-style running commentary of their actions and thoughts.
Inner speech 7 onwards	Language used more effectively in understanding those around them. Speech when solving problems become silent *inner* conversation, or *monologue*.

Since language is our means of communicating cultural knowledge, it is extremely important in this theory. Vygotsky was particularly interested in the relationship between language and thought. This relationship goes through a set of developmental stages.

Before 2 years, language is separate from thought, but by the age of 3, children are beginning to influence each other. By 7 years they are using language more extensively and effectively when solving problems.

QUESTION TIME

Describe and evaluate Vygotsky's theory of cognitive development. (9 + 16 marks)

ASK AN EXAMINER

In addition to these points here, you can add material from other areas to bulk up your evaluation. E.g., McNaughton and Leyland, application to education, and even contrasts with alternative theories.

The development of thinking

Although not a stage theory like Piaget's, Vygotsky identified that the process of concept formation went through four stages.

STAGES IN CONCEPT FORMATION	
Stage 1: Vague syncretic	Little or no understanding of concepts. Problems solved by trial and error.
Stage 2: Complexes	Children begin to use non-random strategies to solve problems but are not successful in discovering the concepts.
Stage 3: Potential concept	Systematic strategies used, but the focus is on only one concept at a time.
Stage 4: Mature concept	Systematic strategies used simultaneously to solve problems.

The zone of proximal development

For Vygotsky, group or collaborative working is extremely important in developing and using language skills. He used the term *zone of proximal development* to describe the difference between what a child can do on their own and what they can achieve through collaboration.

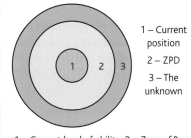

1 – Current position
2 – ZPD
3 – The unknown

1 – Current level of ability. 2 – *Zone of Proximal Development* through which child must move to improve ability. 3 – Region of ability currently out of reach: this becomes the new ZPD once the current ZPD has been crossed.

Scaffolding
» This is support for moving the child through the ZPD until they are more able (Wood et al, 1976).
» McNaughton and Leyland (1990) experimented with jigsaws of increasing difficulty. The amount of help (scaffolding) mothers gave their children was directly related to the difficulty of the jigsaw. Below the child's ZPD, 'helping' behaviour was more like 'joining in with the task'. A harder jigsaw within the child's ZPD required more 'assistance and guidance' from the mother until the child's ability improved as the ZPD was crossed.

Evaluation of Vygotsky's theory

1. Individual differences

Group working may be beneficial to some, but not all:

Blaye et al (1991) – Using a task where children worked alone or in pairs on a problem-solving task they found great variation in whether pair or group working was most appropriate, with at least 30% of those working alone performing just as well as those in groups.

Bennett and Dunne (1991) – Competitiveness between students is something which can be beneficial but group work discourages this.

2. Over-emphasis on social factors

Other theorists (e.g. Piaget) argue that self-discovery and experimentation are central to development, rather than interaction with others.

3. The role of the teacher

The theory emphasises the role of the teacher in providing the right amount of scaffolding at just the right time. This is fine, e.g. when there are only few children in a class, but when numbers increase and each individual child needs different levels of support we can see how unlikely it is that the teacher can provide this.

Applying Bruner's theory to Education

Spiral curriculum

Rather than information being taught in large chunks before moving on, it is taught is smaller pieces which are repeatedly revisited. This suits individual learning speed and interests and provides opportunities to master skills. Instruction must be *honest* within the spiral, returning to earlier concepts over and over again until everything is absolutely clear. This is a little like 'careful scaffolding'.

» DiBassio et al (1999) – A spiral approach was more successful than a regular curriculum approach to teaching chemistry, especially with the most complex concepts being taught.

» Whysong et al (2008) –The spiral approach was found to be an advantage when teaching ethics to university students.

Reciprocal teaching and learning

Palinscar and Brown developed a technique based on the spiral curriculum which is useful for understanding written text. A group reads through a piece of text together, then a 'discussion leader' summarises what has just been read. Then members critically discuss the summary, followed by a re-read of the text by the group.

» Marston et al (1995) – Reciprocal teaching was found to be advantageous in a situation with a computer-based learning package, benefiting communication skills and comprehension.

» Klinger and Vaughn (1996) – Bilingual students were helped by this technique to better understand English.

Motivation to learn

If we understand why a child wants to learn then we are better placed to help them do so. Motives for learning change with age, but what is important is that children feel they are participants in their education, not just receiving instruction.

» Brophy (1987) – Motivation to learn is developed through experience of learning, so having the correct environment to provide this experience is essential.

Intuitive thinking

Experts often act on 'feelings' or 'hunches' when solving problems, and this *intuitive* thinking should be encouraged. It is more important to have an intuitive understanding than a detailed knowledge of something, e.g. mathematical knowledge is less important than an intuitive understanding of what to do with numbers. If teachers act intuitively in helping ('scaffolding') students, then students are more likely to learn to act on intuition. This learning is likely to make a child feel a little unsure of themselves.

Applications from Piaget and Vygotsky's theories

Bruner draws heavily on the ideas of Vygotsky: e.g. he emphasises the importance of active instruction and the use of scaffolding and the ZPD.

If you are asked a question on the application of a theory to education, then as well as presenting how the theory is applied you must be prepared to be evaluative in your answer. You can do this most easily by using research studies which back up or criticise particular points.

Discuss the application to education of two or more theories of cognitive development.
(9 + 16 marks)

SECTION 2: DEVELOPMENT OF MORAL UNDERSTANDING

This refers to how we come to learn right from wrong, to empathise with other people, and to feel guilty.

KOHLBERG'S THEORY OF MORAL UNDERSTANDING

Moral development is closely related to cognitive development. Kohlberg investigated moral development by presenting children with stories that described a moral dilemma and asking them what they would do.

From their responses he said that moral understanding developed through three levels, each with two stages:

LEVEL 1 PRE-CONVENTIONAL MORALITY	LEVEL 2 CONVENTIONAL MORALITY	LEVEL 3 POST-CONVENTIONAL MORALITY
Stage 1 – Punishment and obedience orientation Moral decisions based on whether punished or not. If punished, it must be bad; if rewarded it must be good.	*Stage 3 – Expectations, relationships and conformity* Moral decisions made based on norms of a group. If the family behaves in a certain way then it is fine to do so. The concept of 'naughty' is developed.	*Stage 5 – Social contact* Behaviour should be such that the maximum good is achieved by the maximum number of people; the 'law' becomes known to the child, but they know it can be changed or bent if necessary. Basic human rights are understood.
Stage 2 – Individualism, instrumental purpose and exchange Decisions made in their own interest. If it feels nice, it is fine. An understanding of the notion of fairness is developed.	*Stage 4 – Social systems and conscience* Moral decisions based on *intent* are developed. If a person did not *mean* to spill milk, then it is not as bad as if they did mean to do it.	*Stage 6 – Universal ethical principles* Own ethical standards are applied. Conscience dictates whether to break the law or not.

Evaluating Kohlberg's theory
» Colby et al (1983) – A 27-year longitudinal study (male P's were tested six times during this period) supported the idea that we pass through stages of moral development in the same order.
» Eckensberger (1983) – A meta-analysis of research suggests that people appear to move through the same stages in the same order in different cultures.
» Fergusson et al (1991) – Kohlberg's theory is based on Western thinking and does not relate to non-Western ideas of morality and justice. They found that Northern Irish children scored differently from Nigerian children of the same age, who were brought up to be more obedient than the Irish group. In short, the theory is culturally biased.
» Gilligan (1982) – The theory is gender biased, and is based on the 'rule-based' male understanding of morality. She says that women regard morality more in terms of ethics and care. The theory does not relate to women as strongly as it does to men.
» Conley et al (1997) – Tested Gilligan's idea that, when given more realistic dilemmas, people responded differently than in Kohlberg's theory. They found that how people responded to a dilemma regarding a sexually transmitted disease was partly dependent on experience of the problem. Individual differences as well as the reality of the dilemma need to be considered when understanding moral decisions.
» Rest and Narvaez (1991) – It is not always possible to predict how a person will respond from the level of moral development they are in. They suggest that whether a person behaves morally depends on a lot of factors, including their moral sensitivity, motivation and moral strength.

QUESTION TIME

Discuss research into the development of moral understanding. (9 + 16 marks)

QUESTION TIME

(a) Outline Kohlberg's theory of the development of moral understanding. (9 marks)
(b) Evaluate Kohlberg's theory outlined in (a). (16 marks)

DEVELOPMENT OF THE CHILD'S SENSE OF SELF: THEORY OF MIND

ToM is our understanding of others as having their own thoughts, beliefs, emotions and intentions. This understanding allows us to make inferences about others' knowledge, behaviour and motivations.

Researching ToM: false belief tasks

The most famous is the Sally-Anne task by Wimmer and Perner (1983). Correctly understanding a false-belief task like this requires a theory of mind, an ability to look at the world from someone else's perspective.

The Sally–Anne Task

Step 1: Sally and Anne are introduced to the participant.

Step 2: Sally places a marble into her basket in full view of Anne.

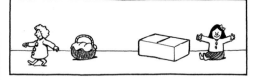

Step 3: Sally leaves the room.

Step 4: Anne takes the marble from the basket and moves it into the box.

Step 5: Sally returns. The participant is asked "Where will Sally look for her marble?"

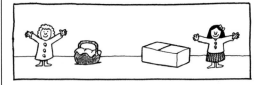

Children between 2 and 3 would say 'Sally will look in the box' even though Sally could not have known that. 4 year olds say she will look in the basket, as they 'understand' Sally's mind and pass the task.

Milligan et al (2007) – In a meta-analysis involving over 9000 children, they found a significant relationship between false-belief task performance and language ability, supporting the idea that ToM develops as part of a broader range of cognitive skills.

Charman et al (2002) – Ability with language might explain why girls are better at false-belief tasks than boys, since they have more advanced language.

Ruffman et al (1999) – Parenting style influences false-belief task performance. Responses of mothers requiring infants to think about others are most beneficial in developing these skills.

Meins et al (1998) – Quality of attachment, related to parenting style, also influences false-belief task performance. Securely attached children are treated by parents as having their own mental states and so their performance improves on false-belief tasks as they grow older.

Baron-Cohen's research

Autistic children seem to lack a ToM.

His research has involved investigating when children develop ToM, e.g. Baron-Cohen et al (1983):

» Three groups of children given the Sally-Anne task. Group 1 – diagnosed with Autistic Spectrum Disorder (ASD); Group 2 – Down's syndrome children; Group 3 – age-matched 'normal' children.
» Around 85% of Down's and normal children completed the task correctly, whilst only 20% of the ASD children could do so.
» The task difficulty experienced by the ASD group must have been due to differences in social cognition, not intelligence, because they had similar levels of measured intelligence to the Down's children.

ASK AN EXAMINER

Baron-Cohen is specifically mentioned in the specification as someone whose research you need to know about. Make sure then that you are able to say something about his research on ToM with autistic children.

QUESTION TIME ?

Discuss the development of a child's sense of self. (9 + 16 marks)

Evaluating Theory of Mind

Influence of culture →

Calaghan et al (2005) – Previous cross-cultural research was flawed because different false-belief tasks were used, raising questions about reliability. Using the same task, they found children passed false-belief tasks by 5 years in all cultures they tested. This suggests that ToM can be applied universally.

Influence of siblings →

McAlistair and Peterson (2006) – Siblings may influence ability on false-belief tasks. A longitudinal study lasting 14 months in Australia showed that having brothers and sisters was very important, as it forced children to interact more with others in the family unit, thus encouraging ToM. It seems our family environment influences ToM.

False belief with every-day objects →

Hogfrede et al (1986) – Using a Smarties tube task instead of the Sally-Anne task, ToM was seen to develop at around 4 years of age.

Criticisms of false-belief tasks

Success may not be due to ToM but to another general intellectual skill, e.g. language. Older children do better on false-belief tasks because they are better with language, i.e. they understand the task better (Lewis and Osborne, 1990).

Onishi and Baillargeon (2005) believe that false-belief tasks over-estimate the age at which ToM appears. 15-month-old infants (who cannot speak) show surprise when they witness a person searching for a moved object to find it is unexpectedly not there. They claim that if tested correctly even very young children can show theory of mind, supporting the idea that performance in traditional false-belief tasks is related to language development.

ASK AN EXAMINER

Both these pieces of research say that false-belief tasks such as the Smarties and Sally-Anne tasks are not measures of ToM as they rely heavily on language skills. If a task does not measure what it says it measures, in this case ToM, then its validity is questioned. This 'language' criticism is really a question of task validity. This is an effective way of evaluating theory of mind research.

QUESTION TIME ?

(a) Outline what is meant by 'Theory of Mind'. (4 marks)
(b) Discuss research into Theory of Mind. (21 marks)

ASK AN EXAMINER

Whilst you could bring ToM into a general question on the development of a sense of self, be aware that you could also get an exam question just on Theory of Mind.

HOW WELL DO I KNOW IT?	NOT AT ALL	MAYBE	OK	WELL	SUPERBLY
SECTION 1: DEVELOPMENT OF THINKING					
Piaget's theory					
Vygotsky's theory					
Bruner's theory					
Application of Piaget's theory					
Application of Vygotsky's theory					
Application of Bruner's theory					
SECTION 2: DEVELOPMENT OF MORAL UNDERSTANDING					
Kohlberg's theory of moral understanding					
Eisenberg's theory of pro-social reasoning					
SECTION 3: DEVELOPMENT OF SOCIAL COGNITION					
Development of a child's sense of self					
Theory of Mind					
Development of children's understanding of others (Selman's theory)					
Biological explanations of social cognition (mirror neurons)					

Psychopathology

WHAT YOU NEED TO KNOW

You will be expected to:

- Demonstrate knowledge and understanding of ONE of the following disorders:
  » Schizophrenia
  » Depression
  » Anxiety disorders – phobia
  » Anxiety disorders – obsessive compulsive disorder
- Apply knowledge and understanding of classification and diagnosis to the chosen disorder

For the chosen disorder you should be familiar with the following:

- Clinical characteristics
- Issues surrounding the classification and diagnosis, including reliability and validity
- Biological explanations for the disorder
- Psychological explanations for the disorder
- Biological therapies for the disorder, including their evaluation in terms of appropriateness and effectiveness
- Psychological therapies for the disorder, including their evaluation in terms of appropriateness and effectiveness

SCHIZOPHRENIA

CLINICAL CHARACTERISTICS OF SCHIZOPHRENIA

A severe debilitating psychotic disorder: sufferers lose touch with reality. Crow (1980) distinguishes between two types:

Type 1 (Positive symptoms) Something is added to the sufferer's personality, e.g. auditory or visual hallucinations.

Type 2: (Negative symptoms) Something is taken away, e.g. there is a lack of emotion or very limited use of speech.

Diagnostic criteria in DSM-IV

To be diagnosed with schizophrenia a person must show the following:

1. *Characteristic symptoms*
   Two or more of:
   • Delusions
   • Hallucinations
   • Disorganised speech
   • Grossly disorganised or catatonic behaviour.

2. *Social/occupational dysfunction*
   Below normal functioning in such things as relationships and work.

3. *Duration*
   Continuous signs of disturbance for six months.

Classification systems distinguish between different subtypes of schizophrenia, although this has little bearing on treatment.

SUBTYPES OF SCHIZOPHRENIA	
Paranoid	Presence of delusions or auditory hallucinations.
Disorganised (Hebephrenic)	Difficulty in responding to the real world. Behaviour and speech disorganised and unpredictable. Flat affect (limited expression of emotion) or inappropriate emotion (laughing at road accident).
Catatonic	Severe motor problems. May freeze up entirely, or may show excessive motor physical activity.
Undifferentiated	Those that do not neatly fit the other categories.
Residual	Someone who has shown symptoms, in the past, but no positive symptoms (see types) for 12 months. Often seen as a transition stage before a full diagnosis of schizophrenia. May show negative symptoms in the 12 month period.

Onset is most common in mid to late adolescence and occurs in about 0.4% of the population. It is more frequent in urban areas of a lower socioeconomic class.

ISSUES SURROUNDING CLASSIFICATION AND DIAGNOSIS

» The main tools used in classification and diagnosis are DSM and ICD (produced by the American Psychiatric Association and World Health Organisation).

» These classify disorders into groups and types, making it easier for problems to be identified.

» By sharing a common diagnostic tool and a standard method of identifying problems, communication between professionals should be much more effective and the risk of professional bias and misinterpretation is reduced.

» Classification however raises a number of controversial issues.

Issue: LABELLING

1. Diagnosis can result in a hard-to-remove label.
   • Modern classification means you do not 'recover'. Experience of negative symptoms is labelled 'residual schizophrenia'; and no symptoms as 'schizophrenia in remission'.

2. Having been diagnosed with a mental problem often means that this has to be disclosed in future.
   • e.g. on job and insurance applications.

3. The diagnosis therefore carries the extra responsibilities of potential stigma.

If you are asked for clinical characteristics in the exam you won't have to write in much detail (it would probably be worth around 4 or 5 marks), so what is here is more than enough.

Discuss issues surrounding the classification and diagnosis of schizophrenia. (9 + 16 marks)

Issue: SUBJECTIVITY

1. Focusing on *categorising* a person there is a danger that important individual differences are overlooked, e.g.:
   • Varying degrees to which people can experience the same disorder.
   • The degree to which the schizophrenia is having an impact on life.
2. Opinion and judgement is still needed in diagnosis – thus there is a possible influence of beliefs and biases, e.g.:
   • What behaviours constitute a symptom of schizophrenia and which do not?
   • What is a mild symptom and what is an uncharacteristic mood swing?

Issue: VALIDITY

1. How valid is the system of classification and diagnosis:
   • does it reflect the true nature of the problems?
   • does it accurately reflect the prognosis?
   • does it predict the success of treatments?
2. Because schizophrenia shares many symptoms with other disorders, Schneider (1959) argues that the content of the symptom is more important than the symptom itself, e.g., the type of hallucination rather than having them per se.
3. Schizophrenia cannot be diagnosed if an existing mood disorder or developmental disorder has been diagnosed, or if there are organic origins. Diagnosis is complicated by having to rule these things out.

Validity: the problem of co-morbidity

Some individuals do not fit neatly into the categories created. Instead of acknowledging limitations of the diagnosis method, clinicians often diagnose two separate disorders.

Schizophrenia has such a strong co-morbidity with mood disorders that it is considered a fundamental characteristic. Buckley et al (2009) identify the following co-morbidities with schizophrenia, and suggest that these co-morbidities might represent sub-types of schizophrenia: 15% for panic disorder; 29% for post traumatic stress disorder; 23% for obsessive-compulsive disorder; 50% for depression; 47% have a lifetime diagnosis of co-morbid substance abuse

Issue: RELIABILITY

1. In this context, we refer to inter-rater reliability: to what extent would two clinicians arrive at the same diagnosis?
2. Research has suggested inter-rater reliability is quite low. Beck et al (1961):
   • Looked at the reliability of two psychiatrists considering the same 154 patients.
   • Found that there was only 54% agreement in diagnosis.

Why lack of reliability?

Even with medical records available, interviews are important; and these rely on potentially inaccurate retrospective data, patient's memory.

Limited time and resources available to health professionals. Meehl (1977) said diagnosis is best if clinicians:
» pay close attention to medical records
» are serious about diagnosis
» really use classification systems
» consider all available evidence.

Unfortunately, this is not possible in modern pressured health systems.

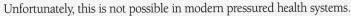

ASK AN EXAMINER

Five issues are presented here, enough to give an impression of both breadth and depth in an exam answer.

Reliability, validity and subjectivity: On being sane in insane places

Rosenhan et al (1972) found that 'normal' people could get themselves diagnosed with schizophrenia and admitted to psychiatric hospital merely by claiming they could hear voices.

In a follow-up study they checked diagnosis reliability by warning hospitals to expect fake patients within the next three months. 41 patients were suspected, 19 of them diagnosed by two staff members. In fact, there were no such fake patients.

Issue: CULTURAL RELATIVISM

» The concept of abnormality varies between cultures and subcultures.
» Without acknowledging the influence of culture, individuals risk being wrongly regarded as abnormal: e.g. different cultures express emotion in different ways.
» There are also disorders which are very culturally specific (known as culture bound syndromes).

Culture: Language issues

Diagnosis involves social intercourse.

Problems can arise if patient and clinician do not share the same language.

Customs may also vary.

A lack of understanding of language and customs can lead to misdiagnosis: e.g. different cultures grieve in different ways – when does grief become abnormal?

Culture-bound syndromes

Amok (Malaysia) – The *pengamok* suddenly withdraws, then bursts into a murderous rage, attacking the people around him with whatever weapon is available. He does not stop until he is overpowered or killed; if the former, he falls into a sleep or stupor, often awakening with no knowledge of his violent acts.

Tabanka (Trinidad) – Depression in men abandoned by their wives, associated with high rate of suicide.

Anorexia nervosa (N. America, W. Europe) – Chronic weight loss brought on by self-starvation.

BIOLOGICAL EXPLANATIONS OF SCHIZOPHRENIA

Genetic explanations of schizophrenia

Family studies

Gottesman (1991) in a meta-analysis looked at rates of schizophrenia in MZs and DZs and found that an MZ twin was much more likely to get it if the other twin was a sufferer than was the case for DZ twins (see table).

The more genes relatives share, the more likely they are both to suffer with schizophrenia if one of them is diagnosed.

Relationship		Concordance (%)
Unrelated	General population	1
	Spouse	2
3rd degree relative	First cousin	2
2nd degree relative	Uncle/aunt	2
	Nephew/niece	4
	Grandchild	5
	Half-sibling	6
1st degree relative	Sibling	9
	Non-identical twin (DZ)	17
	Identical twin (MZ)	48

Adapted from Gottesman (1991)

Adoption studies

Adoption studies allow the separation of genetic and environmental influences – e.g. children born to schizophrenic parents but adopted into non-schizophrenic ones should have a higher than normal risk of the disorder.

Kety et al (1988) found that 32% of adoptees separated from a schizophrenic biological parent contracted the disorder, compared to 18% separated from non-schizophrenic parents, indicating the importance of genetics.

Kendler et al (1994) found that those adopted by a schizophrenic parent were no more likely to be diagnosed than members of the general population, suggesting the environment has little influence.

Evaluation of genetic explanations

Shared environment – Even DZ twins show an increased incidence of schizophrenia relative to the general public if one twin is diagnosed. Shared environment must therefore play a role, not just genetics, as DZ twins are not genetically identical. As adopted twins, also, are often adopted by families with similar backgrounds or even within the same family, a very similar environment is common.

Other influences – If one MZ twin is schizophrenic there is indeed a good chance of the other being diagnosed; but how much this is due to another, as yet undiscovered reason is unclear. The problem is not entirely due to genetics, so the role of other factors needs to be considered.

Multiple genes – Miyamoto et al (2003) say that it is likely that many genes influence the disorder. Identifying one has been impossible.

Other disorders – Heston (1970) says that if one twin has schizophrenia there is a 90% chance of the other twin having *some kind* of mental disorder. This suggests a predisposition for suffering with mental problems, not a clear genetic cause for a single disorder.

Neurochemical explanations of schizophrenia

The symptoms of schizophrenia are caused by the over-production of the neurotransmitter, dopamine (Snyder, 1976).

Theory arose following observations that an overdose of leisure drugs that enhance the activity of dopamine (e.g. LSD, amphetamine) can produce symptoms indistinguishable from schizophrenia. An overdose of amphetamines can produce something called amphetamine psychosis.

Also, drugs to treat Parkinson's disease, such as L-Dopa (which increase dopamine levels) can, when given in too high doses, produce schizophrenic-like symptoms.

Evaluation of the dopamine hypothesis

Drug effects – Evidence for the involvement of dopamine comes from the effects of drugs which change dopamine levels, (e.g. amphetamines and L-Dopa increase dopamine and can bring on schizophrenic-like symptoms).

Post-mortem studies – Studies with dopamine in the brains of schizophrenics are done after they have died and because of this we cannot tell if increased dopamine levels cause schizophrenia or if they are caused by schizophrenia changing the brain.

Brain scans – PET scans which track dopamine levels in living patients suggest that it is an important neurotransmitter but do not support the notion that its overproduction is the sole cause of schizophrenia.

Individual differences – Not every schizophrenic treated with dopamine-controlling drugs responds; it may be only some types or subtypes of schizophrenia that are affected by dopamine levels, e.g. type 1.

Neuroanatomical explanations of schizophrenia

Many brain areas have been implicated in schizophrenia, but only a few areas consistently so.

Ventricles appear to be as much as 15% larger in schizophrenics, especially in those with type 2 (Torrey, 2002). It is not larger ventricles as such, however, that cause the problem, but the loss of adjacent brain tissue.

Lambert and Kinsey (2005) argue that the larger ventricles could be because sufferers have smaller frontal and temporal lobes. The larger the ventricles, the less likely that symptoms would ease and become more manageable.

Molina et al (2005) found that hypofrontality (reduced brain tissue and activity in the frontal lobes) is an indication of later development of schizophrenia.

BIOLOGICAL THERAPIES FOR SCHIZOPHRENIA

It can be a bit daunting when confronted with the names of drugs, but a bit of effort learning them can make an exam answer look really knowledgeable!

Drug therapy

The most common and effective therapy for the treatment of schizophrenia.

These antipsychotics were discovered when it was noted that drugs used to calm people prior to hospital surgery also alleviated positive symptoms.

Most anti-psychotic drugs work by blocking the effects of the neurotransmitter dopamine.

There are three categories of antipsychotics:

» *Typical/conventional* (such as chlorpromazine, the oldest type of drug).
» *Less typical/conventional* (such as pimozide, which have effects on particular symptoms, often used as a last resort when other drugs fail).
» *Atypical* (such as risperidone, which are the most effective over a broad range of symptoms with lower risks of relapse and fewer side effects).

Evaluation of drug therapy

Appropriateness

Symptoms or cause? – Drugs treat the symptoms not the cause, because the cause is unknown. Drug therapy for schizophrenia has been likened to putting a cold flannel on someone's head when they have a fever.

Relapse – Relapse is common if drugs are discontinued, meaning that antipsychotics may be a lifetime prescription. Because of this, dependency and tolerance develops.

Side effects – e.g. about a quarter of people will suffer disordered movement. Side effects are why about 50% stop taking their drugs in the first year, leading to relapse. Newer drugs have fewer side effects however.

Individual differences – Not all sufferers respond in the same way – only around 30% react favourably.

Effectiveness

Help – For most, the symptoms are calmed; and for many the problem is cured.

Not all symptoms – Antispsychotics only seem to help positive symptoms; negative symptoms need other drugs and/or psychological therapies.

Beneficial side effects – Silverman et al (1987) claim that antipsychotics not only reduce symptoms but also increase levels of thinking and attention.

The best treatment available – Antipsychotics are the single most effective treatment for schizophrenia.

Make sure that you learn about both drug therapy and psychosurgery: you are expected to know about two biological therapies and you need these in a bit of depth. You can use psychological therapies as a contrast to add to the evaluation.

Outline and evaluate one psychological therapy and one biological therapy for schizophrenia. (9 + 16 marks)

You will notice that therapies are evaluated in term of effectiveness and appropriateness. Take care! These terms might be included in the wording of the exam question. Use the terms to organise your learning and include them in your evaluation whether you are asked for them or not. That way you have it covered!

(a) Outline and evaluate one psychological therapy for schizophrenia. (4 + 8 marks)
(b) Discuss issues surrounding the classification and diagnosis of schizophrenia. (5 + 8 marks)

Psychosurgery

Psychosurgery involves damaging a part of the brain to change behaviour.

Treatment was developed in the 1930s with attempts to separate the frontal lobes from the rest of the brain (frontal lobotomy). It was noticed that symptoms of schizophrenia reduced or disappeared.

More efficient methods of lobotomising were developed and the procedure applied more widely, with ultimately tens of thousands of operations conducted before it waned in popularity.

Nowadays psychosurgery is used only in very exceptional circumstances.

Evaluation of psychosurgery

Appropriateness

Abnormal frontal lobes – Research shows abnormal frontal lobe functioning in schizophrenics so there is some support for the idea of reducing this to control symptoms.

Justifiable? – It is, however, a very drastic and permanent treatment and it is debatable whether such procedures can ever be justified.

Side effects – Whilst schizophrenic symptoms may reduce, serious side effects have been recorded, such as loss of memory, emotional disturbance, personality change, loss of inhibition. In some people, the side effects were a greater problem than the original condition.

Effectiveness

Tooth and Newton (1961) reported on psychosurgery carried out between 1942 and 1954. Few sufferers (4%) had died of the surgery, and at least 69% showed improvement of some kind, 41% significantly so. It is therefore often very effective. However, just as a good stiff whisky can help reduce anxiety, so too does psychosurgery reduce the symptoms of schizophrenia. It is the equivalent of making an anxious person permanently drunk, since the symptoms are not removed, they are suppressed, permanently.

(a) Outline one biological explanation of schizophrenia. (4 marks)
(b) Outline and evaluate one psychological therapy for schizophrenia. (21 marks)

PSYCHOLOGICAL THERAPIES FOR SCHIZOPHRENIA

Behavioural therapy

This therapy has been used in conjunction with drugs to help sufferers with their behaviour.

Token economy is the most common technique, most often used in institutions:

» Based on operant conditioning, sufferers are rewarded for not displaying unwanted behaviour and as therapy progresses they are rewarded for acceptable non-schizophrenic behaviour.
» Reward comes in the form of 'tokens' which can be exchanged for benefits or treats, e.g. sweets, music.

Evaluation of behavioural therapy

Appropriateness

More freedom – Token economy has been useful in many institutions, giving sufferers more freedom rather than control by confinement.

Behaviour management – It does not deal with the schizophrenia but is a technique for managing behaviour.

For institutions – Because behaviour has to be monitored and rewarded, token economy is most appropriate for use within institutional settings.

HOW WELL DO I KNOW IT?	NOT AT ALL	MAYBE	OK	WELL	SUPERBLY
SCHIZOPHRENIA					
Clinical characteristics of schizophrenia					
Issues of classification and diagnosis of schizophrenia: reliability					
Issues of classification and diagnosis of schizophrenia: validity					
Biological explanations of schizophrenia: genetics					
Biological explanations of schizophrenia: neurochemical					
Biological explanations of schizophrenia: neuroanatomical					
Psychological explanations of schizophrenia: behavioural					
Psychological explanations of schizophrenia: cognitive					
Psychological explanations of schizophrenia: psychodynamic					
Biological therapy: Drugs – appropriateness and effectiveness					
Biological therapies: Psychosurgery – appropriateness and effectiveness					
Psychological therapy: behavioural – appropriateness and effectiveness					
Psychological therapy: psychodynamic – appropriateness and effectiveness					
Psychological therapy: cognitive-behavioural – appropriateness and effectiveness					

DEPRESSION

CLINICAL CHARACTERISTICS OF DEPRESSION

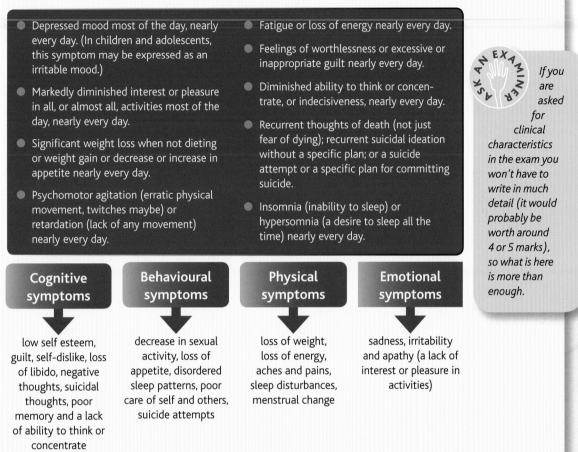

- Depressed mood most of the day, nearly every day. (In children and adolescents, this symptom may be expressed as an irritable mood.)

- Markedly diminished interest or pleasure in all, or almost all, activities most of the day, nearly every day.

- Significant weight loss when not dieting or weight gain or decrease or increase in appetite nearly every day.

- Psychomotor agitation (erratic physical movement, twitches maybe) or retardation (lack of any movement) nearly every day.

- Fatigue or loss of energy nearly every day.

- Feelings of worthlessness or excessive or inappropriate guilt nearly every day.

- Diminished ability to think or concentrate, or indecisiveness, nearly every day.

- Recurrent thoughts of death (not just fear of dying); recurrent suicidal ideation without a specific plan; or a suicide attempt or a specific plan for committing suicide.

- Insomnia (inability to sleep) or hypersomnia (a desire to sleep all the time) nearly every day.

ASK AN EXAMINER — *If you are asked for clinical characteristics in the exam you won't have to write in much detail (it would probably be worth around 4 or 5 marks), so what is here is more than enough.*

Cognitive symptoms	Behavioural symptoms	Physical symptoms	Emotional symptoms
low self esteem, guilt, self-dislike, loss of libido, negative thoughts, suicidal thoughts, poor memory and a lack of ability to think or concentrate	decrease in sexual activity, loss of appetite, disordered sleep patterns, poor care of self and others, suicide attempts	loss of weight, loss of energy, aches and pains, sleep disturbances, menstrual change	sadness, irritability and apathy (a lack of interest or pleasure in activities)

ISSUES SURROUNDING CLASSIFICATION AND DIAGNOSIS

» The main tools used in classification and diagnosis are DSM and ICD (produced by the American Psychiatric Association and World Health Organisation).

» These classify disorders into groups and types, making it easier for problems to be identified.

» By sharing a common diagnostic tool and a standard method of identifying problems, communication between professionals should be much more effective and the risk of professional bias and misinterpretation is reduced.

» Classification however raises a number of controversial issues.

Issue: SUBJECTIVITY

1. By focusing on *categorising* a person there is a danger that important individual differences are overlooked, e.g.:
   - Varying degrees to which people can experience the same disorder.
   - The degree to which the depression is having an impact on life.

2. Opinion and judgement is still needed in diagnosis: thus there is a possible influence of beliefs and biases, e.g. when does feeling very down become a clinical depression?

ASK AN EXAMINER — *Five issues are presented here, enough to give an impression of both breadth and depth in an exam answer.*

QUESTION TIME — *Discuss issues surrounding the classification and diagnosis of depression. (9 + 16 marks)*

(a) Outline the clinical characteristics of depression. (4 marks)
(b) Outline one biological explanation for depression (5 marks)
(c) Consider issues surrounding the classification and diagnosis of depression. (16 marks)

Issue: LABELLING

1. Diagnosis can result in a hard-to-remove label.
   - e.g. a depressive may always carry the stigma of having suffered with this problem.
2. Having been diagnosed with a mental problem often means that this has to be disclosed in future.
   - e.g. on job and insurance applications.
3. The diagnosis therefore carries the extra responsibilities of potential stigma.

Issue: VALIDITY

How valid is the system of classification and diagnosis:
- does it reflect the true nature of the problems?
- does it accurately reflect the prognosis?
- does it predict the success of treatments?

There are many types of depression and it can be difficult for clinicians to tell the difference between them, especially working under pressure. As many as 25% of people with depression have 'double depression' (more than one kind at the same time).

Validity: the problem of co-morbidity

Some individuals do not fit neatly into the categories created.

Instead of acknowledging limitations of the diagnosis method, clinicians often diagnose two separate disorders.
- Kessler et al (1996) – the chance of someone with a form of MDD suffering from an anxiety disorder is about 58% and about 74% for any disorder at all.

Co-morbid disorders	Percentage of people also suffering with depression
Generalised anxiety disorder	17%
Agoraphobia	16%
Specific phobia	24%
Social phobia	27%
Panic disorder	10%
Post-traumatic stress disorder	19.5%

Issue: RELIABILITY

1. In this context, we refer to inter-rater reliability: to what extent would two clinicians arrive at the same diagnosis?
2. Research has suggested inter-rater reliability is quite low:
   - Beck et al (1961)
     - Looked at the reliability of two psychiatrists considering the same 154 patients.
     - There was only 54% agreement in diagnosis.

Why lack of reliability?

Even with medical records available, interviews are important – and these rely on potentially inaccurate retrospective data, patient's memory.

Limited time and resources available to health professionals.

Meehl (1977) said diagnosis is best if clinicians:
- pay close attention to medical records
- are serious about diagnosis
- really use classification systems
- consider all available evidence.

Unfortunately, this is not possible in modern pressured health systems.

Issue: CULTURAL RELATIVISM

» The concept of abnormality varies between cultures and subcultures.
» Without acknowledging the influence of culture, individuals risk being wrongly regarded as abnormal: e.g. different cultures express emotion in different ways.
» Some disorders are very culturally specific (known as culture bound syndromes). E.g. Parker et al (2001) point out that China has low rates of depression, not because it doesn't exist there, but because they deny it or express it as a physical illness. However, exposure to Western influence is changing this.

Culture: Language issues

» Diagnosis involves social intercourse.
» Problems can arise if patient and clinician do not share the same language.
» Customs may also vary.
» A lack of understanding of language and customs can lead to misdiagnosis, e.g. different cultures grieve in different ways – when does grief become abnormal?

Culture-bound syndromes

Amok (Malaysia) – The *pengamok* suddenly withdraws, then bursts into a murderous rage, attacking the people around him with whatever weapon is available. He does not stop until he is overpowered or killed; if the former, he falls into a sleep or stupor, often awakening with no knowledge of his violent acts.

Tabanka (Trinidad) – Depression in men abandoned by their wives, associated with high rate of suicide.

Anorexia nervosa (N. America, W. Europe) – Chronic weight loss brought on by self-starvation.

BIOLOGICAL EXPLANATIONS OF DEPRESSION

Genetic explanations

Those with a parent or sibling with depression are up to 3 times more likely to suffer it themselves, suggesting a genetic component.

Twin studies

The greater the genetic similarity, the more likely two people are to suffer depression.

McGuffin et al (1996) – Chance of one MZ twin suffering is 46% if their identical twin suffers, compared to 20% in DZ twins.

Serotonin decreasing gene

Serotonin is a neurotransmitter important in mood regulation, low levels of which are associated with depression.

Caron and Zhang (2005) – A gene responsible for reducing serotonin is 10 times more likely in depressives. Those with the gene do not respond to antidepressants and 65% have relatives with depression.

Evaluating Genetic explanations

Genes and familial inheritance – If genes were the only reason for depression, identical twins would both be certain to suffer if one did, but this is not the case. Also, children of parents with depression are only slightly more likely to develop the problem than the rest of the population. Genes and familial inheritance are not the whole story.

Gender differences – Genes are more influential in the development of female depression. Kendler et al (2006) studied over 15 thousand pairs of male/female twins and showed heritability was higher in females.

(a) Outline two or more biological explanations for depression. (9 marks)
(b) Evaluate biological explanations of depression. (16 marks)

(a) Outline and evaluate one biological explanation of depression. (5 + 8 marks)
(b) Discuss psychological explanations of depression. (5 + 8 marks)

Neurochemical explanations

Neurochemicals are substances used by brain cells to communicate. We have over a hundred different neurochemicals and several have been implicated in depression, especially serotonin and noradrenaline.

Catecholamine hypothesis

» One type of catecholamine is noradrenaline, low levels of which are associated with depression.
» Discovery of this was by accident – the drug reserpine, used to lower blood-pressure, also reduces noradrenaline levels in the brain. It was noticed that those taking the drug also often suffered with depression. Increasing noradrenaline levels reduced their depression.

Serotonin hypothesis

» Low levels of serotonin cause depression.
» Genetic studies have implicated a serotonin reducing gene in depression.
» Serotonin is known to affect mood dramatically: MDMA (ecstasy) for instance creates a euphoric effect by increasing serotonin.
» Tricyclic drugs sometimes used to treat depression prevent 'reuptake' of serotonin in the brain, meaning that more of it is available for use. Commonly prescribed drugs called selective serotonin reuptake inhibitors (e.g. Prozac) are focused solely on altering levels of serotonin.

Evaluation of the catecholamine hypothesis

Individual differences – Low noradrenaline does not affect everyone in the same way. Some depressives prescribed drugs to increase noradrenaline do not respond with reduced depression as might be expected.

Increased levels in the brain – Noradrenaline levels can be increased by preventing the *reuptake* of the drug by the synapse. Versiani et al (1999) and Elkin et al (1996) showed that when reuptake is blocked or *inhibited*, thus making more noradrenaline available to the brain, this has a much greater effect on depression than does a placebo.

Evaluation of the serotonin hypothesis

Serotonin and mood – There is good evidence that increasing serotonin improves mood, supporting the serotonin hypothesis. This can happen with prescription or recreational drugs.

Placebo effect – A placebo effect occurs when an inert substance generates the effect a real drug might. Kirsch et al (2002) say that SSRI drugs are no more effective than placebos and regular exercise is more effective in reducing the symptoms of depression than anti-depressants.

Dependence – The huge increase in use of antidepressants may be a good thing since people are seeking treatment for their depression. On the other hand, it could be showing that we are becoming dependent on the drugs rather than seeking other methods to manage depression.

Neuroendochrine explanation

Pariante (2007) – Depression is characterised by overactivity in the HPA system (involved in our response to stress).

1. The hypothalamus releases corticotrophin-releasing hormone (CRH) when stressed.
2. CRH travels to the pituitary gland, which releases adreno-corticotrophic hormone (ACTH).
3. ACTH travels to the adreno-cortex which activates the release of cortico-steroids – most importantly, cortisol.
4. The hypothalamus monitors cortisol levels. When these are high enough, the stress response is lowered. When too low, more CRH is released, which results in more cortisol.

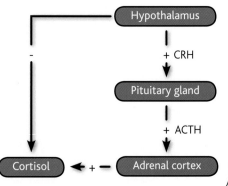

Evaluation of the neuroendocrine explanation

Cause or effect? – Taking antidepressants is correlated with a reduction in CRH but it is not clear whether the drugs reduce the depression and therefore cause a reduction in CRH or whether they cause a reduction in CRH and therefore a reduction in depression.

High and low levels influence depression – The neuroendocrine explanation says that very high levels of cortisol are associated with depression, but so too are very low levels. Those with Cushing's syndrome have high levels; those with Addison's syndrome have low levels after treatment, but both show increased levels of depression, so the relationship between cortisol and depression is far from clear.

Bao et al (2008) – Injecting CRH into the brains of animals can generate depression-like symptoms. This can also account for higher female rates of depression as oestrogen can stimulate the release of CRH, while androgens (male hormones) suppress it: thus women are more likely to be depressed.

Bennett (2008) – Exposure to stress and stress hormones while in the womb can result in a loss of synapses in the pre-frontal cortex, an area that does not function properly in depressed people.

Davison et al (2002) – The hippocampus, responsible in part for ACTH levels, itself responsible for cortisol levels, does not function properly in the depressed.

Some say that the increased levels of CRH may actually result in a reduction in serotonin (see *serotonin hypothesis*) which is actually the reason for the person's depression.

PSYCHOLOGICAL EXPLANATIONS

Cognitive-behavioural explanation

Seligman (1974) – People who have bad experiences may feel that they cannot avoid them and so stop trying to – they *learn* to be helpless (learned helplessness).

This is related to *attributional style*. Abramson (1978) says that attributions have three dimensions:

1. *internal-external* – Is the person to blame (internal) or is the blame outside the control of the person (external)?

2. *stable-unstable* – If a failure is seen as a one-off the person is making an unstable attribution. If a single failure is seen as inevitable, as it will happen all the time, the attribution is stable.

3. *global-specific* – If a failure in one area is seen as representative of the person's life in general it is a global attribution. If failure is attributed to the specific circumstances of the event, rather than life in general, the attribution is specific.

A person who makes internal, stable and global attributions is more likely to develop learned helplessness and so depression.

Evaluation of the cognitive-behavioural explanation

Cross-species comparisons – The original theory was developed by observing dogs that, when faced with unavoidable shocks, just gave up trying to escape them. Human emotional behaviour is much more complex than this, so extending a theory developed with shocks and dogs to depression in humans may lack validity.

Human study – Hiroto and Seligman (1975) replicated the original study, with humans – but shocks were replaced with a loud noise. One group experienced uncontrollable noise that could not be stopped; another could control the noise. In a second condition unexpected noise that could be stopped was presented. Those who had originally experienced uncontrollable noise took longer to stop the noise than the others, indicating helplessness.

Electroconvulsive therapy (ECT)

Originated in the 1930s with the observation that people with epilepsy do not seem to suffer mental illness. Logically therefore, creating a seizure similar to epilepsy should alleviate symptoms of mental illness.

A small electrical current, just large enough to bring on a 'fit' or convulsion, is passed across the brain of a person anaesthetised and given muscle relaxant.

The shock is brief, lasting less than a second, and usually applied to the right hand side to minimise loss of language memory (located in the left side of the brain).

It is generally only employed where drugs have failed in very severe cases of depression.

Evaluation of ECT

Appropriateness

Memory loss – Bilateral ECT can impair memory and language. Rogers et al (1993) say that about 30% found ECT distressing and reported severe memory loss.

Not well understood – Why it works is unclear. There is some evidence that it can actually repair some brain activity and there is no evidence that the brain is damaged. There is no evidence that accepted primary reasons for depression such as serotonin levels are influenced at all. It is argued that using something that is so badly understood is inadvisable.

Ethics: Informed consent – It is unlikely that a very severely depressed person is able to give informed consent at all. In England in 1999, 11340 had the treatment, about 15% of whom did not give their consent to the treatment (Johnstone, 2003).

Fast acting – When it does work it does so very quickly. Waiting for weeks for drugs to work with a suicidal depressed person carries risks and ECT can be said therefore to have saved many lives.

Effectiveness

Works for most – Greenblatt et al (1964) report that ECT is effective in 8 out of 10 cases of depression.

Not a cure – Whilst many patients initially benefit, further medical treatment is sometimes required, including drugs and further ECT, so ECT is not a permanent cure.

Works best for some types of depression – Buchan et al (1992) compared the effects of 'real' ECT with 'sham' ECT and found that ECT did have some beneficial effects but only for those sufferers who also had delusional symptoms (which is quite rare). For the 'average' depressed person, ECT has few benefits.

Short lasting benefits – Schwartz (1995) says that 85% helped with ECT eventually relapse, and Breggin (1997) says that any benefit experienced does not last more than 4 weeks.

(a) Outline one biological explanation of depression. (4 marks)
(b) Outline and evaluate one psychological therapy for depression. (21 marks)

(a) Outline and evaluate one psychological therapy for depression. (4 + 8 marks)
(b) Discuss issues surrounding the classification and diagnosis of depression. (5 + 8 marks)

You will notice that therapies are evaluated in term of effectiveness and appropriateness. Take care! These terms might be included in the wording of the exam question. Use the terms to organise your learning and include them in your evaluation whether you are asked for them or not. That way you have it covered!

PSYCHOLOGICAL THERAPIES

Cognitive behavioural therapy (CBT)

Assumes that mental disorders are the product of abnormal thoughts and feelings.

There are several forms of CBT but they all aim to help sufferers address their own dysfunctional emotions, thought processes, and the behaviours that result.

One form, rational-emotive therapy, says that depressed thoughts are a result of an irrational 'internal' dialogue, which leads to abnormal behaviour, and aims to replace these with more rational thoughts.

Beck's cognitive behavioural therapy argues that disorders are primarily due to 'errors of logic' and aims to address these to reduce depression.

CBT is relatively brief, usually lasting less than 20 sessions. The thought processes are evaluated, challenged and assessed. Optimistic thinking and training strategies designed to help with anxiety are introduced where appropriate. Changes in cognition will lead to changes in dysfunctional behaviour.

Evaluation of CBT

Appropriateness

Not an immediate cure – It can take months for a person to benefit from CBT. This is not something a severely depressed person may be able to wait for.

Motivation required – CBT takes time and effort, and since a symptom is lack of motivation, depressed people may not wish to embark on this form of treatment.

Expensive and time consuming – Compared to anti-depressants, CBT is relatively expensive and is not always available on the NHS. It also takes time out of a person's schedule that can be very hard to arrange.

No side effects – Unlike drugs, it has no significant side effects.

Cause not symptoms – The cause of the depression is addressed, not just the symptoms, so it can be effective in the long-term and can help the person learn life-skills that can be applied in other stressful, and potentially depression-inducing, situations.

Effectiveness

At least as effective as other treatments – It has been shown to be at least as effective as drugs (Rush 1977), especially over periods of more than a year.

Low relapse rate – Whilst the relapse rate with drugs can be as high as 50%, the long term benefits of CBT are good and the relapse rate is relatively low (Hensley et al, 2004).

Combined treatment – Whilst CBT has been found to be at least as effective as drugs in preventing relapse over a number of years, Kupfer and Frank (2001) claim that a combination of CBT and drugs is the most effective form of treatment.

(a) Discuss psychological therapies for any one anxiety disorder. (5 + 8 marks)
(b) Outline and evaluate one or more biological therapies for any one anxiety disorder. (4 + 8 marks)

ASK AN EXAMINER
Some exam questions have what is called a partial performance criterion. *That is, if you are asked to do more than one thing but only actually do one, then you will be penalised. This usually means that your maximum mark reduces to about two thirds of the available marks. You have been warned – answer the question clearly!*

(a) Outline two psychological therapies for depression. (9 marks)
(b) Evaluate one psychological therapy for depression in terms of its appropriateness and effectiveness. (16 marks)

ANXIETY DISORDERS – PHOBIA

CLINICAL CHARACTERISTICS OF PHOBIA

Phobia comes from the Greek 'phobos' meaning 'fear'. It is an 'obsessive, unreasonable, persistent fear triggered by a specific object or situation' (Neale, 2008). It is estimated 6% to 7% of the population suffer from these irrational fears. The DSM identifies three main types of phobia.

PHOBIA	DETAILS
1. Specific phobia	Four types of phobias of objects or situations. 1. *Natural environment type* (Heights, Water). 2. *Animal type* (Spiders, Dogs, Cats). 3. *Situational type* (Flying, Trains etc.). 4. *Medical type* (Medical procedures, Dentistry, Blood).
2. Social phobia	Fear of performing some kind of action in front of others, often in situations others are unlikely to think twice about, e.g. travelling on the bus, eating and drinking.
3. Agoraphobia	Fear of being incapacitated by a panic attack in places where escape would be difficult or embarrassing. Agoraphobics avoid public places, preferring a 'safe' place such as their home.

If you are asked for clinical characteristics in the exam you won't have to write in much detail (it would probably be worth around 4 or 5 marks), so what is here is more than enough.

ISSUES SURROUNDING CLASSIFICATION AND DIAGNOSIS

» The main tools used in classification and diagnosis are DSM and ICD (produced by the American Psychiatric Association and World Health Organisation).
» These classify disorders into groups and types, making it easier for problems to be identified.
» By sharing a common diagnostic tool and a standard method of identifying problems, communication between professionals should be much more effective and the risk of professional bias and misinterpretation is reduced.
» Classification, however, raises a number of controversial issues.

Issue: LABELLING

1. Diagnosis can result in a hard-to-remove label.
   • e.g. an agoraphobic may always carry the stigma of having suffered with this problem.
2. Having been diagnosed with a mental problem often means that this has to be disclosed in future.
   • e.g. on job and insurance applications.
3. The diagnosis therefore carries the extra responsibilities of potential stigma.

Issue: SUBJECTIVITY

1. By focusing on *categorising* a person there is a danger that important individual differences are overlooked, e.g.:
   • Varying degrees to which people can experience the same disorder.
   • The degree to which the phobia is having an impact on life.
2. Opinion and judgement is still needed in diagnosis; thus there is a possible influence of beliefs and biases, e.g.:
   • What is a fear and what is a true phobia?
   • Is a child with a fear of dogs more credible than a man with a fear of buttons?

Five issues are presented here, enough to give an impression of both breadth and depth in an exam answer.

Discuss issues surrounding the classification and diagnosis of phobic disorders. (9 + 16 marks)

Issue: VALIDITY

How valid is the system of classification and diagnosis:

- does it reflect the true nature of the problems?
- does it accurately reflect the prognosis?
- does it predict the success of treatments?

Validity: the problem of co-morbidity

Some individuals do not fit neatly into the categories created. Instead of acknowledging limitations of diagnosis method, clinicians often diagnose two separate disorders.

Neurotic disorders have high co-morbidity, since the various anxiety disorders:
- share symptoms, e.g. panic
- share causal features, e.g. cognitive factors.

Issue: RELIABILITY

1. In this context, we refer to inter-rater reliability: to what extent would two clinicians arrive at the same diagnosis?

2. Research has suggested inter-rater reliability is quite low:
   - Beck et al (1961)
     - Looked at the reliability of two psychiatrists considering 154 patients.
     - There was only 54% agreement in diagnosis.

Why lack of reliability?

Even with medical records available, interviews are important – and these rely on potentially inaccurate retrospective data, patient's memory.

Limited time and resources available to health professionals.

Meehl (1977) said diagnosis is best if clinicians:
- pay close attention to medical records
- are serious about diagnosis
- really use classification systems
- consider all available evidence.

Unfortunately, this is not possible in today's pressured health system.

Issue: CULTURAL RELATIVISM

» The concept of abnormality varies between cultures and subcultures.
» Unless we acknowledge the influence of culture, individuals risk being regarded as abnormal: e.g. different cultures express emotion in different ways.
» There are also disorders which are very culturally specific (known as culture-bound syndromes).

Culture: Language issues

» Diagnosis involves social intercourse.
» Problems can arise if patient and clinician do not share the same language.
» Customs may also vary.
» A lack of understanding of language and customs can lead to misdiagnosis: e.g. different cultures grieve in different ways – when does grief become abnormal?

Culture-bound syndromes

Amok (Malaysia) – The *pengamok* suddenly withdraws, then bursts into a murderous rage, attacking the people around him with whatever weapon is available. He does not stop until he is overpowered or killed; if the former, he falls into a sleep or stupor, often awakening with no knowledge of his violent acts.

Tabanka (Trinidad) – Depression in men abandoned by their wives, associated with high rate of suicide.

Anorexia nervosa (N. America, W. Europe) – Chronic weight loss brought on by self-starvation.

PSYCHOLOGICAL EXPLANATIONS

Behavioural explanations

The phobia is acquired through classical conditioning and maintained through operant conditioning.

Acquiring a phobia

Because an emotion is being conditioned rather than a behaviour, the conditioned response is referred to as a conditioned *emotional* response.

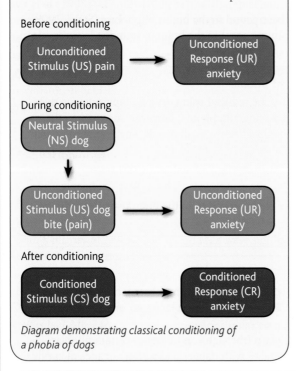

Diagram demonstrating classical conditioning of a phobia of dogs

Don't be afraid to use diagrams in your examination answers! The classical conditioning diagram outlines nicely how phobias develop, also using an example. To draw this and then explain what is going on in the diagram produces an effective outline.

Maintaining a phobia

Operant conditioning maintains a phobia through negative reinforcement.

Avoiding the feared object or situation reduces anxiety, which is rewarding.

This increases likelihood of engaging in this anxiety-reducing behaviour again.

You encountered the behavioural approach at AS level so it should be familiar to you. If you need a reminder, more on the principles of classical and operant conditioning can be found in the Intelligence and Learning chapter.

Evaluation of behavioural explanations of phobia

Some phobias are more common than others – Behavioural explanations do not say why some phobias are easier to acquire than others. Car phobia should be very common in the western world according to behavioural learning explanations, but it is not. Preparedness theory may explain why. In addition to this, Kleinknecht (1982) says that the many safe experiences we have with cars outweigh those that are negative and we have very few experiences with snakes and large hairy spiders upon which to assess their scariness. The amount and balance of positive/negative outcomes of experiences may influence phobia.

Scared of sharks? Ever seen one up close? – Few phobics have had a negative experience with their phobic object, and the learning theory cannot fully explain this. One of the authors of this study guide has never crashed in a plane but has a huge fear of flying nonetheless!

Unpredictability and controllability – Mineka (1985) identifies the unpredictability, uncertainty and controllability of a stimulus as important in whether a phobia will be formed. The less we have experienced the stimulus, and the less understanding we have of its behaviour, the more likely we are to become phobic of it. It is unpredictability which predisposes us to fear. E.g. we can be afraid of unpredictable lightning but rarely of (controlled) electrical sockets.

Watson and Rayner (1920) – A phobia of rats was generated in Little Albert by pairing the presentation of the rat with a very loud noise. After only three presentations Albert began to show phobia-like responses to the rat.

Social learning explanation

Social learning theory focuses on observational learning and imitation of models. Phobias are learned by watching others' reactions (vicarious learning). E.g. a phobia of snakes would be learned from watching a parent (a 'model') showing fear of snakes.

Evaluation of the social learning explanation of phobia

Observational learning – Monkeys reared in captivity were not scared of toy crocodiles, rabbits, snakes and flowers. They watched films of adults showing a fear response to these objects, and afterward showed fear to the snake and crocodile toys only, showing vicarious learning. Cook and Mineka (1990) concluded that this was because they had not evolved a predisposition to be scared of the flower and rabbit, but a dormant fear of the more 'dangerous' animals was activated by the film.

Vicarious learning not always important – Those with social phobia did not report any vicarious learning of their phobia (Hoffman et al 1995). Similarly not everyone who witnesses people displaying a fear response to things develops a phobia.

Parent-offspring similarities – Mineka et al (1985) showed that the offspring of monkeys demonstrated almost identical phobias to their parents and the phobia was still strong after 6 months.

Cognitive explanations

Phobia occurs because of faulty thinking in which the focus is on negative outcomes and faulty predictions. E.g. from the fact that planes may crash and survival is unlikely, the phobic would predict that boarding a plane would result in a dangerous and potentially fatal experience. Errors of logic also mean that we expect the same bad experience every time we encounter the object of our phobia (every dog will bite us, every plane will crash etc.).

Beck (1985) said that the concern of experiencing anxiety is often at least as much as the fear of the object of phobia, e.g. the *worry* that a panic attack will occur in a public space in agoraphobics. Irrational beliefs contribute, e.g. a spider phobic might fear that spiders are going to chase them.

Evaluation of cognitive explanations of phobia

The likelihood of the event happening – Those with a phobia of dogs were compared with those without the phobia. 50% of both phobics and non-phobics remembered a negative incident with a dog in their lives; 50% said that they had had one but could not recall it. DiNardo et al (1985) concluded it was the *prediction of likelihood* of the negative event occurring that mattered. Those with the phobia focused on the likelihood of it happening again; those without the phobia did not focus on this.

Overestimation of number – When shown pictures of trees and snakes, snake phobics reported seeing many more snakes than did non-phobics, showing a distortion of their cognitive processing (Tomarken, 1989).

Conscious processing is not necessary – Phobic people do not need to be aware that they have processed the image of the phobic object to show a fear response. Images shown *very* quickly elicit fearful responses (increased heart rate, blood pressure etc.) even though the phobic is unable to name the item they have seen (Ohman and Soares, 1994).

Three psychological explanations for phobia are presented here. Learn the behavioural one (because it is the best explanation for phobia that we have) and at least one other. In an exam question which does not specify a number of psychological explanations, doing three can give you more scope to achieve those evaluative marks.

Describe and evaluate psychological explanations for any one anxiety disorder. (9 + 16 marks)

BIOLOGICAL THERAPIES FOR PHOBIA

Drug therapies

There is really only one biological therapy for phobia, and this is drug therapy. However, the specification requires you to know about more than one biological therapy. Get around this by writing about each kind of drug therapy, making it look as though they are separate therapies!

Drug therapy: Benzodiazepines

These anxiolytics (anxiety reducers) increase the amount of gamma aminobutyric acid (GABA) in the body, which is how the body 'calms' neurological activity. The drug also achieves its calming effect by mimicking GABA and tricking the brain into thinking that less activity is needed.

QUESTION TIME ?

Outline and evaluate one psychological therapy and one biological therapy for any one anxiety disorder. (9 + 16 marks)

Drug therapy: Beta-blockers

These are often given to social-phobics or those about to do something like stage acting or public speaking. They enhance calmness by working on heart rate, and blocking the effect of adrenaline on the person's physiology, making them feel calmer.

Drug therapy: Monoamine oxidase inhibitors (MAOIs)

These anti-depressants work very well for some phobias, better in some cases than benzodiazepines. They block the production of monoamine oxidase, which is used to break down dopamine, serotonin and noradrenaline, which then remain in the system of the sufferer for longer. This can have a positive effect.

Evaluation of drug therapy

Appropriateness

Problems with side effects – Drugs may produce fatigue, co-ordination problems and drowsiness among other things. Side effects are sometimes severe: e.g. MAOIs may produce fatal reactions to red wine.

Price and availability – The drugs are cheap and easily available, which is good as people can get treatment easily. It is also bad in that drugs are often the first and only source of treatment and are over-prescribed where other treatments may be beneficial to the sufferer.

A shot in the dark – It is often unclear why the drugs work, and they do not work with everyone. Until the biology of phobia is understood, drug therapy may never be more than a preventative 'shot in the dark'.

Dependency – Benzodiazepines and MAOIs can lead to physiological dependency.

Effectiveness

It is not always clear which drugs will work, and why, and for what phobias. E.g. MAOIs have 50–80% success in treating social phobias but are not much better than a placebo at treating specific phobias (Seligman, 1994).

Clinical studies (e.g. Furmark et al, 2002) have shown that drugs can be just as effective as CBT in reducing phobias in both the short and long-term.

1. Benzodiazepines – Not as effective as MAOIs in treating social phobias. May not be good for use long term, as the high doses needed produce undesirable side effects and subsequent rebound of symptoms.

2. MAOIs – Can be better than some anxiolytics, being effective in 60 to 80% of cases and just as good as cognitive behavioural therapy (Heimberg et al, 1980). They can, though, have serious side effects such as increased blood pressure and stroke, especially if taken alongside certain foods.

3. Beta Blockers – Very fast acting and useful as the stressful event can be anticipated by the phobic. They reduce the phobia since their use allows the sufferer to carry out the stressful task in the future, and as confidence grows the drug need reduces.

PSYCHOLOGICAL THERAPIES

Systematic desensitisation

The principles of classical conditioning are used to reduce anxieties to the phobic object.

It is important to the success of the therapy that the client is at first taught to relax (*reciprocal inhibition* – you cannot be anxious and relaxed at the same time).

Beginning at the bottom, a sufferer is gradually moved up through an *anxiety hierarchy*.

At each level the client remains relaxed, until eventually the highest point in the hierarchy can be reached in a relaxed state.

You covered systematic desensitisation at AS level! What you did then is entirely relevant now.

(a) Discuss psychological therapies for any one anxiety disorder. (5 + 8 marks)
(b) Outline and evaluate one or more biological therapies for any one anxiety disorder. (4 + 8 marks)

Evaluation of systematic desensitisation

Appropriateness

Virtual reality (VR) – This can be effective in treating phobias as a person is exposed in a safe environment. Choy et al (2007) say VR is effective for some phobias such as heights and flying, but less so in others, such as phobias for specific animals.

Real life exposure – Exposure to objects of phobia in real life is called *in-vivo* desensitisation and can result in the treatment being discontinued mid-term because it is so stressful (Choy et al, 2007). Barlow and Durrand (1989) say this can actually make the phobia worse.

Co-morbidity – Agoraphobia is often co-morbid with panic disorder and so desensitisation is unlikely to have the desired reducing effect on the phobia.

Effectiveness

McGrath et al (1990) – Systematic desensitisation is effective in treating 75% of phobias.

Craske and Barlow (1993) – Even though many psychologists feel this therapy is inappropriate for agoraphobia, improvements were observed in 50 to 85% of agoraphobics in their study. There was however a 50% relapse from a slight improvement.

Wolfe (2005) – Therapy consistently effective in helping people make eventual contact with the phobic object.

Menzies and Clarke (1993) – No great improvement of phobic symptoms after therapy, but better than no treatment at all.

(a) Outline one biological explanation of any one anxiety disorder. (4 marks)
(b) Outline and evaluate one psychological therapy for any one anxiety disorder. (21 marks)

Make sure you learn enough about psychological therapies, to be able to describe them in an exam – this is how you will earn your descriptive marks. Evaluative marks come from looking at the appropriateness and effectiveness of the therapies.

(a) Outline and evaluate one psychological therapy for any one anxiety disorder. (4 + 8 marks)
(b) Discuss issues surrounding the classification and diagnosis of any one anxiety disorder. (5 + 8 marks)

You covered CBT at AS level! What you did then is entirely relevant now.

Cognitive behavioural therapy (CBT)

Abnormal thoughts result in the phobia response so CBT aims to address this.

Therapy begins by identifying the faulty thinking. These abnormal thoughts are then challenged and addressed, so that sufferers see how different thinking and a logical approach might be appropriate.

They will be required to practise statements which challenge present cognitions. Over time, altered cognitions will result in changes to dysfunctional (phobic) behaviour.

Discuss psychological therapies for any one anxiety disorder. (9 + 16 marks)

Evaluation of CBT

Appropriateness

Lack of patient insight – CBT aims to train people to understand that their problem is irrational, but phobics generally already know this, and yet still have the fear of the object. Why is unclear.

Time and money – CBT takes time and can be expensive, and this must be considered. Running out of money half way through treatment and stopping it can be damaging and cause greater problems. If the phobia is something the person experiences on a daily basis a long treatment may not be desirable.

Cause, not symptoms; and no side effects – Unlike drugs, there are no real side effects; and it is the problem that is treated, not just the symptoms.

Effectiveness

Rational emotive therapy (RET) – Ellis (2005) and Cowan and Brunero (2008) say that RET (a form of CBT) can be successful in treating at least some forms of phobia.

Virtual situations – Wallach et al (2009) say that CBT can be carried out in safe, 'virtual' environments where a stimulus can be presented 'virtually', for people to practise their coping skills. As well as for specific phobias, a virtual reality helmet can be used to train skills to help with social phobia. In addition to the safe, controllable environment, another advantage is that 50% fewer phobics discontinue virtual treatment.

Evidence from scanning – Schienle et al (2009) used fMRI scanning to assess the long term effects of CBT. Spider phobics who reported improvements following CBT were compared with non-phobics in their reactions to pictures of phobic objects six months later. Self reports and behavioural responses indicated improvements. fMRI scans indicated effects of CBT on the activity in the orbito frontal cortex (involved in emotion-related learning in the brain) in those showing the most positive outcomes.

The diathesis-stress model

» The cause of phobia is an interaction between biology and environment.
» A person may have a biological predisposition to develop a phobia but it may never develop unless something in the person's environment triggers it.
» Cook and Mineka (1990) argue that we have evolved predispositions to be afraid of certain things that might have been threatening to the survival of our ancestors (e.g. snakes). Something in the environment must however trigger the phobia.
» Explanations for phobia therefore need not be simply psychological or biological, but a combination of the two.

The diathesis-stress model is very useful to learn. Because it focuses on an interaction between biology and psychology it can be used to earn evaluative marks in essays on either approach. Learn it well and use it wisely!

*(a) Outline clinical characteristics of any one anxiety disorder. (4 marks)
(b) Discuss biological therapies for any one anxiety disorder. (21 marks)*

TWO USEFUL THEORIES

Preparedness	This is a biological 'genetic' theory and is explained in terms of evolution. Preparedness theory says that we have an innate disposition to phobias of things that would, in our past, have posed a threat to our well-being and survival. Seligman says we are 'prepared' to learn certain phobias, and this preparedness is passed down genetically. There has been sufficient time in terms of evolution for us to learn phobias to things such as heights but not enough yet to learn phobias of cars, hence car-phobia is largely non-existent.
	Seligman (1971) found that people can become phobic about certain stimuli, such as spiders, after only 3 or 4 exposures. Other things, such as flowers, could not generate a phobia, supporting the theory that we may be prepared to be phobic about some stimuli but not others.
	Bennett-Levy and Marteau (1984) support the theory, showing that we are phobic of some animals and not others, and this depends on the appearance of the animal, suggesting an innate basis for fear of ugly animals.
	Davey et al (1998) – ratings of 'disgust' of animals correlate with fear of them. These ratings are similar in different cultures.
Diathesis-stress	This theory has one foot in biology and one in psychology. The diethesis is the biological predisposition to a phobia. The stress is something that brings on the phobia.
	For instance, we may be pre-disposed to be fearful of spiders, but we may not experience the phobia until something happens in our lives to 'trigger' the phobia. This 'stress' may be in terms of observational learning. It could be that we experience someone else being frightened of spiders, and this leads us to experience the phobia ourselves.
	Cook and Mineka (1990) – the predisposition to the phobia is passed down through generations in terms of evolution. A 'trigger' or stressor in the environment is required to bring on the phobia.

Media psychology

You are expected to develop knowledge, understanding and critical thinking in relation to the topic Media psychology.

This includes applying knowledge and understanding of research methods, approaches, issues and debates where appropriate. You must also show an appreciation of the relationship between research, policy and practices in applying psychology in everyday life.

WHAT YOU NEED TO KNOW

MEDIA INFLUENCES ON SOCIAL BEHAVIOUR
- Explanations of media influences on pro- and anti-social behaviour
- The effects of video games and computers on young people

PERSUASION, ATTITUDE AND CHANGE
- Persuasion and attitude change, including Hovland-Yale and Elaboration Likelihood models
- The influence of attitudes on decision making, including roles of cognitive consistency/dissonance and self-perception
- Explanations for the effectiveness of television in persuasion

THE PSYCHOLOGY OF 'CELEBRITY'
- The attraction of 'celebrity', including social psychological and evolutionary explanations
- Research into intense fandom, e.g. celebrity worship, stalking

SECTION 1: MEDIA INFLUENCES ON SOCIAL BEHAVIOUR

Rideout et al (2003) found 80% of parents said that their children under 6 years of age imitate the behaviour they see on television. This behaviour can be anti-social or pro-social. Most of the imitated behaviour appears, interestingly, to be pro-social.

EXPLANATIONS OF MEDIA INFLUENCES ON PRO-SOCIAL BEHAVIOUR

Pro-social behaviour is 'that which is desirable and which in some way benefits the individual and society at large' (Rushton, 1979), so might include helping behaviour.

Social modelling: Exposure to appropriate models may influence behaviour.

Sprafkin et al (1975) – One group of children watched an episode of *Lassie*; another group watched an episode of *The Brady Bunch*. In a competitive game that followed, in which the children could win a prize, distressed puppies were encountered. Those who had watched *Lassie* comforted the puppies, even though it meant that they might not win the prize: a 'positive social norm' was learned from watching *Lassie*.

Empathy: The ability to feel emotions experienced by other people. The pro-social effect of media depends on how much people can identify with characters in the media.

Yancey et al (2002) – Young children identify with characters experienced in the media, and 40% of adolescents name a media figure as one they identify with.

Duck (1990) – Teenagers can identify media figures they would most like to resemble.

Parental influence: Parents can enhance the positive effects of the media or reduce the effects of harmful media.

Singer (1998) – Parents who watch programmes showing pro-social behaviour can help children by discussing and explaining the content.

Coates and Hartup (1969) – Children understood and remembered more of a model's behaviour when it was explained by a parent.

McKenna and Ossoff (1998) – Children remembered violence in a film rather than the moral message, although they understood that there was a message to be learned. Parents could help by explaining and drawing attention to the pro-social behaviour.

General learning model: A complex interaction of personal and situational variables influences learning from the media.

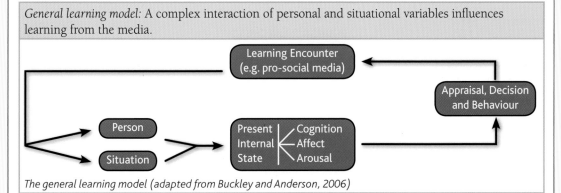

The general learning model (adapted from Buckley and Anderson, 2006)

Personal and situational variables influence how we think, our attitude, mood and how excited and aggressive we may feel. We then 'appraise' the situation and make decisions about our behaviour in relation to that experienced in the media. This can then lead to learning and the cycle begins again. The more cycles, the more likely a person is to learn the pro-social behaviour.

Greitmeyer (2009) – Participants listened to songs with pro-social lyrics or neutral lyrics. Then they completed sentences and word fragments. Those who listened to pro-social lyrics used more pro-social words, evidence that pro-social tendencies had been fostered by exposure to the pro-social media.

EXPLANATIONS OF MEDIA INFLUENCES ON ANTI-SOCIAL BEHAVIOUR

Anti-social behaviour is 'virtually any intimidating or threatening behaviour that scares you or damages your quality of life'. Such behaviour is seen widely on television at almost every moment. The question for us is whether it influences our behaviour when exposed to it – and evidence seems to be that it does.

» Huesmann et al (2003) – Strong positive correlations found between exposure to aggressive television previously and levels of physical aggression in adults

» Bushman and Anderson (2001) – This correlation is nearly as strong as that between smoking and lung cancer.

Observational learning and imitation – Bandura showed that children 'model' behaviour by watching others behave. This is called 'vicarious' learning.

Bandura et al (1963) – Children were 'frustrated' by having their toys removed. Some then watched a film of an adult being aggressive to a 'bobo' punch-bag doll. When shown back into a toy-room containing a bobo doll, those who had watched the film behaved more aggressively towards it than those who had not watched the film.

Hicks (1968) – Aggression towards a bobo doll could be reproduced 6 to 8 months later and so imitation can be long lasting.

Barr et al (2007) – Children as young as one can imitate behaviour seen on TV.

Steuer et al (1971) – Children who had watched violent TV behaved more aggressively in their break-time play than those who had not.

Excitation transfer – Arousal in one emotional state (fear) can lead (be transferred) to arousal in a different state (aggression).

Donnerstein and Berkowitz (1981) – Male participants, having watched one of 3 types of film, were later given the chance to 'retaliate' against a woman (a stooge researcher) who had annoyed them, by giving her 'electric shocks'. Those who had previously watched a violent sex film gave higher shocks than those who had watched a sex film or a violent film. The sexual and aggressive emotion appeared to add together.

Uhlmann and Swanson (2004) – Self-image can change with as little as 10 minutes' exposure to a violent game, with participants regarding themselves as having more violent traits than before the game. Attitude change can be fast and additive, building up each time a person is exposed to emotional stimuli.

Emotional desensitisation: The more violence we see, the less arousing it gets, so our own aggression becomes less inhibited.

Drabman and Thomas (1974) – Viewing a violent film made children less responsive to the next violent film they saw, possibly encouraging a sense of indifference when violent acts are witnessed.

Linz et al (1989) – Repeated exposure to pornography made people less likely to label images seen later as pornographic.

Cognitive priming: Aggressive cues can trigger aggressive thoughts and feelings.

Josephson (1987) – The behaviour of boys who had previously watched aggressive films was rated as more violent while playing hockey than that of those who had not watched violent films.

Anderson et al (2003) – Violent song lyrics stimulate violent thoughts. Desmond (1987), however, showed that only about a third of young people could accurately describe the meanings of popular songs. Other research (Ballard and Coates, 1995) showed no effect of violent lyrics, but the songs were performed in a way that made the lyrics largely incomprehensible, reducing the validity of the research.

Individual differences: Some are influenced more than others. These differences are mediated by age, pre-existing tendencies and gender.

Pre-existing tendencies: Those with anti-social characteristics are more likely to be influenced than others (Anderson, 2003). Supported by Leyens et al (1975) who found more aggressive behaviour following exposure to aggressive films in previously-rated aggressive children in a correctional institution.

Age: The greatest influence of the media is on young children. After that it is unclear. Some research shows greater influence on 30 year olds than on those of 22 or 16. A methodological problem here is that aggressive behaviour is often measured in young people, but aggressive 'thoughts' in older people, and these are not the same thing and not comparable.

Gender: Recent research shows no difference of gender at all, possibly due to increasing female aggression seen in the media.

EFFECTS OF VIDEO GAMES AND COMPUTERS ON YOUNG PEOPLE

Stone and Gentile (2008) say effects are on 5 clear dimensions seen in the table below.

Dimension	Effects
Amount	Appears most related to displacement effects, such as poorer performance at school and obesity due to less activity.
Content	Effects are specific to the content of the game: e.g. reading games improve reading and aggressive games increase aggression.
Context	Effects of content may be changed by context of game play, e.g. the social contexts of MMO (massively multi-player on-line) games where people interact in virtual environments.
Structure	Effects are influenced by how the game is structured: e.g. games that require constant scanning of the screen improve visual attention skills.
Mechanics	Related to the mechanical devices used, so the greatest effects will be seen when the devices are most 'real', e.g. playing a shooting game with a pistol rather than a keyboard.

Dimensions and effects of video games, adapted from Stone and Gentile (2008)

Effects of computers and video games on aggressive behaviour
The fear is that fantasy and reality will blur as games get more realistic and technology allows greater 'immersion'.

Anderson et al (2007) – The severity of punishment of characters delivered in a game was greater if children had previously played a violent video game.

Grüsser et al (2007) – A questionnaire sample of 'pathological' or 'extreme' gamers showed only a mild link between their gaming and aggressive tendencies. However, the types of games played were not recorded.

Peng et al (2008) – Only those with more violent personalities in the first place showed more violence within a game.

Positive effects of computers and video games
Cognitive skills, such as attention and spatial abilities, can be improved with gaming. *Tetris*, for instance, can improve spatial skills (Sims and Meyer, 2002).

De-Lin Sun et al (2008) – Difficult to unravel the positive and negative effects of gaming as they are experienced simultaneously. May be that the positive effects last longer than the negative ones.

Karni and Sagi et al (2003) – Cognitive experiences while gaming can lead to changes in the brain.

Gentile et al (2007) – Playing pro-social games increased pro-social behaviour.

Lanningham-Foster et al (2006) – Energy expended with active video games was three times that of playing traditional video games, so they need not foster obesity, although much more energy is expended playing traditional sports such as football.

Social effects of video games and computers
Computers are used for more than just games. The internet and social networking are extremely widely used also.

Nie and Erbring (2000) – More internet use means less time socialising with friends and family.

Padilla-Walker et al (2009) – Video-game use leads to poorer relationships with parents and peers.

Young (1998) – People can become psychologically dependent (addicted) to the internet and so relationships in the real world may suffer.

Hartmann (1998) – Heavy internet users spent less time with friends and family and suffered increased loneliness even though much of their internet time was spent socially in chatrooms or on social network sites.

Valkenburg and Peter (2009) – Most adolescents actually use the internet to nurture existing friendships, not make new ones. Communication facilities (voice and video) are improving everyday and the internet can help people feel less shy, encouraging self-disclosure and actually improving the development of relationships.

SECTION 2: PERSUASION, ATTITUDE AND CHANGE

PERSUASION AND ATTITUDE CHANGE

Attitudes have three, inter-related components.

1. Cognitive: Our thoughts and beliefs about a person, subject or object

2. Affective: How positive or negative we feel about our attitude

3. Behavioural: How we act, based on the cognitive components

If the media can change our beliefs about something, they can change our attitude and possibly our behaviour.

The Elaboration likelihood model (ELM)

Described by Petty and Cacioppo (1983), the ELM aims to explain processes leading to persuasion. According to the ELM there are two routes to persuasion.

Changes through the *central route* are said to be longer lasting than changes through the *peripheral route*.

ELABORATION LIKELIHOOD MODEL (ELM)

Central Route	Recipients take an active part in the process and this requires motivation and attention. Effort is made with cognitive thinking. Careful consideration is given to the core of the message. Because of the effort put into the thinking, the central route can produce more permanent attitude change. The more personally relevant the message is, the more motivated recipients will be to engage with it. Reasonably well-informed, intelligent people may be best targeted with the central route.
Peripheral Route	Less mental effort than the central route is required. People are swayed by superficial things. Elaboration will be low. Peripheral cues can include attractiveness and likability of the messenger. If people not too involved, or motivated, or if easily distracted, the peripheral route may be more appropriate than the central route. It is better for ill-informed recipients.

The ELM and persuasive advertising

The ELM describes 5 factors influencing the persuasiveness of advertising. These can be seen in the table.

Resisting persuasion can be difficult, but can be done once the strategies of persuasive advertising are understood.

Counterargument: Internally, to ourselves, we may argue things like 'Does it really work that well?' or 'Is it really that good?'

Reactance: When told what to do, 'Cross road here!' we may react by saying 'I will not! I'll cross where I like!'

Forewarning: We may remind ourselves that it is an advert designed to sell things people don't really want. If we do this, our defences to the persuasive arguments are strengthened.

ELM AND PERSUASIVE ADVERTISING

1. Message repetition	The more often a message is presented, the more chance there is to evaluate it. This type of elaboration will lead to a more favourable attitude as long as boredom is avoided.
2. Prior knowledge	The more a person already knows about a product, the more they bring to the message themselves and the more they are able to think about it and relate the new information to already existing knowledge.
3. Self-referencing	Elaboration is best when the message can be referenced to the recipient themselves, as the new information can be more easily fitted into existing knowledge.
4. Arousal	Increases in arousal reduces our capacity to deal with the new information. Because of this, complex arguments become less influential, and less demanding peripheral information is focused on.
5. Media type	People are less likely to read something that is not of interest to them, so printed adverts are less likely to be influential than TV adverts that are presented whether the person likes it or not, to all senses.

Evolutionary explanations

Evolution states that behaviour that remains widespread today will have once had a useful survival purpose.

Entertainment as play theory – Vorderer (2001)

Entertainment experiences have a lot in common with play. Play has an evolutionary purpose. It engages us in exercise and allows us to practise skills that may be needed for life. Media were used in the form of Rock art over 40 thousand years ago, showing stories and plots indicating that energy was directed towards imagination and creativity.

Leisure time theory – Zillman (2000)

As communication and hunting/cultivation skills developed, more leisure time was available. Over thousands of years, the time available grew and was put to good use in developing a culture of entertainment.

Ornamental mind theory

Females choose to mate with males showing attractive traits. Through generations these traits are passed on. Miller (2000) says that the male brain is an 'ornament' used to attract females. Celebrity is the result of generations of sexual selection of males with creative, interesting minds. Most readers of celebrity media are females, and this could provide support for the theory.

Gossip theory – McAndrew (2008)

Exchanging information about people who are not present (gossip) is universal to human nature. Celebrities are a rich and available source for this. It can carry important information that may make someone more powerful than another; and shared secrets are a good way to build groups and show trust, just as grooming does in primates. Knowing who is doing what with whom may help ensure survival.

RESEARCH INTO INTENSE FANDOM

Celebrity worship

Some fans are vaguely interested in celebrities; others seem to 'worship' them, the fandom affecting their whole lives. The *Celebrity Attitude Scale* (Maltby et al, 2002) describes different levels of fandom.

Erotomania (Houran et al, 2005)

The belief that someone (in this case a celebrity) secretly has sexual feelings for them.

Poor body image (Maltby et al, 2005)

Strong association in females between poor-body image and intense celebrity worship. The association tends to disappear in adulthood.

CELEBRITY ATTITUDE SCALE (CAS)	
Entertainment-Social Approximately 20% of fans tested: McCutcheon et al (2003)	Attraction to celebrity is for their entertainment value, because it provides social functions such as talking to friends.
Intense-Personal Approximately 10% of fans tested: McCutcheon et al (2003)	Strong, intensive, compulsive and almost obsessional feelings towards their favourite celebrity are generated.
Borderline Pathological Approximately 1% of fans tested: McCutcheon et al (2003)	Uncontrollable fantasies and behaviours relating to the celebrity are developed.

Absorption-addiction hypothesis (McCutcheon et al, 2002)

Explains how parasocial relations can become abnormal. It may be that some people become absorbed and embroiled in their parasocial relationship because they have difficulties with their own identities. The absorbtion is an attempt to gain this identity and it has addictive characteristics so that more and more extreme celebrity-worship, and other extreme parasocial relationship traits, are demonstrated.

Stalking

Regarded by some as an extreme form of celebrity worship, stalking is a dangerous obsession. It can be 'private' where there has been a previous relationship between the stalker and the victim, or 'public' where there has not.

Attachment theory of stalking

There is a body of evidence to suggest that early attachment difficulties can lead to social and emotional problems in later life. Someone forming insecure attachments as a child tends to form less secure adult relationships. Kienlen (1998) says that the motivations of stalkers are different, depending on the kind of insecure attachment they have.

MOTIVATIONS OF DIFFERENT TYPES OF STALKER (KIENLEN 1998)	
'Preoccupied' stalker	Poor self-image, constantly seeking approval from others. Results from a real or imagined rejection. Stalking is attempt to restore a positive sense of self.
'Fearful' stalker	Poor self-image, sees others as unsupportive. Stalking is a result of a cycle of wanting to have someone boost self-image, but always rejecting them because of lack of trust.
'Dismissing' stalker	Distant and aloof, allowing the maintenance of an inflated self-image. Stalking may, for instance, be a revenge because of a perceived maltreatment in their own relationship.

Kienlen et al (1997) – Majority of stalkers in a jail had experienced childhood attachment problems, and had lost a personal relationship just prior to the onset of the stalking

Lewis et al (2001) – Stalkers have personality traits typical of insecure attachment

McCutcheon et al (2006) – In a sample of students, those that had experienced childhood insecure attachment were more likely to excuse celebrity stalking than those that had not.

Rational goal pursuit theory of stalking

The goal here is to attain a certain type of relationship. If the relationship is thwarted, people try harder. If the effort is too great the goal is abandoned. In stalking, the rejection magnifies the efforts of the stalker, leading to further feelings spurring their actions on.

Goals are in a hierarchy. Lower goals (eat healthily) are needed to attain higher goals (get fit) and still higher goals (be attractive to others) and even higher goals (be attractive to, and marry a millionaire).

In celebrity stalking, a lower order goal (to be in a relationship with a celebrity) is linked with a higher order goal (to feel good about myself). The lower goal is blocked and the stalker constantly thinks about the unfulfilled goal. Because it is linked somehow to a feeling of self-worth, the obsessional thoughts result in very negative feelings. Efforts at attaining the original goal (a relationship with the celebrity) are doubled, and the stalking continues and worsens.

HOW WELL DO I KNOW IT?	NOT AT ALL	MAYBE	OK	WELL	SUPERBLY
MEDIA PSYCHOLOGY					
Explanations of media influences on pro-social behaviour					
Explanations of media influences on anti-social behaviour					
Effects of computers and video games on young people					
Persuasion and attitude change: Hovland-Yale model					
Persuasion and attitude change: Elaboration likelihood model					
Influence of attitudes on decision making: Role of cognitive dissonance					
Influence of attitudes on decision making: Role of self-perception					
Explanations for effectiveness of television in persuasion					
The attraction of 'celebrity': Social psychological explanation					
The attraction of 'celebrity': Evolutionary explanation					
Research into intense fandom: Celebrity worship					
Research into intense fandom: Stalking					

The psychology of addictive behaviour

You are expected to develop knowledge, understanding and critical thinking in relation to the topic of Addictive behaviour.

This includes applying knowledge and understanding of research methods, approaches, issues and debates where appropriate. You must also show an appreciation of the relationship between research, policy and practices in applying psychology in everyday life.

WHAT YOU NEED TO KNOW

MODELS OF ADDICTIVE BEHAVIOUR

- Biological, cognitive and learning models of addiction, including explanations for initiation, maintenance and relapse
- Explanations for specific addictions, including smoking and gambling

FACTORS AFFECTING ADDICTIVE BEHAVIOUR

- Vulnerability to addiction including self-esteem, attributions for addiction and social context of addiction
- The role of media in addictive behaviour

REDUCING ADDICTIVE BEHAVIOUR

- Models of prevention, including theory of reasoned action and theory of planned behaviour
- Types of intervention, including biological, psychological, public health interventions and legislation, and their effectiveness

Cognitive model of addiction

People initiate, maintain and relapse because of the way that they think. Beck (2001) identifies this 'vicious circle' to explain addiction:

```
    - >  Low Mood  - >  Using (smoking or gambling)  - - - 
   |                                                        |
   |                                                        |
    - - - -  Financial, Medical, Social Problems  < - - - -
```

Key concepts:

» *Coping* – Addictive behaviour helps people 'cope' with stress for 3 reasons:

1. *Mood regulation* – Maintains a more positive mood.
2. *Performance enhancement* – Addict may feel more alert and capable of carrying out tasks.
3. *Distraction* – Activity distracts them from less pleasant aspects of their life.

» *Expectancy* – The more positive we 'expect' the behaviour to make us feel, the more likely we are to engage in it and vice versa.

• What is expected can influence the experience: more positive expectations can *improve* the experience of the behaviour.
• Expectancies need not be correct. Expecting alcohol to improve sexual arousal increases drinking when actually it has the reverse effect!

» *Self-efficacy* – Self belief in our ability to deal with a behaviour.

• High self-belief in ability to give up can make the behaviour more likely.

SMOKING: COGNITIVE EXPLANATION

Initiation	• *Expectancy* – A smoker may believe that it makes them look attractive or helps them lose weight, for instance. • *Performance enhancement* – Can help the person concentrate and therefore perform more efficiently (Heishman, 1999). • *Boredom* – Smoking may relieve boredom. • *Self-efficacy* – May believe that even though the habit is highly addictive, they are strong enough to give up whatever they want.
Maintenance	• *Vicious circle* – For instance, smoking begins to alleviate stress, causes illness, creating stress, which is dealt with by smoking. • *Smoking ban* – Not being able to attend public spaces without smoking can cause huge stress, so the person stays at home, which in turn causes social problems and stress, maintaining their habit. • *Self-efficacy* – people feel unable to cope with withdrawal symptoms. • *Expectancy* – expecting the withdrawal period to be horrible may deter a person from quitting.
Relapse	• *Coping* – Returning to smoking immediately helps the person cope with negative withdrawal symptoms. • *Self-efficacy* – They've given up once and so feel able to do so again. • *Expectancy* – They expect the next time they give up to be as simple as it was this time.

Marlatt's relapse model (1985)

High-risk situations cause relapses. A 'coping response' in these situations increases self-belief (self-efficacy) in our ability to cope. Not using a 'coping response' reduces self-efficacy and increases the expected positive outcome of the behaviour, and cravings. This leads to an initial relapse, called a 'lapse'. The person experiences 'cognitive dissonance' ('I don't want to smoke, yet I smoked'), guilt and reduced self-esteem that in turn can lead to a full relapse.

GAMBLING: COGNITIVE EXPLANATION

Initiation	● *Positive feelings* – Gambling may provide positive feelings and a buzz of excitement.
	● *Environment* – The environment of the bookmakers or the race track may be appealing and provide additional positive feelings.
	● *Boredom* – Gambling may relieve boredom.
Maintenance	● *Vicious circle* – For instance, gambling begins to raise mood; financial problems follow, creating the need to raise mood and funds.
	● *Positive interpretation* – Occasional wins and excitement may be interpreted as indicators that their behaviour is not a problem.
	● *Not regarded as a problem* – Many gamble, without realising it, on fruit machines or with the national lottery.
	● *Expectancy* – Expecting the possibility of a huge payout maintains the behaviour.
Relapse	● *Low withdrawal* – Physical withdrawal symptoms are not too bad and so the gambler expects to be able to give up easily when they return.
	● *Excitement* – Life without the buzz of gambling may seem extremely boring and dull so they return to their habit.

Learning model of addiction

Addictive behaviours are explained in terms of classical and operant conditioning and social learning.

Key concepts

» *Classical conditioning* – Famously identified by Pavlov with his dogs that responded with salivation (Conditioned response) to the sound of a bell (Conditioned stimulus). This followed the dogs' salivating (Unconditioned response) when presented with the bell (Conditioned stimulus) and food (Unconditioned stimulus) in numerous training sessions.

» *Operant conditioning* – We learn because we are rewarded for our behaviour: if a negative feeling improves, or punishment stops, when the behaviour happens.

» *Cue-reactivity theory* – Addicts react similarly to the behaviour when presented with material and paraphernalia associated with their problem. Smokers may react to matches or ashtrays; gamblers may react to betting slips and betting shops. These cues act as conditioned stimuli (see classical conditioning).

» *Vicarious reinforcement* – Bandura said we engage in social learning through vicarious reinforcement, which happens when we watch others we admire or look up to engaging in a behaviour. For instance, if we want to be like someone who happens to smoke, then we may, ourselves, start smoking.

GAMBLING: LEARNING EXPLANATION

Initiation	● *Observation of others* – Watching others have fun and win may lead to a first bet.
	● *Excitement* – Excitement is associated with the activity.
Maintenance	● *Rewards* – financial or physical (excitement) rewards only continue while gambling and so the behaviour is maintained.
	● *Partial reinforcement* – Winning only occasionally provides 'partial reinforcement', which produces long lasting learned behaviours.
	● *Inconsistency of negative feelings* – Combining regular negative feelings or neutral feelings with gambling is very hard as gambling is so easy to engage in. Extinguishing the learned behaviour is therefore extremely difficult.
Relapse	● *Cue reactivity* – Seeing or handling items associated with gambling generates a craving and similar cues are everywhere, so relapse is extremely hard to resist.

ASK AN EXAMINER

You should be familiar with learning theory from AS and perhaps elsewhere on the A2 course. If you need a summary of the theory, it can be found in the Intelligence and Learning section.

SMOKING: LEARNING EXPLANATION

Initiation	● *Positive feelings* – May associate positive feelings with the behaviour, or negative feelings (name calling, teasing) may stop when smoking begins. ● *Ritual* – The ritual of smoking (handling and smelling the pack, tapping the cigarette to pack the tobacco a little) can all provide positive feelings.
Maintenance	● *Peers* – When friends and peers smoke, being around them is hard unless smoking continues. ● *Daily ritual* – Smoking at certain times of the day becomes a ritual that is hard to give up. These times include after eating, or with the first coffee of the day.
Relapse	● *Cue reactivity* – Seeing or handling a lighter can be enough to generate a craving and similar cues are everywhere, so relapse is extremely hard to resist.

SECTION 2: FACTORS AFFECTING ADDICTIVE BEHAVIOUR

VULNERABILITY TO ADDICTION

Some people are more prone to become addicted to smoking and gambling than others. Three factors affecting addiction are vulnerability, attributions for addiction and social context.

1. Vulnerability – Self-esteem

Self-esteem is our feeling of our own self-worth. It is a feature of our personality. Those with low self-esteem may feel weak, and lack confidence. When self-respect, self-worth and self-regard are low, self-esteem is damaged.

Reaction to criticism

Negative criticisms of behaviour or performance can result in weakened self-esteem.

Perceived ability to succeed

Low self-esteem means that the perception of ability to succeed or achieve positive results is very low. Tasks are regarded as intimidating rather than as challenges and abilities are doubted. They may exhibit a 'negative' attitude or outlook.

Self-esteem in gambling and smoking

» Vulnerability to peer pressure increases when self-esteem drops.
» Pressure to start smoking to be part of an attractive group is harder to resist.
» 'Expectancy' of how group membership will change things is important.
» May believe that gambling will make the person feel better about themselves.
» Gambling may offer a way out of an undesirable, dead-end existence.
» Criticism by society of gambling and smoking makes them feel worse and so the behaviour is continued when self-worth drops further.
» The challenge of giving up seems insurmountable and so the behaviour is maintained.

2. Attributions for addiction

Attribution theory (Kelley 1967) looks at how people explain things and how they ascribe causes for things. The concept of 'control' is very important.

Internal attribution: 'I smoke and/or gamble because I am weak and pathetic. It is my fault'. The person's own inadequacies are blamed.

External attribution: 'I smoke and/or gamble because the government makes the behaviour too easy to engage in'. Others' behaviour is blamed.

SMOKING – INTERNAL ATTRIBUTIONS	
Initiation	I started to smoke because I lack willpower.
Maintenance	I am too weak and scared to give up.
Relapse	I am just hopeless.

GAMBLING – INTERNAL ATTRIBUTIONS	
Initiation	I found it really exciting, I loved that feeling.
Maintenance	I am too weak and scared to give up.
Relapse	The cravings got too much for me. I am just hopeless.

SMOKING – EXTERNAL ATTRIBUTIONS	
Initiation	Others pressured me.
Maintenance	Society demands we are thin. Smoking maintains my weight.
Relapse	Pressures of life and the need to work to maintain an acceptable lifestyle forced me to start again.

GAMBLING – EXTERNAL ATTRIBUTIONS	
Initiation	Not my fault, no one told me it was addictive.
Maintenance	If the government didn't put national lottery places everywhere it would be easy to give up.
Relapse	The bank will not lend me money to pay my rent, so I have to gamble.

3. Social context

Access to money can help people deal with addictions through rehab and good professional help. Less wealthy people lack these resources. Other social aspects also influence addictive behaviour, including parents, life-experiences, social environmental cues and peer pressure.

Parents

Lader and Matheson (1991) – If parents smoke, children are more likely to smoke.

Murray et al (1984) – If parents are anti-smoking, children are 7 times less likely to smoke.

Wardle et al (2000) – Problem gamblers are more likely to have had gambling parents.

Life-experiences

Stressful and unpleasant life experiences may make smoking more likely.

Protective and warm families may be protective and make addictions less likely.

Turner et al (2002) – Early experience of ADHD may result in gambling behaviour.

Turner et al (2002) – Unpleasant life experiences often precede gambling behaviour.

Theory of Planned Behaviour (TPB)

This is similar to the TRA, but adds the issue of 'control', to recognise that all actions and behaviours are not entirely under our control.

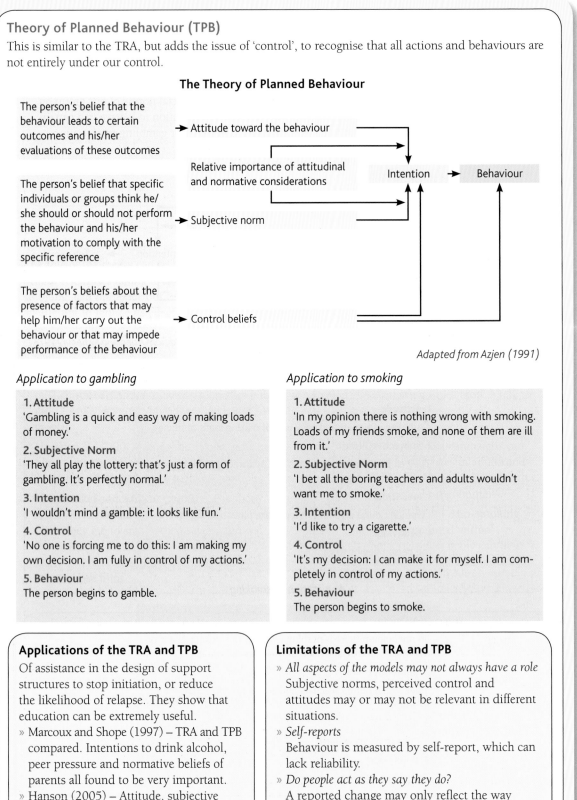

The Theory of Planned Behaviour

The person's belief that the behaviour leads to certain outcomes and his/her evaluations of these outcomes → Attitude toward the behaviour

Relative importance of attitudinal and normative considerations

Intention → Behaviour

The person's belief that specific individuals or groups think he/she should or should not perform the behaviour and his/her motivation to comply with the specific reference → Subjective norm

The person's beliefs about the presence of factors that may help him/her carry out the behaviour or that may impede performance of the behaviour → Control beliefs

Adapted from Azjen (1991)

Application to gambling

1. Attitude
'Gambling is a quick and easy way of making loads of money.'

2. Subjective Norm
'They all play the lottery: that's just a form of gambling. It's perfectly normal.'

3. Intention
'I wouldn't mind a gamble: it looks like fun.'

4. Control
'No one is forcing me to do this: I am making my own decision. I am fully in control of my actions.'

5. Behaviour
The person begins to gamble.

Application to smoking

1. Attitude
'In my opinion there is nothing wrong with smoking. Loads of my friends smoke, and none of them are ill from it.'

2. Subjective Norm
'I bet all the boring teachers and adults wouldn't want me to smoke.'

3. Intention
'I'd like to try a cigarette.'

4. Control
'It's my decision: I can make it for myself. I am completely in control of my actions.'

5. Behaviour
The person begins to smoke.

Applications of the TRA and TPB

Of assistance in the design of support structures to stop initiation, or reduce the likelihood of relapse. They show that education can be extremely useful.

» Marcoux and Shope (1997) – TRA and TPB compared. Intentions to drink alcohol, peer pressure and normative beliefs of parents all found to be very important.
» Hanson (2005) – Attitude, subjective norm, and perceived behavioural control all predicted smoking behaviour amongst African-American girls.

Limitations of the TRA and TPB

» *All aspects of the models may not always have a role*
Subjective norms, perceived control and attitudes may or may not be relevant in different situations.
» *Self-reports*
Behaviour is measured by self-report, which can lack reliability.
» *Do people act as they say they do?*
A reported change may only reflect the way someone is *expressing* himself or herself: it may not actually reflect how the person was actually *thinking*.

TYPES OF INTERVENTION

Biological interventions

Drug treatment

This can be done in three ways: the first is to provide a replacement for the 'high' experienced; the second is to block the biological effect of the behaviour; and the third is to immunise people against the biological effects of their behaviour.

---

1. An alternative treatment – Agonist substitution
The best known is replacing heroin with the safer methadone. Safer alternatives to nicotine can be used similarly. Gambling has been shown to have similar effects on the brain as amphetamine, and using a controlled dose of amphetamine can reduce the urge to gamble. Critics argue that replacing one drug with another is not the answer in the long run. The person is still dependent.

2. An alternative drug – Antagonist substitution
A drug is given that blocks the effect of nicotine or the physiological effects of gambling. Typically, a drug can be taken that blocks the rewarding effects stimulated by neurotransmitters such as dopamine. Hollander et al (2000) showed this to be effective in reducing gambling behaviour in problem gamblers.

---

3. Immunotherapy – drug immunisation
Carrera et al (1995) stimulated rats' immune systems to produce antibodies important in resisting cocaine addiction. The effects of the cocaine were reduced, and so the rats were effectively immunised against the drug. Similar techniques can immunise against the effects of nicotine.

Psychological interventions

Cognitive behavioural therapy (CBT)

The client is helped to think differently about the problem object or behaviour. The principles of CBT are seen in many psychological interventions:

---

1. Relapse prevention
Strategies to enhance self-control can be taught. The positive and negative aspects of relapse can be explored, and self-monitoring of cravings is encouraged to catch them quickly before they become an insurmountable problem. Situations where the danger of relapse is high are identified – these may be race-tracks, or places where people smoke – and coping strategies are put in place.

» Carroll et al (1994) – The positive results can be relatively long-lasting, over a year from the end of treatment

---

2. The matrix model
A range of aspects of therapy is used, including issues of relapse prevention, group and family therapy. This depends on the individual and the addiction.

» Huber et al (1997) – This approach increases self-worth and positive outlook. Education, attitudes and approaches of addicts and their family members are all addressed and this seems to help.

3. Addiction counselling

The focus is on stopping the addictive behaviour. Related issues (financial, family, friends etc.) are also addressed. Coping strategies can be encouraged for longer-term support.

» McLellan et al (1993) – show addiction counselling to be highly effective especially when combined with employment and family services.

» Hazel et al (2006) – Telephone addiction counselling for smoking was valuable in helping people quit but not very effective in preventing relapse.

» Reid et al (1999) – Telephone counselling is useful when combined with other therapies such as biological therapies.

» Bryant-Jefferies (2005) – Addiction counselling can be helpful for problem gamblers.

4. Motivational enhancement therapy

Addicts are encouraged to become involved in their treatment and seek help. Coping strategies and techniques to increase motivation and drive are used.

» Stephens et al (1994) – very effective in cases of alcohol and marijuana abuse.

Public health interventions and legislation

Drugs

Laws and licences control drugs in most countries. The classification of each drug changes as scientific evidence, or government opinion, changes. Using, possessing and distributing different drugs carry different penalties. Age restrictions are also in place for the purchase and use of 'legal' drugs.

The Smoking Ban

It is now illegal to smoke in enclosed public spaces throughout the UK. The effects of the smoking ban in Scotland have been assessed as follows.

» Dundee researchers showed that symptoms of passive smoking in bar workers fell from 80% before the ban to less that 50% two months after the ban.

» Pell et al (2008) report a year on year drop of 17% in hospital admissions for heart attack following the ban in Scotland.

» Semple et al (2007) investigated non-smoking workers and found a 75% reduction in cotinine in their saliva, an indication that reliably less nicotine has entered the body.

Smoking legislation like this can help people quit. Increases in calls to quitting help lines were seen before the ban came into place, and attempts to quit following the ban also increased. Relapse can be reduced, as smoking activity is less prevalent and obvious in society, so cravings become less frequent.

Gambling legislation

The 2007 gambling act restricts the advertising of nearly all gambling activities. The importance and effectiveness of the legislation preventing the building of huge super casinos in the UK is seen in the removal of legislation allowing their construction, effectively removing the possibility of hundreds of thousands of jobs associated with the industry.

Public gambling is covered by the gambling act, but private gambling is not, and people may play for things other than money, limiting the effectiveness of the legislation.

Age restrictions are in place to help prevent younger people, regarded as vulnerable, from taking part in this addictive activity. The placement of gambling machines and access to gambling is highly restricted for this reason.

Public health interventions where harm is done to others

This principle was established in 2004. Where a company or industry is harming others, the government can legislate against them. This might include junk food and alcohol, but most importantly for us it can include smoking and gambling. In addition, government cannot legally make employers help employees quit but can publicly encourage them to allow workers, without losing pay, to attend 'stop smoking' sessions.

Effectiveness

Governments must weigh up the costs of introducing legislation. It can be devastatingly effective, but the costs can be serious. Not allowing large casinos can hugely increase poverty in an area and increase unemployment.

» Gomel et al (1993) – Craving and stress levels amongst workers, following the smoking ban in Australia, were hugely increased and even though they may have reported that they did not smoke, blood tests showed that they were still smoking.

» Ogden (2000) – Price increases may well help reduce smoking amongst children and adolescents, but a smoking ban in public places may result in increased smoking elsewhere such as the home, potentially more harmful to children of smokers.

» Weiss et al (2008) – Some smokers have a gene that makes them more prone to smoking if they begin before 17. In future, identifying subgroups like this can help the government target health legislation to greatest effect.

» Fowler and Christakis (2008) – Social context is important. A friend quitting smoking increases the chances of someone in their group quitting by over 30%. A spouse quitting increases the chances of the partner quitting by over 65%. Education is hugely important.

» Albarracin et al (2009) – Those watching campaigns designed to help people lose weight actually ate more. This suggests that the message, however clear, may have a very different result from the one intended.

SECTION 1: THEORETICAL AND METHODOLOGICAL ISSUES IN THE STUDY OF ANOMALOUS EXPERIENCE

ISSUES OF PSEUDOSCIENCE AND SCIENTIFIC FRAUD

Anomalistic Psychology is the study of extraordinary experiences or behaviours that are often described as 'paranormal'. These are summarised in the table as conflicting with 'principles' set out by Broad in 1953.

EXAMPLES OF BROAD'S 'LIMITING PRINCIPLES' AND EXPERIENCES THAT SEEM TO CONTRADICT THEM

BROAD'S PRINCIPLE	APPARENT EXCEPTIONS
Causes must come before effects.	Premonitions, such as dreams that refer to (are caused by?) a future event.
A person's mind cannot produce any direct change in the material world except those caused via the brain/sensorimotor system.	Psychokinetic events, where people claim to have moved or distorted some object through an act of will.
Any mental event is an event in the brain of a living body.	Out-of-body experiences, where the centre of experience seems to be located away from the body. Near-death experiences, where mental events seem to occur when the brain is inactive. Mediumship communications purportedly from deceased persons.
All knowledge of the world comes to us through our conventional senses or by inference from known facts.	Telepathy, where people seem to know directly what is in the mind of another person.

Issues of Pseudoscience

Pseudoscience literally means 'a false science'. A pseudoscience has three principles, identified by Kurtz (1985):

1. Failure to use rigorous experimental methods.	*Parapsychology fails to use rigorous experimental methods* Rigorous and well-controlled experiments are used in parapsychology (See ESP, and PK research for examples).
2. Claiming positive results even though replication has been impossible.	*Parapsychology claims positive results even though replication has been impossible* Replications are attempted and often achieved. The criticism is made that replications are often made by small groups of like-minded researchers, weakening their perceived reliability. Also, just because an effect is possible, it does not mean it will happen every time. Statistics are used to analyse the results and they often show reliable evidence.
3. Lacking a coherent theoretical framework to explain observations (for instance, the claims of astrologers that stars may have an effect on humans even though they are so very far away).	*Parapsychology lacks a coherent theoretical framework to explain the observations made* Just because there is no generally accepted set of theories to explain and tie the phenomena together, this does not exclude parapsychology from being a science. As Edge (1986) points out, there is a rich network or core knowledge and of accepted, tried and tested procedures, and a range of theories that are useful to parapsychologists in helping them address their results. Really, the problem is that there are too many theories and they are developing all the time. Advances in brain science, and our understanding of perceptual processes, appear almost daily and these continue to add to the tools at the parapsychologists' fingertips.

SOME OF THE CHARACTERISTICS OF SCIENCE AND PSEUDOSCIENCE

Science	Pseudoscience
Findings are expressed primarily through scientific journals that are peer-reviewed and maintain rigorous standards for honesty and accuracy.	Literature is aimed at the general public. There is no review, no standards, no pre-publication verification, no demand for accuracy and precision.
Replicable results are demanded; experiments must be precisely described so that they can be replicated exactly or improved upon.	Results cannot be replicated and therefore not verified. Studies, if any, are always so vaguely described that one can't figure out what was done or how it was done.
Failures are searched for and studied closely, because incorrect theories can often make correct predictions by accident, but no correct theory will make incorrect predictions.	Failures are ignored, excused, hidden, lied about, discounted, explained away, rationalised, forgotten, avoided at all costs.
Over time, more and more is learned about the physical processes under study.	No physical phenomena or processes are ever found or studied. No progress is made; nothing concrete is learned.
Convinces by appeal to the evidence, by arguments based upon logical and/or statistical reasoning, by making the best case the data permit. Old ideas are abandoned when new evidence contradicts them.	Convinces by appeal to faith and belief. Pseudoscience has a strong quasi-religious element: it tries to convert, not to convince. You are to believe in spite of the facts, not because of them. The original idea is never abandoned, whatever the evidence.
Does not advocate or market unproven practices or products.	Questionable products marketed (such as books, courses, and dietary supplements) and/or pseudoscientific services (such as horoscopes, character readings, spirit messages, and predictions).

Adapted from http://www.quackwatch.com/01QuackeryRelatedTopics/pseudo.html

Issues of scientific fraud

Fraud means wholesale cheating and lying about results. There are issues of fraud in all walks of life, including science, but parapsychology is no more prone to it than any other social science.

Historical 'paranormal' fraud
The 'occult' and the existence of the 'paranormal' were extremely popular interests in the last century, even more so than now.

Fake photographic evidence
Evidence of faked photos (using 'double exposure' methods whereby a 'ghostly image' could be super-imposed onto a normal picture) was widespread. Think of it like an old-fashioned Photoshop technique.

Table tipping
Parties where a séance was held where those present touched a table, and it seemed, during the séance, to move on its own. These parties were very popular amongst Victorians. Alas, the tables were mechanically moved, or moved by the person that held the party.

Michael Faraday
Faraday was most famous for developing our understanding of electricity. He turned his mind to 'table tipping' by inventing a table with two tops. Between the tops were marbles. If the fingers moved the table the top part only would move because of the marbles. If the table itself moved then the top would not move independently. As soon as those present realised what was happening, the table, surprisingly, stopped moving at all. Evidence, from an early parapsychologist, of a fraud, or at least of 'fraudulent' claims.

Claims of fraud in parapsychological investigations
Sceptics, and others who do not find the claims of those reporting issues such as psychokinesis and ESP convincing, often identify the results as fraudulent. However, there is little evidence of wholesale fraud in the area. Where fraud has been claimed to explain studies, mechanisms by which the fraud may have taken place are usually impossible to identify.

CONTROVERSIES RELATING TO THE GANZFELD STUDIES OF ESP AND STUDIES OF PSYCHOKINESIS

Extra sensory perception (ESP) refers to perception without the usual sensory stimulation, whilst psychokinesis refers to the power to move something without using physical force.

Ganzfeld studies

Ganzfeld means 'total field'. Think of it as sensory deprivation of sorts.

» *The visual field:* Half ping-pong balls are placed over the eyes. Red or pink light is shone through them. Eyes are kept open to experience the same pink or red light. Participants get used to the light, 'habituating' to it and often report no visual experience at all.

» *Sensory hunger:* Once habituated, participant feels as though no perceptual stimuli are received at all. Perceptual system 'hunts' for internally generated stimuli that feel like mild, dream-like hallucinations.

» *Procedure:* Recruitment is in pairs. One is the 'receiver' who wears the ping-pong balls in isolation, one the 'sender' who watches randomly selected video clips in a separate room. The procedure lasts about 30 minutes. The receiver removes the ping-pong balls, and watches 4 clips, one of which was 'sent' during the procedure, and 'ranks' them for familiarity. This is the 'judging' section of the experiment. There is a 1 in 4 possibility (25%) of getting the right clip purely by chance.

Honorton (1985) – used manual Ganzfeld studies (with cards, not video clips) and claimed a very large, 55% success rate.

Criticisms – Hyman (1985) – once taken into account, Hyman said that 3 simple criticisms reduce the success rate to chance:

GANZFELD: HYMAN'S CRITICISMS	
Inadequate randomisation	People are likely to be biased in their ESP responses, and in experimenters choosing the stimuli to present, preferring to choose otherwise familiar objects and images perhaps, or those presented in a particular position in a sequence. Randomisation must be carefully done to avoid this. Manual card shuffling, and a human, non-random chooser, is inadequate and bias may creep in.
Security	There is the possibility of cheating. The sender and receiver must be carefully monitored to ensure this does not happen.
Selective analysis and reporting	Selectively choosing some results and not others for analysis, and not including those that showed no ESP, can influence data analysis and give misleading results. Trying many different types of analysis until one shows the desired result is also misleading.

However, even when a single analysis is done on all studies, the result is still highly significant, and Blackmore's review of the parapsychology community suggested that just as many non-results were found as positive results, so careful selection of the result did not seem to be happening.

Automated Ganzfeld

Bem and Honorton (1994) – replaced the experimenter with a computer, used decoys during the judging period, and recorded all ratings throughout judging, not just those relating to the target: they found a good hit rate in 329 trials involving 240 receivers and 8 different experimenters. This is significantly greater than chance.

Milton and Wiseman (1999) – reviews of research showed that those using the new automated Ganzfeld and applying the careful changes showed an overall hit rate of 27%, not significantly different from what would be expected by chance.

Standardness: Ratings of 'standardness of the procedure' were introduced by those using the Ganzfeld technique, in an attempt to counter arguments that judgments of how 'standard' a procedure was were biased. When Bem et al (2001) did this, they found that when the 'non-standard' studies were removed, the result fell to 24%, very close to chance.

Alternative studies of ESP

Zener card studies

Rhine began the original work with cards designed by Karl Zener, now known as the Zener card deck.

The Zener card deck

Using the deck, a participant guesses the identity of each card. There is a 1 in 5 chance of getting the answer right. This allows the experimenter to make statistical calculations of how unlikely a performance is to be due to chance. Rhine's results were impressive, showing significantly better than chance results on many different occasions – results that were published as evidence of ESP.

Dream ESP – the Maimonides approach

Typically, ESP experiences happen not in a laboratory but during dreaming, or just at the point of sleeping or waking. During sleep people experience periods of rapid eye movement (REM) that coincide with mental alertness, and if awoken now people are likely to report dreaming. The Maimonides technique placed a 'sender' in a remote room who had preciously interacted with the participant, who was asleep in a sound proof room. The 'sender' attempts to mentally 'transmit' to the sleeper images selected at random by the researchers. In the morning the participant is given a collection of images and told to rank them in order of 'familiarity'. If the target was in the top half of the rank it is a 'hit'; if in the bottom half it is a 'miss'.

Ullman et al (1966) – 7 hits and 1 miss were recorded. Strong evidence, according to the criteria Ullman decided on, for ESP.

Ullman and Krippner (1969) – 8 hits and no misses were recorded. Even stronger evidence for ESP.

Sherwood and Roe (2003) – 21 previous studies showed 14 with above chance ESP results and 6 below chance. When combined the results are slightly greater than chance, thus supporting the claims that ESP can be measured in this way. However, the findings are significantly lower than the original Ullman studies.

Studies have been criticised for 'data mining' (using different statistical tests until something is found) and not using a common methodology, which makes comparison with other studies problematic.

MIGHT EXPERIMENTERS INFLUENCE ESP STUDIES?

Attitude of the experimenter

Honorton et al (1975) – Researchers who were friendly to the participants were more likely to record ESP than those who were hostile.

Schmeidler (1995) – If sceptical, researchers were less likely to find evidence of ESP then if they were themselves 'believers'. It is possible that this belief is revealed in some way to the participants, thereby altering the perceived ESP 'ability' and attitude to it.

'Psi-conductivity'

Researchers may be considered as 'psi-conductive' or 'psi-inhibitory', with 'psi' referring to the type of information or energy transfer studied in parapsychology. Conductive researchers tend to find ESP, inhibitory ones do not, suggesting that the findings are more to do with who conducts the research than with the participants being studied. Some argue that only psi-conductive researchers should carry out the research, but that means independent scientific evaluation cannot be made and so validity is harmed, and the scientific approach destroyed.

Possible participant-experimenter psi interaction

It may be that the participant's 'psi' ability and that of the experimenter interacts somehow. This further confuses matters and makes investigations even harder

What you really need to know about is Ganzfeld – you could get a question specifically on this. However, an understanding of other research might come in useful in more general questions on ESP and research methodology.

Psychokinesis (PK) studies

This means 'motion produced by the mind'. Early studies were related to large changes and levitation. Research these day is usually into 'micro PK', meaning the attempt to influence an object at even a tiny level that requires a delicate instrument to measure the movement.

» *Dice throwing:* Investigations into whether people can influence the number a dice shows once thrown were made by Rhine in the 1930s. A machine that eliminated any skill in rolling the dice was used. Very tiny paranormal effects were claimed, but methodological problems were identified with the procedure used. For instance, some numbers are biased to fall upwards. Tiny weight differences on each face because of paint used or holes drilled to make the 'spots' will become statistically important over many thousands of throws.

Ferrari (1991) – Very tiny differences between a control, where no influence was attempted, and an experimental condition, where a PK agent attempted to influence dice throws, were found.

» *Random number generators (RNG):* Mechanical machines that generate random numbers were used. Possible PK influencing on the machines was investigated.

Radin and Nelson (1989) – Over 600 RNG procedures were selected and compared in a meta-analysis. A tiny, but significantly reliable effect of PK was found. The researchers claim this as evidence of PK.

Bösch et al (2006) – a larger meta-analysis also showed a tiny but significant PK effect.

PK – The parapsychologists' view

Radin and Nelson (1989) used a meta-analysis to find 'evidence' of PK. A small number of very positive results that went into the analysis could have had a huge effect, suggesting a result when really there was none. There is also less likelihood that a non-significant result (one where PK was not found) would ever be published by a journal editor – and so it would be likely to be filed away and forgotten. This means that the positive results appear more significant than they really are.

Steinkamp et al (2002) – A larger meta-analysis found no evidence at all of PK.

Wilson and Shadish (2006) – The effects found by Bösch et al (2006) are so tiny that even a tiny methodological flaw in the experiments used would heavily influence the result.

» *Correlation and cause:* PK and the RNG results are correlations. This does not suggest a cause.

» *Occam's Razor:* William of Occam stated that when faced with two explanations the one to accept should be the simplest. Things not known to exist (such as paranormal powers) should not unless absolutely necessary be thought of as existing when building an explanation of something. Chance is the simplest explanation and so the results are more likely to be explained by chance than something we do not know about.

Distant mental influence on living systems (DMILS)

» One form of PK is where one person has an influence at a distance on the physiology of another organism – this is a form of macro-PK.

» Research has involved such things as whether a person can influence the behaviour of animals and plants, distant healing, and the feeling of being stared at.

» The feeling of being stared at appears culturally universal and therefore may have a basis in fact.

» Typically, research into remote staring involves a 'sender' watching a 'receiver' who is isolated in another room. Some aspect of the receiver's physiology is measured to see if it changes when staring occurs. Some findings support such an effect, e.g. Baud et al (1993).

» However, such research is criticised: e.g. Baker (2000) says that it is vulnerable to experimenter effects, and that the measurements are too subtle. Wiseman and Schlitz (1997) concluded that sceptical researchers found no evidence for remote staring effects, whilst non-sceptical researchers did, even though the procedures were identical.

SECTION 2: FACTORS UNDERLYING ANOMALOUS EXPERIENCE

Cognitive factors underlying anomalous experience

Critical thinking

Belief in the paranormal may be a default position when people do not have the critical thinking ability to work out what they have just experienced.

Memory and probability estimates

When something appears to happen by chance an estimation of probability is called for. 'What are the odds of THAT happening!'. In general people are very poor at this.

Diaconis and Mosteller (1989) – It is the case that with large numbers of events, something odd or difficult to explain will certainly happen.

Russell and Jones (1980) – When shown ESP results that contradict and support their opinion, participants are more likely to remember the ones that support, or *confirm* their opinion. This is called a *confirmation bias*.

French (2002) – We all dream every night. By chance, some dreams may 'come true'. If a paranormal dream has a 1 in 10,000 chance of coming true, 3.6% of the population (that's 2 million people!) should have at least one very improbable dream each year.

Cognitive deficits hypothesis

The believer is regarded as irrational, illogical, uncritical and unthinking.

French (1992) – Much research has been done investigating whether believers score worse than non-believers on a range of cognitive tasks. There is great disagreement however.

Killen et al (1974) – IQ correlated *negatively* with paranormal belief.

Watt and Wiseman (2002) – No relationship found between IQ and paranormal belief.

Jones et al (1977) – IQ *positively* correlated with paranormal belief!

Otis and Alcock (1982) – Humanities students (e.g. History) show higher paranormal belief than science students. It may be that general ignorance of the scientific approach, not general cognitive ability, influences paranormal belief.

It is a really good idea to develop a sound understanding of probability and coincidence. They are core ideas in psychology. You will be better able to understand why people often readily turn to paranormal explanations for their difficult-to-understand experiences. Just as importantly however, you need to know about probability (from the Psychological Research and Scientific Method section) too. One bit of learning and two parts of the specification covered – a bargain!

Illusions of causality and the psychology of coincidence

Blackmore identifies illusions of form, memory, pattern, control and connection as being responsible for paranormal experiences. Our understanding of 'coincidence' is terribly important here.

Blackmore and Troscianko (1985) – Those that hold paranormal beliefs are more likely to interpret coincidences as meaningful than those who do not.

ILLUSIONS OF CAUSALITY	
Illusions of Form	Some see shapes that are not really there, increasing the likelihood of a paranormal experience.
Illusions of Memory	We select memories and reconstruct them from fragments. This makes it possible that events are mis-remembered.
Illusions of Pattern and Randomness	We seek patterns all the time. We may see one when in fact the stimuli are random, identifying the experience as paranormal.
Illusions of Control	When a coincidence between an event and a person's behaviour happens, a person may assume that they are in control of the event.
Illusions of Connection	Some things happen by chance, but we naturally seek links and causal relationships between things, making paranormal experience more likely.

Personality factors underlying anomalous experience

Some people are more prone to experiencing anomalous and paranormal behaviour than others, and this may be due to personality. Groth-Marnat and Pegden (1998) describe the three characteristics in the table nearby as relevant here.

PERSONALITY CHARACTERISTICS RELATED TO PARANORMAL BELIEFS	
Locus of control	The more external the 'locus' (location) of control the less we feel we ourselves are in control. Personalities regarding the locus as more external are more likely to have some paranormal beliefs and associated characteristics, such as superstitious beliefs. Tobacyk et al (1988) linked superstition with higher external locus of control.
Sensation seeking	Some people actively seek excitement, and often look for new and novel experiences. Paranormal experiences may fulfil these needs. Kumar et al (1983) found evidence that sensation seekers were more likely to hold paranormal beliefs.
Creativity	Creativity is positively correlated with paranormal beliefs. Gianotti et al (2001) found that creative people could identify more links between word pairs than non-creative people, and that the most original and creative links came from those with paranormal beliefs.

Need for control and locus of control

Paranormal belief is increased as anxiety increases. Locus of control is described in the table as a personality characteristic. When experiencing an anxious situation, believing we are in control can alleviate anxiety; as the psychodynamic functions hypothesis describes, control reduces unpredictability.

Sanderson et al (1989) – Fewer panic attacks were experienced amongst people who thought they had control over stress-inducing stimuli.

Dudley (1999) – Paranormal beliefs were greater in those solving unsolvable puzzles, where there was no control of the solution, than solvable puzzles.

Roe and Bell (2007) – Measured locus (perceived position) of control in terms of internal to the person (they have control) or external (they do not have control). Their paranormal belief was related to anxiety, and this in turn was related to expectancy of things happening to them in the future and their perceived control over events.

Tobacyk et al (1988) – Locus of control is also positively related to beliefs in superstition and witchcraft.

Psychodynamic functions hypothesis

Some are prone to see life as chaotic and unpredictable. This causes anxiety. Anomalous beliefs develop to alleviate the anxiety.

McGarry and Newberry (1981) – Students who viewed the world as largely unpredictable and unfair were more likely to hold paranormal beliefs.

Keinan (1991) – Those under threat of military action during the Gulf War, an unpredictable time for them, were more likely to engage in magical thinking.

The psychology of superstition

A superstition is the belief that something affects something else even though there is no basis for the belief. Some are more superstitious than others.

Skinner (1947) – A superstition is explained as a false association between a reinforcer and a response. For instance, you had a good experience when you wore a particular pair of pants on a date, and so you wear them on every date now as your 'lucky pants'.

Kida (2006) – Superstitions arise in uncontrollable, uncertain and random circumstances, as do other paranormal beliefs, and so are also related to locus of control.

Whitson and Galinsky (2008) – Misperceptions result in superstitions. A misperception satisfies a need for control and arises when there is little control.

Biological factors underlying anomalous experience

Some people appear to show biological reactions to environmental stimuli such as 'geomagnetism', the magnetic field that surrounds us. Geomagnetic activity can stimulate the temporal lobes, producing similar effects to the 'haunting' experience, such as 'sensing' a presence.

Gearhart and Persinger (1986) – claim that hauntings seem to be related to increased geomagnetic activity.

Wiseman et al (2003) – South Bridge Vaults in Edinburgh were investigated. Those parts of the vaults in which more haunting experiences were recorded also had greater fluctuations in the geomagnetic field.

ASK AN EXAMINER

More biological factors underlying anomalous experience are described later on, where we summarise research on out of body experienced and near-death experiences.

Functions of paranormal beliefs and related beliefs – cultural significance

Religion
» Schmeidler (1985) says that one reason for experiencing paranormal beliefs could be cultural norms.
» E.g. a religious person may be more open to mystical explanations or ones where no or limited proof is presented.
» A paranormal belief in this case may serve to explain why something happens when we may not immediately understand the reasons: e.g. a religion may explain the death of a loved one as 'part of God's plan' – religious beliefs can help us to make sense of things and justify why they happen.
» However, belief in the paranormal as such does not seem to be related to particular cultures, although the spreading influence of the media may partly explain high levels of paranormal belief seen in many countries.

The media
There is a long history of the paranormal in media, such as films, books and magazines. It is not unusual in films to find characters able to interact with the dead, see the future or transform into magical or terrifying creatures. Video games make use of imaginary creatures very successfully. A belief in the paranormal in these cases allows us to suspend disbelief and enjoy the possibility of imaginary creatures and environments. It can allow us to live out a fantasy when we would not otherwise be able to.

The Psychodynamic functions hypothesis
Paranormal belief serves to reduce anxiety by providing answers in a world otherwise seen as disorganised and chaotic. Unpredictable things now feel more controllable. McGarry and Newberry (1981) found that those more likely to hold paranormal beliefs were those who viewed the world as largely unpredictable. Keinan (1991) found that those under threat of military action during the Gulf War were more likely to engage in magical thinking.

The psychology of deception and self-deception

The behaviour and so-called 'skills and gifts' of psychics impress and influence many people. Haraldsson (1985) found that 83% of those surveyed who had attended a séance found the experience useful. However, Schouten (1994) found that the likelihood of a correct statement about a matter unknown from a psychic was no greater than chance.

The apparent 'psychic skills' of mediums have been explained by psychologists.

Deception and research into psychic mediumship

Setting the scene
People are encouraged to regard what is said in a certain way e.g. 'I only see parts of a puzzle and they may be muddled. It is for you to put them together', suggesting that the audience is encouraged to reorganise, rearrange and add information to the reading to try and help it make sense when in fact the material is incomplete, and quite random.

Using the correct language
Barnum statements are statements which appear personal but which apply to many people. When used in a psychic reading they can encourage belief in the paranormal, deceiving people into believing that the psychic knows something about them. We are also more likely to remember statements that refer to us than those that do not. This is to do with 'selectivity of attention'.

 ASK AN EXAMINER

You need to know specifically about psychic mediumship and deception/self deception, so it makes sense that they are both included together here.

Top down processing
This means to make sense of what we experience by applying it to information we may have experienced in the past. When a psychic leaves gaps in the information for us to make sense of, we do so with our own information that makes sense to us. E.g. a reading from a psychic that describes images of coins falling and people trapped beneath houses may be interpreted in any number of ways; but when we are told it refers to a global 'financial crisis' and our fear of losing our house because we have less and less money to spend, it all makes sense to us and we are unable to regard the random, ambiguous images in any other way thereafter.

Cold reading and fishing
Cold reading involves taking advantage of information given up during interaction ('fishing') and developing it. E.g. an opening statement is made and the psychic responds to how the person responds. A statement such as 'You are worried about money' may elicit a yes or no response. Rich people tend not to be. This tells the psychic something about them that allows them to assume a great deal about their lifestyle.

Research into psychic healing

Also known as distant healing, psychic healing aims to influence people's physical systems, hopefully to make them feel better in some way. There are many approaches, including Reiki, prayer and therapeutic touch. Austin et al (2000) estimate that there are 14,000 psychic healers working in the UK.

Schouten (1993) found that patients' ratings of 'subjective' health (they were still in pain but they found it easier to deal with now) were much greater than for objective measures (pain was actually reduced). This suggests that, if anything, psychic healing can help with an attitude to pain rather than the pain itself.

Placebo

A placebo is an inert treatment that does not tackle the problem directly, but may have an effect because the person *thinks* they are being treated. It may be a sugar pill, or it may be the use of equipment that does nothing at all.

Radin (1997) estimated that between 20 and 40% of the results of clinical drug trials may be because of placebo effects. It follows that psychic healing may well have an effect not because it is doing anything to the illness, but because the person feels they are being treated.

Regression to the mean

Consider the example of arthritis, the painful swelling of the joints that many experience. Most days in a year are 'typical' days. On a typical day in a typical year a sufferer will not feel good or bad, just 'ok'. Suffering will be at 'mean' or average level. When they feel good (or better than average) they would not seek treatment, there's no need. They will only seek treatment when they feel bad. When feeling really bad, the only way to go is to get better. So, any treatment applied at this stage, of whatever kind (apple juggling, Reiki or balloon-animal-making therapy) is certain to result in a movement back from 'feeling really bad' towards feeling 'ok' or 'average'. In this way, people 'regress' or move back towards the 'mean' of their experience. By this explanation, psychic healing has no effect whatsoever. An improvement is a simple regression from the unusual 'feeling terrible' towards the most common, average feeling.

Research into out-of-body experiences (OBE)

An OBE is when the person experiences themselves outside their own body. They may see their own body from above, or from a distance. According to Blanke (2004) OBE experiences are common across cultures, suggesting that they are something to do with our biology.

Biological explanations

» Blanke and Arzy (2005) – More common in those who experience epilepsy and migraine.
» Devinsky et al (1989) – Those experiencing OBE have been described as having damage in the temporal or parietal lobes.
» De Ridder et al (2007) – Stimulation of a point of the brain in the temporoparietal region (see diagram) generates OBE-like experiences. It is thought that this is because this part of the brain in involved in integrating information from and about the body when generating an internal map of 'self-perception'.

Research into near death experiences (NDE)

A person coming close to death may experience deep peace, well-being, separation from the body and, variously, passing through a tunnel, towards a light or into a beautiful garden. Parnia et al (2007) says that 10–20% of cardiac arrest survivors report an NDE.

Cultural factors in NDE

» Schorer (1985) – North American NDEs involve moccasins, snakes, eagles, bows and arrows.

» Pasricha and Stevenson (1986) – Western NDEs involve the person at the centre of them, seemingly able to decide whether to return to the body or not, whilst Asian Indian NDEs report being controlled. This appears to reflect the collectivist and individualistic cultural differences.

Biological explanations

The positive feelings of well-being etc. are explained in terms of release of endorphins, powerful naturally-produced pain killers.

» Whinnery (1997) – Jet pilots experiencing extreme manoeuvres with huge G-forces often 'pass out' and experience NDE-like symptoms of moving towards a light, or through a tunnel.

» Blackmore (1993) – Some brain cells are more sensitive to a lack of oxygen than others. Typically, these cells fire *more* with less oxygen and so the person's experiences at this time are richer. Eventually, as oxygen levels get lower and lower in the visual cortex, the experience would be like moving towards a light that gets bigger and bigger and eventually envelopes a person, as if moving down a tunnel towards a light.

HOW WELL DO I KNOW IT?	NOT AT ALL	MAYBE	OK	WELL	SUPERBLY
ANOMALISTIC PSYCHOLOGY					
Issues of pseudoscience					
Issues of scientific fraud					
Controversies relating to Ganzfeld studies of ESP					
Controversies relating to studies of psychokinesis					
Cognitive factors underlying anomalous experience					
Personality factors underlying anomalous experience					
Biological factors underlying anomalous experience					
Function of paranormal beliefs and related beliefs including their cultural significance					
Psychology of deception and self-deception					
Psychology of superstition					
Psychology of coincidence					
Research into psychic healing					
Research into out-of-body and near-death experiences					
Research into psychic mediumship					

Psychological Research and Scientific Methods

WHAT YOU NEED TO KNOW

This section builds on the knowledge and skills of research methods developed at AS level.

You are expected to be able to understand the application of scientific method in psychology, design investigations, understand how to analyse and interpret data arising from such investigations, and report on practical investigations.

THE APPLICATIONS OF SCIENTIFIC METHOD IN PSYCHOLOGY
- The major features of science
- The scientific process, including theory construction, hypothesis testing, use of empirical methods, generation of laws/principles
- Validating new knowledge and the role of peer review

DESIGNING PSYCHOLOGICAL INVESTIGATIONS
- Selection and application of appropriate research methods
- Sampling strategies
- Issues of reliability, including types of reliability, assessment of reliability, improving reliability
- Assessing and improving validity (internal and external)
- Ethical considerations in design and conduct of psychological research

REPORTING INVESTIGATIONS
- Appropriate selection of graphical representations
- Probability and significance, including the interpretation of significance and Type 1/Type 2 errors
- Choosing the correct statistical test, including levels of measurement
- Inferential analysis, including Spearman's Rho, Wilcoxon, Mann-Whitney, chi-square
- Analysing and interpreting of qualitative data
- Conventions of reporting on psychological investigations

A good deal of what you need to know about psychological research and scientific method was covered in your AS course. Some of this will be summarised here, but you really must bring with you to A2 all that you have learned previously, since exam questions will cover ALL that you have learned on this topic and not just those parts that are new at A2. Only a summary of key points is presented in this chapter – use your main textbook to flesh out the details if necessary.

WHAT YOU SHOULD ALREADY KNOW FROM AS PSYCHOLOGY

METHODS AND TECHNIQUES

- Experimental method, including laboratory, field and natural experiments
- Studies using a correlational analysis
- Observational techniques
- Self-report techniques including questionnaire and interview
- Case studies

INVESTIGATION DESIGN

- Aims
- Hypotheses, including directional and non-directional
- Experimental design (independent groups, repeated measures and matched pairs)
- Design of naturalistic observations, including the development and use of behavioural categories
- Design of questionnaires and interviews
- Operationalisation of variables, including independent and dependent variables
- Pilot studies
- Control of extraneous variables
- Reliability and validity
- Awareness of the British Psychological Society (BPS) Code of Ethics
- Ethical issues and ways in which psychologists deal with them
- Selection of participants and sampling techniques, including random, opportunity and volunteer sampling.
- Demand characteristics and investigator effects

DATA ANALYSIS AND PRESENTATION

- Presentation and interpretation of quantitative data including graphs, scattergrams and tables
- Analysis and interpretation of quantitative data
- Measures of central tendency including mean, median and mode
- Measures of dispersion including ranges and standard deviation
- Analysis and interpretation of correlational data
- Positive and negative correlations and the interpretation of correlation coefficients
- Presentation of qualitative data
- Processes involved in content analysis

SECTION 1: APPLICATIONS OF SCIENTIFIC METHOD IN PSYCHOLOGY

In the exam you might be asked about the features of science (e.g. replicability and objectivity) or you might be asked about the scientific process (e.g. theory construction, hypothesis testing, and the generation of laws/principles). Make sure you are familiar with what a science is!

THE MAJOR FEATURES OF SCIENCE AND THE SCIENTIFIC PROCESS

KEY PHRASES	DEFINITION	HOW IS THIS USEFUL TO ME?
Hypothesis Testing	How the scientific method progresses. Statements are made, and procedures designed to test whether the statements can be supported or not. If we are able to 'reject' an hypothesis, it is because the procedure has proved it to be incorrect. Hypotheses may predict a change in direction (skinny men sleep less than fat men) or they may not (skinny and fat men sleep for different amounts of time).	Ask yourself, have the researchers rejected or accepted the null hypothesis incorrectly? If so they have made a *type 1* or *type 2* error.
Replicability	Carrying out good research at a different time should generate the same result. If it does, it has *replicability*.	Has the research been carried out more than once? If so, did it always produce the same result? If not, it is not '*reliable*'.
Objectivity	Objective research does not depend on the identity of the researcher. A subjective researcher may be looking for particular things. If you *want* to believe in UFOs, your research on the topic may be *subjective*. If you could not care less whether they existed, it would be *objective*.	The lower the objectivity, the higher the potential *bias* of the result. Look to see who carried out the research, and who paid them to do it! If a publisher funds research on education, the result may favour their products for instance, and so would not be objective.
Empirical Method	A method of data collection that allows us to reach a conclusion. This allows the development of existing theories or the design of new ones.	Was the study empirical? Did it develop an existing theory? Could the original theory be evaluated in some way as a result of the study?
Deductive Reasoning	We can *deduce* from the results of an empirical study whether the hypothesis is supported or not. This is *hypothetico-deductive* reasoning.	A study that cannot be tested like this is not regarded as *scientific*. The testability of the findings is crucial.

(continued)

THE MAJOR FEATURES OF SCIENCE AND THE SCIENTIFIC PROCESS

KEY PHRASES	DEFINITION	HOW IS THIS USEFUL TO ME?
Theory Construction	Theories are developed by constant hypothetico-deductive testing and retesting. They should all be falsifiable by a well-designed experiment.	Unfalsifiability of a theory (such as Freud's) means it is not testable and not scientific.
Laws and Principles	A law is something that ALWAYS happens. Newton identified a few in physics! With enough evidence for a theory, it may eventually be described as a law.	Some may describe the existence of the subconscious as a principle or law. If you do not think this is the case, then any research that does so can be questioned.
Inductive Reasoning	If something *usually* happens we can *induce* that it will happen. We may *induce* that the next swan we see will be white. They usually are.	Conclusions based on this type of reasoning are *generalisations* and so may be weak. Swans are *sometimes* black!
Parsimony	There may be two answers to the same experimental question. If this is the case, we should select the *least complex explanation*. This is called '*Occam's Razor*'.	Could there be a simpler explanation for the results? If so, point it out and cite Occam's Razor as a reason for doing so!
Karl Popper	Philosopher whose thinking led to the concept of hypothesis testing and the experimental method as we know it.	If a theory, like Freud's, is untestable, Popper's thinking directly attacks it as being unscientific. Quote Popper's philosophy where you identify this.
Thomas Kuhn	Philosopher who believed scientific progression is based on assumptions and laws. If these laws and assumptions change, science takes a different direction. This is called *paradigm shift*.	Old research based on the theory that the world was flat is now outmoded due to the knowledge that it is, in fact, round. Does the research in question work under very old-fashioned incorrect assumptions?
Peer Review	Process of knowledge validation where academics evaluate their peers' work before it is sent for publication in journals for public viewing.	If something has not been peer-reviewed by other academics it may not be trustworthy.

SECTION 2: DESIGNING PSYCHOLOGICAL INVESTIGATIONS

Designing psychological investigations

ASK AN EXAMINER

In the table, notice how each type of research method and design option has been identified as having good and bad points, which we have described as pros and cons. This is an extremely useful thing to know! Once you have identified the type of design under discussion you can easily identify the problems and benefits associated with it. Not only that – you can even suggest alternative approaches to the design that could be considered for future research.

DESIGNING PSYCHOLOGICAL INVESTIGATIONS – DESIGN OPTIONS

KEY PHRASES	DEFINITION	PROS	CONS
Repeated Measures (RM)	Each person carries out the procedure with each level of the IV.	No problems of individual differences, such as fitness and age. Can use a much smaller sample than IG.	Possible for order effects. Person may get better (practice) or they may get worse (fatigue).
Independent Groups (IG)	Each level of the IV is carried out by a separate group of participants.	Absolutely no order effects such as practice or fatigue.	Huge problems of individual differences. Those in one group may be different from those in another and this may account for the results.
Matched Pairs	An IG study where members of each group are *matched* with members of the other group.	Controls for individual differences in each group.	Impossible to match perfectly. Even identical twins have different desires, experiences and skills.
Lab Experiment	Carried out in controlled *laboratory* settings.	Good ones have *replicability, generalisability, reliability and validity*. Environmental variables can be carefully controlled.	Can be said to lack ecological validity. Because of the highly controlled environment the results may not relate to the real world.
Field Experiment	Like a lab experiment but in more *real life* conditions.	Real world offers ecological validity.	Often fantastically expensive and time consuming to carry out
Natural Experiment	The effects of naturally occurring independent variable (e.g. a war, extreme weather, etc.) are investigated.	High in ecological validity, no or few *demand characteristics*.	No control over the IV and so high chance of unwanted issues (confounding variables) influencing the experiment.
Quasi Experiment	If you can't manipulate the IV (e.g. comparing Americans and English people).	Can make use of naturally occurring, easy to identify variables, and so easy to ensure membership of different groups.	Matching other variables in each group is difficult or impossible. Cannot be certain that any results are because of your observed variable.
Case Study	Careful and systematic investigation of an individual or single organisation.	Extremely detailed data.	Very low generalisability, and data from the past or from those with brain damage may not be very reliable.

(continued)

DESIGNING PSYCHOLOGICAL INVESTIGATIONS – DESIGN OPTIONS

KEY PHRASES	DEFINITION	PROS	CONS
Observational Method	Where researchers observe the behaviour of others.	At first glance easy to apply and can provide detailed and rich data. What to look for (*behaviour checklist*) can be as detailed or as wide as necessary.	May be biased. Subjectivity and skill of the observer must be considered. If the *behaviour checklist* is wrong, important behaviour will go unrecorded.
Observational Technique	You can use observation as a technique in many designs so it can be a method or a technique.	Can be used in a wide variety of settings. Is hugely flexible.	Open to same criticism as Observational Method. Requires great skill to be done properly.
Content Analysis	A kind of observational method but the content of text or film is scrutinised rather than the behaviour of individuals.	Useful way of systematically analysing print and film material for a particular type of *behaviour* such as *racism* or other prejudice.	May be subjective depending on the motivation of the researcher doing the analysis. One researcher may, for instance, regard a comment as racist but another may not, so reliability and bias are possible.
Self Report	Questionnaires and interviews. Participants *report* their answers on the questionnaire or to the researcher directly.	Huge amounts of data can be collected simply, easily and relatively inexpensively.	Participants may take part, or lie, to please the researcher or appear more socially acceptable. Also, a participant may provide different answers on different occasions, reducing the reliability of the research.
Correlational Method	A design option where the relationship between two variables (age and intelligence perhaps) is investigated.	Naturally occurring variables can be measured which can lead to future research and the generation of more reliable theories.	Cannot infer cause and effect from correlation. Something we may not have considered may have *caused* the effect we see and we would never know.

In all of these designs, you need to watch out for two things that can cause problems.

Investigator Effects

The experimenter may unintentionally give away what they think or what they would like behaviour to resemble. E.g. when a response is laughed at, the participant knows from the investigator's behaviour that the response they have just given is funny, and so likely to be 'incorrect' in some way.

How to avoid them: Double blind procedure, where neither the participant nor the experimenter knows the demands.

Problems: Ethics may be infringed if neither investigator nor participant knows what is going on in the experimental session.

Demand Characteristics

This is something in the research design which changes the participant's behaviour. E.g., if something about the procedure suggests that a certain response is desirable then the participant may change what they say or do.

How to avoid them: Single blind procedure, where participant does not know the requirements of the study.

Problems: Keeping the participant in the dark about the requirements of the study *may* count as deception and *may* therefore infringe ethics.

Sampling

Sampling is the process of selecting participants to take part in a study. This sample should be representative of the population from which it was chosen in order to generalise the findings.

SAMPLING		
KEY PHRASES	DEFINITION	ISSUES OF GENERALISABILITY AND BIAS
Random	Everyone in the population has the same chance of being chosen to be in the sample.	The minute someone says, 'No, I don't want to be in the sample,' it is no longer random as someone else must be chosen to replace them, so *bias* comes very easily. It is also unlikely that investigators have the contact details of absolutely everyone in the population and the means of contacting them. If choosing participants from the phone book, then only those with phones are in the sample. If the electoral register, then only those registered to vote can be contacted. In both cases, the sample cannot be generalised to be the larger, more inclusive population.
Opportunity	Anyone handy is asked to participate. A notice may be put up, or people grabbed as they pass by.	Typically, students or people from their own social group, and often family, are chosen to take part. These people are least likely to say no and so the sample is biased to a quite narrow population and generalisability is reduced. The motive for taking part must be questioned. Students may take part to impress a lecturer and so demand characteristics may be a real problem. Also, only people who *want* to take part do so. Helpful people often provide a certain type of response. This provides a certain bias, and another restriction on generalisability.
Volunteer	Similar to opportunity sampling. An entirely self-selecting group is used, possibly via a newspaper advert requesting volunteers.	Volunteers are often interested parties, generating a bias. If the sample come from a newspaper advert only those who read that particular newspaper volunteer, and this may be a certain type of person. Readers of *The Guardian*, for instance, are quite different, usually, from *The Sun* readers. Helpful people may volunteer, as may those attempting to get higher marks for being nice to their lecturer! All these issues influence the make up of the sample (bias) and the generalisability of the results to people elsewhere in the population.

Each sampling method has its implications, expressed in terms of generalisability and validity. Generalisability means how well the results can be applied to a different and larger sample, and validity refers here to the extent to which the sampling creates a sample which is representative of the wider population.

Reliability and validity

These are key issues in psychological research. Reliability refers to consistency (e.g. whether the research can be repeated with similar results), so reliability gives us confidence in the results. Validity refers to whether or not a test or research measures what it says it measures.

RELIABILITY & VALIDITY		
KEY PHRASES	**DEFINITION**	**HOW CAN IT BE IMPROVED?**
Observer reliability	If more than one observer is carrying out the observation, reliability is a measure of how closely they agree. If their *ratings of the observed behaviour* correlate highly, they are reliable.	Training the observers more carefully. Making sure they both have a good and similar view of the behaviour to be observed and ensuring they both understand the definitions and identities of the behaviours to be observed will all improve this.
Test reliability	A test to assess a behaviour, perhaps aggressive tendencies, should provide the same score each time it is used on the same person. A high correlation of scores on different presentations of the same test identifies it as reliable.	If test and retests do not correlate highly then a different test might be used, or the test itself might be altered so that correlation is improved.
Internal validity	We must be sure that our results are due to what we think they are. If testing the effects of coffee on concentration, we must be sure that the participant is not full of chocolate too!	Careful research design and instruction to participants can improve this. If fatigue and practice influence the results then internal validity is damaged. We may consider a different research design if necessary.
External validity	High external validity comes where the results can be generalised to a larger population.	Careful sampling can improve external validity. A larger more inclusive sample may be used, or a completely different sampling method employed if necessary.
Ecological validity	If findings relate to *situations* other than those in which the work was carried out. Lab studies, for instance, may have low ecological validity as they may not relate to the world outside the lab.	Some research design options can be prone to low ecological validity. For instance, a researcher may consider developing the research to a field or natural experiment to improve this.
Population validity	High population validity is where the findings relate to the general population.	A massive sample, of 500,000 people, has a higher population validity than a sample of you and two mates. Increase the sample size and widen the range of people from which the sample was drawn to increase the population validity. A similar study carried out elsewhere should, with high population validity, provide a similar result.
Test validity	*Content Validity* – does the test test what it is supposed to? *Face Validity* – does it *seem* to test what it is supposed to? *Predictive Validity* – how well does the test predict ability on the test were it to be taken at another time, perhaps 20 years later?	All three can be improved with careful test design. A hammer, for instance, has *very* low test validity if it is used to test a person's personality. Sometimes an entirely new test must be designed for research to enable researchers to improve test validity.

Demand characteristics, investigator effects, reliability and validity are extremely useful things to consider when you comment on the research you read about. Have these in mind when thinking critically about the methodology used. You can often pick up valuable marks by making one or two effective comments based on these issues when evaluating research.

Ethics

» If researchers do not take account of ethical considerations, their work might not be published and seen by other psychologists. Such researchers may be penalised by their employers and the British Psychological Society (BPS), and in extreme cases they may not be allowed to work again. They could also face legal action from 'harmed' participants, which may lead to fines and ultimately imprisonment.

» People (or, for that matter, animals) treated badly or caused to be afraid or unhappy in any way are likely to provide responses that do not properly reflect their true nature. Results may thus be misleading and therefore lack validity and generalisability.

» A summary of the major ethical considerations is provided below.

ETHICAL ISSUE	DEALING WITH IT	PROBLEMS
Informed consent	Participants need to be told what they are to do and why they are to do it, before they agree to take part in the study.	● Being told about the purpose of a study might make it worthless. ● Obtaining informed consent does not guarantee that a participant understands what they are agreeing to.
Lack of debriefing	After the study is complete, participants must be fully informed about the nature of the study and be given the opportunity to ask any questions they might have.	● Debriefing does not turn the clock back and undo any harm already done. ● It is not always easy to debrief in a way which ensures understanding by all participants.
Deception	Participants should not be deceived unless absolutely necessary. If deception is required, then the benefits of research should outweigh the costs of deception.	● Debriefing can occur but this does not necessarily undo harm done. ● Cost-benefit analysis is problematic – e.g. costs and benefits are not always apparent at the start of the study.
Right to withdraw	Participants should be informed at the start that they are free to end their participation in the study at any time.	● Participants may feel a pressure to remain part of the study, e.g. they might not want to 'spoil' it. ● Participants may feel that sometimes they are unable to withdraw, e.g. when taking part in research is a requirement of being on a university course.
Confidentiality	Any information provided by the participants should remain private and confidential.	● It is not always possible to ensure complete anonymity. ● Participants themselves may reveal their part in the study.
Protection from harm	The safety and well-being of participants must be protected at all times, and this includes physical and mental well-being.	● It is not always possible to accurately predict the risks of taking part in a study in advance. ● What one participant feels is 'harmful' might not be judged in the same way by another.

Ethical issues are extremely important to consider in designing and carrying out research. For this reason, you can expect questions on ethics to crop up regularly in exams. Although you should be familiar with these ethical issues from your AS course, make sure that you can apply your knowledge of them.

SECTION 3: DATA ANALYSIS AND REPORTING ON INVESTIGATIONS

Graphs and tables

The whole point of presenting data in graphs and tables is to make the results easy to understand for others interested in the research. They should therefore be simple, clear and appropriate for the data of data you have.

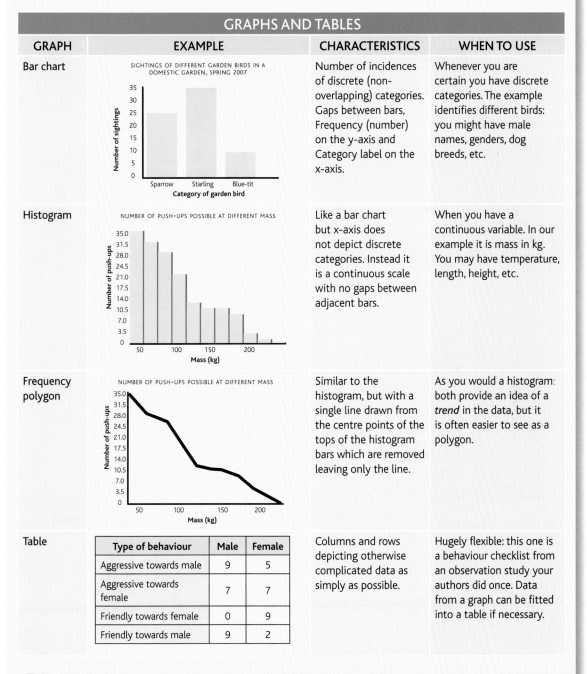

GRAPH	EXAMPLE	CHARACTERISTICS	WHEN TO USE
Bar chart	SIGHTINGS OF DIFFERENT GARDEN BIRDS IN A DOMESTIC GARDEN, SPRING 2007 (Number of sightings vs Category of garden bird: Sparrow, Starling, Blue-tit)	Number of incidences of discrete (non-overlapping) categories. Gaps between bars, Frequency (number) on the y-axis and Category label on the x-axis.	Whenever you are certain you have discrete categories. The example identifies different birds: you might have male names, genders, dog breeds, etc.
Histogram	NUMBER OF PUSH-UPS POSSIBLE AT DIFFERENT MASS (Number of push-ups vs Mass (kg))	Like a bar chart but x-axis does not depict discrete categories. Instead it is a continuous scale with no gaps between adjacent bars.	When you have a continuous variable. In our example it is mass in kg. You may have temperature, length, height, etc.
Frequency polygon	NUMBER OF PUSH-UPS POSSIBLE AT DIFFERENT MASS (Number of push-ups vs Mass (kg))	Similar to the histogram, but with a single line drawn from the centre points of the tops of the histogram bars which are removed leaving only the line.	As you would a histogram: both provide an idea of a *trend* in the data, but it is often easier to see as a polygon.
Table	(behaviour checklist table, see below)	Columns and rows depicting otherwise complicated data as simply as possible.	Hugely flexible: this one is a behaviour checklist from an observation study your authors did once. Data from a graph can be fitted into a table if necessary.

Table example:

Type of behaviour	Male	Female
Aggressive towards male	9	5
Aggressive towards female	7	7
Friendly towards female	0	9
Friendly towards male	9	2

It's unlikely that you'll need to draw a graph. It's more likely that you'll need to be able to identify, read and interpret one, and be able to indicate which sort of graph is appropriate in which circumstance. You might also be asked to read data from a table.

Whilst you won't have to do any calculations in the exam, you are expected to know about these descriptive statistics and what they are useful for.

Descriptive statistics

These summarise your data with very simple numbers.

» When using a MEAN use a STANDARD DEVIATION.

» When using a MEDIAN use a SEMI-INTERQUARTILE RANGE or RANGE.

» When using a MODE use RANGE.

	Mean	Mode	Median	Standard deviation	Range	Semi-interquartile range
Strength	Most power-ful measure of central tendency as it uses all of the data	The best measure to use if you want to know how often things happen	Not heavily influenced by rogue scores	Uses every value in the data set, not heavily distorted by extreme values and is the most sensitive	Takes extreme scores into consideration and is simple to calculate	Less distorted scores than the range
Weakness	One rogue score (large or small) can heavily influence it. For instance, the mean of 3, 4 and 8 is 5. The mean of 3, 4, 8 and 1,005 is **255**. The extreme value has seriously influenced the mean	Sometimes a data set does not have a most common value and sometimes it has lots of common values	Not good for using with small data sets. For instance, if you only have the numbers 1, 17 and 2,000 in your data set the median is 17. Not very informative	The most laborious of the measures of central tendency to calculate	If either of the two scores are extreme, range will be distorted. It tells us little about how spread out or clustered together the data are	Uses only 50% of the data in the calculation and is quite laborious to calculate

Probability, significance testing, and error types

» Probability (*p*) is used in psychological research to refers to how likely it is our results happened by chance.

» When we can reject the idea that our results are due to chance (i.e. we reject the null hypothesis), we can say that our results are *significant*.

» We test for significance using inferential statistics, and it is outcome of these statistical tests which tell us the *p* value.

_p_ is the likelihood that our results occurred by chance

» $p = 1$ means that something is guaranteed to happen.

» $p = 0$ means that something is NEVER going to happen.

» $p = 0.5$ means that there is a 50% chance of it happening (e.g. heads coming up when we toss a coin).

» $p < 0.05$ (*p* is 'less than' 0.05) means that there is less that there is a 5% 'probability' that our results happened by chance. In other words, we can be 95% certain that our results did not occur by chance.

Alpha (α) is the value of _p_ that researchers choose as being as sure as we need to be that our results did not occur by chance.

» Alpha is usually 0.05 (i.e. 95% certain that results did not occur by chance.)

» This means that if the value of *p* given by the statistical test is larger than this we do *not* regard the results as 'significant' since we cannot be certain that they did not occur by chance and so we cannot 'reject' our null-hypothesis.

» Alpha can be 0.01 in cases where we want to be *really* sure (i.e. 99% sure) that we are not making a mistake in rejecting the null hypothesis.

An alpha of 0.05 gives us the best chance of avoiding both type 1 and type 2 errors.

Type 1 error: the 'false positive' error. The null hypothesis is rejected when it is actually true. The less strict the alpha (e.g. $p = 0.1$, or 10%), the more likely this error is.

Type 2 error: the 'false negative' error. The null-hypothesis is accepted when it is actually false. The more strict the alpha (e.g. $p = 0.001$ or 0.1%) then the more likely we are to make this kind of error.

"Do not underestimate the importance of learning about probability, significance, and type1/type 2 errors! They are a crucial aspect of data analysis and you can bet that they will feature frequently in exam questions!"

Choosing a statistical test

Levels of measurement

Different types of measurement can be made in psychological research and this influences the type of statistical test used for analysis.

LEVELS OF MEASUREMENT		
LEVEL OF MEASUREMENT	**DEFINITION**	**EXAMPLE**
Nominal	Where the data can be organised in categories.	An international ecological survey related to global warming may measure the number of different birds spotted on a given day – sparrow, blue-tit, hawk, eagle, buzzard.
Ordinal	The data can be identified as an *order* and can be arranged as such.	In horse racing *Speedy* came first, *Not Bad* came third and *Sleepy* came third.
Interval	Where the data can be arranged in a continuous scale, such as time, weight, temperature or height.	In horse racing, the times of the runners: *Speedy* took 84 seconds, *Not Bad* took 90 seconds and *Sleepy* took 302 seconds.

An understanding of levels of measurement is important for selecting appropriate statistical tests. If you are given an exam question which requires you to select an appropriate test, or even justify the use of a named test, then without this understanding your answer is nothing more than a guess!

» Whilst descriptive tests allow us the *describe* data, inferential statistical tests allow us to *infer* something about the data (i.e. they allow us to *infer* whether our hypotheses are supported or rejected).

» The following decision tree shows you how the appropriate test is selected:

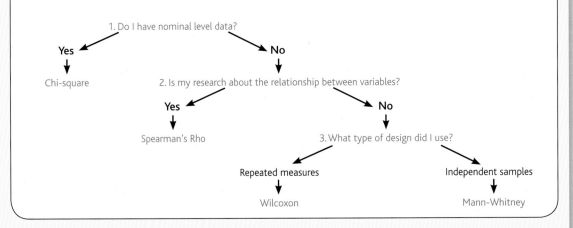

You don't need to be able to do the maths for the exam, so we will not cover them here. You DO need to be able to identify which statistical test is appropriate in which situation, and so we've designed a simple 'tree' diagram to help you with that.

How do we know whether our statistical test suggests a significant result?

» Statistical tests are the only tools which allow researchers to arrive at a *p* value for their research.

» The tests give a *calculated* (or *observed*) *value* which is compared to a number (called a *critical value*) in a statistical table.

» Whether your result is significant (and so allows you to reject the null hypothesis) is decided for each test according to the following rules:

Chi-Squared

You need to know:

» Degrees of freedom = (number of rows − 1) × (number of columns − 1)

» The level of alpha you are using

» Whether your hypothesis was directional (one-tailed) or non-directional (two-tailed)

» The calculated value

The calculated value must be equal to or larger than the number in the table for the result to be significant.

Spearman's Rho

You need to know:

» The level of alpha you are using

» Whether your hypothesis was directional (one-tailed) or non-directional (two-tailed)

» The number of participants who participated (N)

» The calculated value

The calculated value must be equal to or larger than the number in the table for the result to be significant.

Wilcoxon

You need to know:

» The level of alpha you are using

» The number of people who participated

» Whether your hypothesis was directional (one-tailed) or non-directional (two-tailed)

» The calculated value

The number calculated must be less than the number in the table for the result to be significant.

Mann-Whitney

You need to know:

» The smaller of the two numbers you calculated

» The number of participants in each group

» Whether your hypothesis was directional (one-tailed) or non-directional (two-tailed)

» The calculated value

The number calculated must be equal to or less than the number in the table for the result to be significant.

Conventions of reporting on psychological investigations

Once research is conducted it needs to be written up for others to read and review. There are certain conventions that should be followed when reporting psychological research.

SECTION	WHAT IT DOES
Title	Clearly states what the study is about.
Abstract	A short and concise summary of the report (i.e. less than 150 words), containing brief descriptions of aim and method and a summary of results.
Introduction	A description of the background to the research, containing reference to other closely related research.
Aim and hypothesis	The aim is where you state the purpose of the study and the hypothesis is exactly what is being tested.
Method	Describes how the research was carried out, written with sufficient detail to allow replication of the study.
Design	Contains an outline of things like research method used, experimental design, IV, DV, control of extraneous variables, ethical issues.
Participants	Details of the number of participants used, relevant participant details (e.g. age, gender), sampling method adopted, and how participants were allocated to conditions.
Materials/apparatus	Details of the resources used, e.g. questionnaires, stimulus materials, specialised apparatus used.
Procedure	An account of how the study was conducted, detailing instructions to participants, how ethical issues were dealt with (e.g. debriefing) and information about how the data was recorded.
Results	The results of the study reported as descriptive statistics (including tables and graphs) and inferential statistics (the outcomes of statistical tests).
Discussion and conclusion	The results are explained in terms of the aims and hypotheses and related to the background covered in the introduction. Limitations are identified and modifications are recommended. Suggestions for further research are also made.
References	Full details are given of all the research referred to in the investigation, written in a conventional format.

REVISION OF CORE KNOWLEDGE

If you can complete the following tables without referring to notes then you are well on your way to getting a good mark for this question in the exam. Remember, use your memory first and only refer to this section or a main textbook or notes as a last resort. Repeat the task until you can complete it without major error.

THE MAJOR FEATURES OF SCIENCE AND THE SCIENTIFIC PROCESS		
KEY PHRASES	DEFINITION	HOW IS THIS USEFUL TO ME?

(continued)

THE MAJOR FEATURES OF SCIENCE AND THE SCIENTIFIC PROCESS		
KEY PHRASES	DEFINITION	HOW IS THIS USEFUL TO ME?

DESIGNING PSYCHOLOGICAL INVESTIGATIONS – DESIGN OPTIONS			
KEY PHRASES	DEFINITION	PROS	CONS

(continued)

DESIGNING PSYCHOLOGICAL INVESTIGATIONS – DESIGN OPTIONS			
KEY PHRASES	DEFINITION	PROS	CONS

SAMPLING		
KEY PHRASES	DEFINITION	ISSUES OF GENERALISABILITY AND BIAS

RELIABILITY & VALIDITY		
KEY PHRASES	DEFINITION	HOW CAN IT BE IMPROVED?

ETHICAL ISSUE	DEALING WITH IT	PROBLEMS

GRAPHS AND TABLES			
GRAPH	EXAMPLE	CHARACTERISTICS	WHEN TO USE

	Mean	Mode	Median	Standard deviation	Range	Semi-interquartile range
Strength						
Weakness						

LEVELS OF MEASUREMENT		
LEVEL OF MEASUREMENT	DEFINITION	EXAMPLE

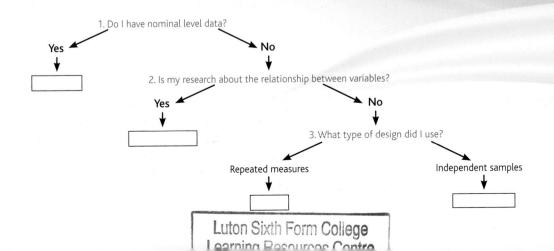

1. Do I have nominal level data?

Yes

No

2. Is my research about the relationship between variables?

Yes

No

3. What type of design did I use?

Repeated measures

Independent samples

GET TO KNOW YOUR EXAM

A2 Psychology consists of two separately examined units, PSYA3 and PSYA4.

PSYA3: Topics in Psychology

Topic selection – There are eight topics, of which you study three. You will identify these on the exam paper by the heading rather than the question number: e.g. a question on aggression will be preceded by the bold header 'Aggression'. Don't bother reading the questions that don't apply to you – it is a waste of precious time and since you haven't studied them you can't answer them anyway!

Question style – As you will have seen from the examples in the chapters, whilst PSYA3 is often referred to as the 'essay' paper, the questions in fact take a number of forms. In addition to single-part 25 mark questions, you will also encounter parted questions. The important thing to remember is that you must answer the question as it is set: for example, do not ignore the fact that the question is in two parts and mistakenly write a single part essay. In all the many thousands of exam papers we have marked we have never seen a candidate advantage themselves by doing this. Furthermore, be very sure only to include material that is relevant to the question – the way that exam papers are marked means that information will not be moved around for you by the examiner. So you will lose marks if you have, for instance, a two part question and put material in part (a) that is relevant to part (b). It pays to read carefully, think and plan before you write! (That is a bit of advice we will be repeating…)

Time limits – The PSYA3 exam lasts for only 90 minutes – that's 30 minutes a question! It's not very long is it? Be assured though, examiners are well aware of what can be expected in this limited time, so they are not expecting a great deal of writing. Your task is not to impress examiners with the *quantity* of words you can produce in 30 minutes, but with the *quality* of an answer you can construct in this time. Examiners also take into account the stress of examination conditions and the impact this has on candidates. We know that the overwhelming temptation in an exam is to blast into overdrive and set about answering a question in frenzied haste, not thinking very much at all, and not taking the trouble to relate your answer to the precise wording of the question. But to repeat – exam success is earned by the quality and relevance of what you write; you don't get marks just for filling the answer book with words.

One final point on timing – you must be disciplined about sticking to 30 minutes an essay. It is easy to see the impact on the third essay of spending 40 minutes each on the first two! One of the most useful things you can do as part of your preparation is to find out how much you can reasonably write in 30 minutes (e.g. by copying something out as fast as you can for that amount of time) and use this valuable information in all your preparation. It will improve the quality of your answers no end.

Issues, debates and approaches (IDA) – It is essential to incorporate issues, debates and approaches *effectively* into your answers. You don't have to write a great deal about any particular issue, debate or approach, but if you want to get into the top band something has to be there in your answer which is identifiably IDA. Quality is the real issue – the more effectively you incorporate IDA into your answer, the further up the mark bands your answer is likely to find itself. We are talking here about the evaluative part of the answer of course. We say this because IDA has to be there, regardless of the structure of the question. For example, if a question is 4+5+16 marks then the IDA should only appear in the 16 mark section. If the question is 4+8 and 4+8 then there needs to be a reference to IDA in both 8 mark sections (although both are part of the same answer it is probably best to nail IDA in both parts, just to be sure).

Read the Issues, Debates and Approaches section in this book. Look at how they have been summarised, and use them like this in your exam answers. You don't have to explain *what* is meant *by* the IDA (e.g. what the nature-nurture debate is) – if you have used an IDA effectively in the right context then you won't have to, as it will be obvious to the reader. We reckon the easiest opportunity to get IDA credit arises when you have described something from a particular approach, for example the behavioural approach. Appropriately comment on the strengths or weaknesses of this approach in the context in which it is being used and hey presto, effective IDA.

PSYA4: Psychopathology, Psychology in Action, and Psychological Research and Scientific Method

Don't worry about IDA in this exam paper – just answer the questions. IDA is built in, so really just forget about it. You have other things to concern you here.

Topic selection and question style – There are three subsections, each putting its own particular demands on you, the examinee.

Psychopathology

This is the subsection that most closely resembles PSYA3 – essay-style questions, maybe parted questions. The mark schemes used by examiners are like those used in PSYA3, so you can take the same kind of approach to answering the questions, minus the IDA.

Psychology in Action

There are three topics and you will have studied one of them. Like everywhere else in your exam, ignore the questions you haven't been taught – you can't do them, even if you think you can.

Your question will have several parts: some will require straightforward knowledge of the topic area whilst others will need the application of psychological knowledge. Do you remember those analysis and application questions from AS, where you had to apply your knowledge to novel situations? Well those types of questions appear again here, but a bit tougher (as they should be – this is now A2!). These are not the kinds of questions you can rote learn for: if you don't know your subject well then you will inevitably struggle. The best preparation is to really learn your stuff and practise as many questions as you can.

Psychological Research and Scientific Method

This is a multi-part question, with each part worth anywhere from 1 to 12 marks. You will have questions testing your knowledge of research and not from your A2 course. Remember your AS Level? If you thought that you could do a mind-dump and leave it behind, then think again. This section tests ALL of your research methods knowledge, including that which you are supposed to have carried with you from the AS. Make no mistake, this is a lot of material and if you have not done enough work on research methods at AS then you have a massive job in front of you compensating for this. Start early and start working earnestly; your performance on this question may well be what makes the difference between grades.

In answering questions, be brief and very direct. Clarity is very important: examiners are reluctant to give full marks for something waffley.

Time limits – the PSYA4 exam lasts 2 hours. This, however, is not necessarily 2 hours of writing. In PSYA4, you have to apply your knowledge; it is perhaps a more *thoughtful* exam than PSYA3. Because of this, PSYA4 has thinking time built in. If you consider that each question has about 30 minutes, like PSYA3, then it is clear that in PSYA4 there is time to spend thinking more about how to answer the question. *Use this time.* We know what happens with lots of students; we've seen it often enough – they blast into the exam paper as though it was a race and then spend half an hour twiddling thumbs at the end, waiting to be let free. This is a very costly thing to do – you have been given thinking time because you really do need to think about your answers very carefully.

The skills assessed in the exam

The A2 examinations aim to assess a number of skills, and knowing what these are is vital to effective preparation and good grades. You will sometimes see these skills referred to as AO1, AO2 and AO3, where 'AO' stands for 'Assessment Objective'.

Knowledge and understanding skills (AO1)

This skill relates to your ability to demonstrate knowledge and understanding of psychology.

Analysis, evaluation and application skills (AO2)

These are about your ability to evaluate and apply your knowledge of psychology.

How science works (AO3)

This refers to your knowledge of how psychology as a science works. Basically it is assessing your knowledge of psychological research.

In practice, AO2 and AO3 are pretty much the same thing and we strongly advise you not to worry about the distinction between them. In the PSYA3 and psychopathology questions, just ensure that you refer to research; if you can use research effectively as evaluation, then all the better.

Plan for success – prepare for the exam

Revision is the process whereby you 'fix' the information in your mind so that you can remember it in the exam. Prior to 'revision' as such, you should have done a lot of hard work, keeping up with your learning, regularly reminding yourself of what has gone before, reading through and organising your material, and filling any gaps in your knowledge. Only when you have done this are you really ready for effective revision.

Revision is an individual thing: what works well for one person might not work so effectively for another. Whatever approach you take, however, revising properly will take time, planning and self-discipline. You have to ask yourself something and answer honestly – how much do you want success and what are you willing to sacrifice for it?

The first steps

You need a place to revise quietly and without disruption. It's not always easy we know, but there is always somewhere you can go for some quality revision time.

Get yourself organised – you can't revise until you've sorted yourself out with material (pens, paper etc.) and learning matter (notes, books etc.). We can assure you that the more organised you are, the more likely you are to get good grades.

Manage your time

Spaced practice is an effective way to approach revision – don't study all the time: take time out to relax and have fun. BUT when you do settle to revise, make sure that you really DO work at it (just sitting there chewing your pen does not constitute real revision …). It is vital that you keep track of your revision. We cannot stress enough the benefits of a revision timetable. Using this you can maintain an awareness of what you need to revise, what you have revised, and what you need to return to. A revision timetable reminds you how little time you have left and how much you still have to do. This can help motivate you to perhaps waste less time and invest more of what you have into revision.

The hard bit

Passively sitting and reading will do you little good when it comes to revision. Some students even seem to think that simply having a book and holding it will cause the contents to somehow seep up their arm. *Learning* is about *doing*; the idea is simple. Learning is not a passive process. *Doing*, however, requires effort and motivation, which is not so simple. There are some things you can do, however, to make your time in revision most effective. Don't take our word for it though – this is all based on sound psychology.

Practice – Skills are acquired through practice, and answering exam questions is a skill. Therefore, the more you practise the better you get. Practise answering questions and planning answers – there are questions in this book to have a go at, and plenty more on the AQA website.

Flashcards – Reduce your notes to key points. These can then be put onto index cards (6"×4" work well). Use colour, embolden/CAPITALISE key words and phrases, use images. Don't be tempted to put too much information on each card – in this regard at least, less is more. Use one side of the card for a single topic. You can carry some cards around with you when complete; and when there are those inevitable lulls in activity you can flick through them. Don't worry if things don't stick straight away: the more often you look at your cards the more familiar the contents will become. There are some flash card summaries in various chapters of this book if you want to see how one might look.

Mind maps – Mind mapping is a very useful strategy for revision, since in creating a mind map you are employing lots of different parts of your brain. You are using words, colours, images, and spatial connections. What is really important about mind maps, however, is something that is often overlooked – the thinking and effort that goes into producing one. You really have to think about the topic to reduce it to a mind map. Once you get the hang of what a good one is they become more straightforward. Various websites explain how to do them, but if you really want to become a skilled mapper then we recommend the book *Mapping Inner Space* by Nancy Margulies.

Useful revision websites

http://www.bbc.co.uk/schools/studentlife/
This site has lots of good advice about revision and exam stress. There are also revision timetables you can download and adapt.

http://mind-mapping.co.uk/mind-maps-examples.htm
A useful source for mind-mapping ideas.

http://www.wikihow.com/revise
Some good revision advice to be found here.

http://www.brainboxx.co.uk/a3_aspects/pages/revision.htm
A good review of revision and memory techniques for revision success.

INDEX